Building Womanist Coalitions

Writing and Teaching in the Spirit of Love

Edited by

GARY L. LEMONS

UNIVERSITY OF ILLINOIS PRESS
Urbana, Chicago, and Springfield

1 2 3 4 5 C P 5 4 3 2 1
∞ This book is printed on acid-free paper.

Library of Congress Cataloging-in-Publication Data
Names: Lemons, Gary L., editor.
Title: Building womanist coalitions: writing and teaching in the spirit of love / edited by Gary L. Lemons.
Description: Urbana: University of Illinois Press, [2019] | Series: Transformations: womanist, feminist, and indigenous studies | Includes bibliographical references and index.
Identifiers: LCCN 2018046036| ISBN 9780252042416 (cloth : alk. paper) | ISBN 9780252084218 (pbk. : alk. paper)
Subjects: LCSH: Feminist theory. | Feminism. | Women's studies.
Classification: LCC HQ1190 .B844 2019 | DDC 305.42—dc23
LC record available at https://lccn.loc.gov/2018046036

Ebook ISBN 978-0-252-05126-5

Contents

Foreword vii
AnaLouise Keating

Introduction: "Womanist Is to Feminist as Purple Is to Lavender": Writing in Solidarity across Shades of Difference 1

PART I: TEACHING IN THE "UNIVERSAL[IST]" SPIRIT OF WOMANISM

1 Spirituality in the Classroom: Some Womanist Reflections 23
Layli Maparyan

2 Coming into Being: Metta to Womanist Teachers 36
Kendra N. Bryant

3 Professing the Liberatory Power of Womanism 53
Gary L. Lemons

4 A Doctored Voice: Resistance, Reading, and Righting as Womanist Pedagogy 70
Ylce Irizarry

PART II: WOMANIST ALLIANCES FOR HUMAN RIGHTS AND SOCIAL JUSTICE

5 Breaking Silence 95
M. Jacqui Alexander and Beverly Guy-Sheftall

6 From Exile to Healing: I "Too" Am a Womanist 123
Susie L.Hoeller

7 Nepantlera as Midwife of Empathy 136
Paul T. Corrigan

8 A Deeper Shade of Consciousness: My Voice Is My Resistance 149
Atika Chaudhary

PART III: SPEAKING AND ACTING OUT IN WOMANIST SOLIDARITY

9 Transgenero Performance: Gender and Transformation in *Mujeres en Ritual* 171
Dora Arreola

10 *Soy Mujer Cuando . . .* A Collective Poem 184
Andrea Assaf

11 Now Is Not the Time for Silence: Writing and Directing *What the Heart Remembers* 188
Fanni V. Green

12 "I Come from a Dream Deferred" 208
Erica C. Sutherlin

13 On Becoming a Feminist 210
Rudolph P. Byrd

14 Compelled by the Spirit: My Journey to Become a Womanist Man 216
M. Thandabantu Iverson

Contributors 235

Index 239

FOREWORD

Womanism for All! The Transformational Power of Radical Love

What does transformation look like? What's the relationship between scholarship, research, pedagogy, and innovative social-justice work? How can we use words, ideas, writing, and reading to provoke progressive individual and collective change? How can we enact transformation in the various aspects of our lives—in our classrooms, our scholarship, our relationships, our daily practices? *Transformations: Womanist, Feminist, and Indigenous Studies* has its origins in these and related questions. Grounded in the belief that radical progressive change—on individual, collective, national, transnational, and planetary levels—is urgently needed and in fact possible (although not easy to achieve), *Transformations* invites authors and readers to transgress the status quo (what Gloria Anzaldúa refers to as "consensus reality") by producing transdisciplinary scholarship informed by women-of-colors theories-praxes and post-oppositional approaches to knowledge and social change.[1]

In *Building Womanist Coalitions* Gary L. Lemons and his contributors have answered this invitation with bold voices and open hearts. They engage deeply with women-of-colors theories-praxes—including, but not limited to, Alice Walker's love-saturated womanism; Gloria Anzaldúa's nepantlera spiritual activism; *This Bridge Called My Back*'s radical self-love and visionary politics; *Colonize This! Young Women of Color on Today's Feminism*'s border-crossing self-definitions; *this bridge we call home*'s transformational identity politics and provocative alliance-making; and the everyday wisdom learned from mothers, sisters, partners, colleagues, educators, and other people in their lives. These engagements demonstrate the profound transformations that women-of-colors' wisdom, teachings, and scholarship make when put into dialogue with mainstream academic disciplines. And, like the authors in *This Bridge Called My Back* and *this bridge we call home*, Lemons and his contributors remind us that theorizing takes many forms—first-person autobiographical narrative, poem, dramatic verse, letters, journal entries, and more.

I was first drawn to Lemons's manuscript because his generous interpretation of womanism as a radically inclusive, spirit-inspired, love-infused, liberatory philosophy and worldview closely resembles my own. Lemons defines and enacts womanism in broad, expansive, invitational terms, creating with this edited collection "a sanctuary where the Spirit of love for womanism may abide." His "sanctuary" includes people of many backgrounds, illustrating that womanism is for everyone—regardless of genders, nationalities, racialized identities, religions, sexualities, and so on. *Building Womanist Coalitions* also embodies womanism's ability to create vibrant, diverse coalitions: "As world-citizens, we characterize the essence of a global community—South Asian, African (American), Middle-Eastern, Canadian, Caribbean, Latina/Chicana, as well as European." As the contributors demonstrate, womanism is available to anyone willing to open their hearts and minds to its wisdom and ethics. To be sure, given the gender-specific nature of the word "womanism," it can seem almost counterintuitive to apply the womanist label to cisgendered men. But as Lemons notes, womanism has enabled him and others to resist "masculinist and misogynistic ideas of manhood" by "lov[ing] ourselves and the womanist within us." Lest you believe that Lemons's decision to embrace womanism was unthinking or overreaching, read his chapter in this volume; walk with him as he wrestles with the sociopolitical implications of identifying with feminism and womanism.

Like feminism and other complex, multifaceted social-justice theories, womanism can be defined in a variety of ways. While all versions honor Spirit (defined broadly) and view black women's wisdom, lives, and words as foundational, they vary considerably in delineating who can or cannot be a womanist, use womanist thought, and create womanist theory.[2] Some versions restrict womanism to cisgender women of African descent; other versions focus primarily on black feminist interventions into Christian theology, offering important critiques of eurocentric, masculinist biases and healing reinterpretations of Biblical narrative. And still other versions define womanism so broadly that they embrace these iterations of womanism and others as well. You'll see a similar diversity in how these various womanisms position themselves in relation to feminism. While some womanists sharply distinguish womanism from feminism, other womanists (like Lemons and many of his contributors) self-define as both womanists *and* feminists. Fortunately, because womanism neither homogenizes nor simplifies, womanists don't need to fully agree with each other—at least, according to the version of womanism that I espouse.

In this book series and within the pages of this book, womanism represents a radically inclusive philosophy and daily practice potentially available to anyone—regardless of personal identity categories (e.g., gender, race, ethnicity, class, religion, sexuality, and so forth). This expansive womanism allows space for contradictions to coexist, jostling each other. Indeed, womanism invites contradictions in and assures us that adequate space and time enables the contradictions to mix, nudge, and speak to each other, initiating additional transformations. To borrow Layli Maparyan's analogy, womanism functions like a big tent so spacious that it includes all family members—regardless of their disagreements with each other.[3] However, this is not an anything-goes inclusion. Although womanism defines kinship broadly and invites everyone into the tent, it stipulates a few ground rules: the willingness to respect others, to listen with humility, and to remain open to the possibility of being changed by our encounters with others.

I attribute womanism's radical inclusiveness to its affirmative, visionary, sacred worldview.

Everything that exists is shaped by and infused with spirit—a creative life force known by many names (soul, God, energy, consciousness, thought, and so on). This shared life force ensures our interconnectedness with all existence; whether we acknowledge or ignore it, we're all interrelated and kin. Or, rephrased in more conventional western academic terms: radically inclusive versions of womanism are grounded in a paradoxical monism positing a world composed entirely of one highly complex, always-morphing "stuff"—a foundational spirit-matter substance that embodies itself as an infinite variety of forms. Because we're all infused with this life-force spirit, we share a commonality—what Anzaldúa describes as "a category of identity wider than any social position or racial label" (*Light* 138). When we acknowledge this shared identity category, we're more willing to take risks and work to connect with others—even (*or especially!*) with those whose lives and experiences differ greatly from our own. We're willing to be radically inclusive.

This radical inclusiveness allows womanists to acknowledge the many differences among us without judging and ranking these differences hierarchically. When we enter the spacious womanist tent, we bring our differences with us—our unique family dynamics and histories; our particular, socially inscribed bodies; our educational backgrounds; and so on. But these differences don't function as rigid walls dividing us from others. Rather, differences become points of connection. As we acknowledge our differences and share our perspectives (*coming to voice*), we create the possibility for building new knowledges, making connections with members of other social groups—without conflating differences between groups or becoming lost in an overarching, homogenizing "umbrella term." Womanism neither denies our personal, social, and/or ancestral roots (*our home communities and early formations*) nor insists that we exclusively embrace them. Instead, womanism encourages us to grow—to recognize and build on our interconnections with others.

Look, for instance, at womanism's relationship to feminism. As contributors demonstrate, you don't need to pick between womanism and feminism. If both resonate, claim them both; borrow, adapt, and apply both womanist and feminist theories. *Building Womanist Coalitions* also demonstrates the synergy made possible with this inclusive approach. Womanism and feminism exist side-by-side and intertwined throughout this book, reminding us that we need multiple tools and perspectives for survival, resistance, and transformation. Lemons moves seamlessly and without comment between feminist and womanist thought. M. Thandabantu Iverson self-defines as "both feminist *and* womanist." Rudolph P. Byrd self-defines as a feminist and urges all men and women to adopt feminism and use feminism's tools to dismantle patriarchy. Fanni Green, identifying as a womanist, explores her collaboration with a self-defined feminist colleague. In these and additional ways, contributors demonstrate that womanism and feminism are spacious enough to accommodate multiple, sometimes contradictory, positions.

Womanism's radical inclusiveness is motivated by expansive love—love of Spirit, love of self, love of others (both human and nonhuman others). Contributors demonstrate some of the many ways that womanist love emboldens us as we think, speak, and act in the world. As Kendra Bryant notes in her epistolary essay, when love infuses our teaching, it creates new possibilities—affirmative student-teacher relationships that ignite students' self-love. Transformed by the love she experienced as a student, she moves forward, passing it on: "It is this loving relationship between student and teacher that I have carried into the classrooms where I teach—with the purpose of reminding my students of their own humanity—and thereby, making more possible the peace the world imagines." Love transforms our relationships with others. Paul T. Corrigan draws on Walker's love-infused definition of womanism and Anzaldúa's theory of nepantleras (transformational, liminal mediators) to suggest a coalitional strategy in which we "recognize others as not wholly other, only when we see—and love—others as ourselves." Love instructs. The love Iverson experienced from key people in his life transformed him: "if I am farther along my path to becoming the liberated man my mother envisioned, it is because of the Spirit of love and the women and men who helped to transform my self-vision." Love inspires. Building on the "universalist love" in Walker's womanism, Chaudhary practices an "all-inclusive love" empowering her to affirm herself and those she encounters.

As indigenous philosophies teach us, language can do real physical-material, psychic, emotional, ontological work in the world.[4] Our words do not simply convey meaning from writers to readers (or speakers to listeners) but also contribute to world-building endeavors. I'm thrilled that the words in this book will be making their way out into the world, assisting and inspiring us as we build new womanist, feminist, loving coalitions.

AnaLouise Keating

Notes

1. As I explain in more detail in *Transformation Now! Toward a Post-Oppositional Politics of Change*, *post-oppositionality* represents relational approaches to knowledge production, social interactions, identity, and transformation that borrow from, but do not become limited by or trapped in, oppositional thought and action.

2. For a discussion of the various strands of womanism, see Layli Maparyan's *The Womanist Idea*, especially chapter one.

3. Maparyan suggested this analogy in an email conversation with me several years ago.

4. I discuss language's causal power in "Living (with) Language." *Hypatia: A Journal of Feminist Philosophy*, 30.3 (2015): 628–635. For indigenous philosophies, Gregory Cajete's *Native Science: Natural Laws of Interdependence*; Craig Womack's "Theorizing American Indian Experience."

Works Cited

Anzaldúa, Gloria. *Light in the Dark/Luz en lo oscuro: Rewriting Identity, Spirituality, Reality*, edited by AnaLouise Keating (Durham: Duke University Press, 2015).

Keating, AnaLouise. *Transformation Now! Toward a Post-Oppositional Politics of Change* (Urbana: University of Illinois Press, 2013).

Maparyan, Layli. *The Womanist Idea* (New York: Routledge, 2011).

Womack, Craig. "Theorizing American Indian Experience." *Reasoning Together: The Native Critics Collective*, edited by Craig Womack, Daniel Heath Justice, and Christopher B. Teuton (Norman: University of Oklahoma Press, 2008), 353–410.

Building Womanist Coalitions

INTRODUCTION

"Womanist Is to Feminist as Purple Is to Lavender"

Writing in Solidarity across Shades of Difference

Womanist: 1. From *womanish*. . . . A black feminist or feminist of color. . . . 2. *Also*: A woman who loves other women, sexually and/or nonsexually. . . . Sometimes loves individual men sexually and/or nonsexually. Committed to survival and wholeness of entire people, male *and* female. . . . Not a separatist. . . . Traditionally universalist, as in: "Mama, why are we brown, pink, and yellow, and our cousins are white, beige, and black?" Ans.: "Well, you know the colored race is just like a flower garden, with every color flower represented." Traditionally capable, as in: "Mama, I'm walking to Canada and I'm taking you and a bunch of other slaves with me." Reply: "It wouldn't be the first time." 3. Loves music. Loves dance. Loves the moon. *Loves* the Spirit. Loves love and food and roundness. Loves struggle. *Loves* the Folk. Loves herself. *Regardless*. 4. Womanist is to feminist as purple is to lavender.

—Alice Walker, *In Search of Our Mothers' Gardens* (1983)

"The womanist idea" [is] a kind of underlying architecture of womanism. . . . The more I reflected on this architecture, however, it increasingly appeared to me not so much as a "theory" or "philosophy" but rather as a worldview, a metaphysics, a methodology, a movement, and a spirit. And as I reflected, the more I came to conclude that "the womanist idea" is actually a potent and necessary intervention upon many of the widely lamented shortfalls of this age in which we live (and, as we so often bemoan, might die).

—Layli Maparyan, *The Womanist Idea* (2012)

Writing Oneself into Being—*Regardless*

Womanism—An Artistic Model for Social Activism

In "Saving the Life that Is Your Own: The Importance of Models in the Artist's Life" (as its title suggests), Alice Walker posits the idea of the necessity for artistic affirmation for creative expression and the devastating loss that comes with its "absence": "The absence of models, in literature as in life, to say nothing of painting, is an occupational hazard for the arts, simply because models in art, in behavior, in growth of spirit and intellect—even if rejected—enrich and enlarge one's view of existence."[1] In all that a womanist *loves*, she models creative expressivity that metaphorically "enlarge[s]" the vision of what it means to be a human being. While Walker does not say that a womanist loves *literature*, who she defines herself to be without it would have no existence. From the antislavery writings of Phillis Wheatley to those of modern and contemporary black/feminists of color, *writing*—across genres—works as a strategic tool of metaphoric artistry to *re*-create themselves in their own words. Writing not only enables a womanist to self-possess images s/he loves, it lays the bridgework for coalitional solidarity for practicing love for social justice across differences of race, gender[s], class, sexualities, culture, nation-state affiliations, abilities, and generation.

In the early 1990s, when I began the research (as a doctoral student at NYU) leading to my writing the book *Womanist Forefathers: Frederick Douglass and W. E. B. Du Bois* (2009)—to the release of *Caught Up in the Spirit! Teaching for Womanist Liberation* (2017)—the idea of womanism has continued to be the "model" for my academic, creative, *and* spiritual expressivity. Conceptualizing *Building Womanist Coalitions: Writing and Teaching in the Spirit of Love* would become yet another representation of my "growth of spirit and intellect . . . enrich[ing] and enlarge[ing my] view of existence"—from an activist viewpoint. Not only have I shown scholarly appreciation for intellectuality, I have also expressed creativity as a painter for most of my life. Alice Walker's employment of the tonal relationship between "purple" and "lavender" to signify an analogous connection between a womanist and a feminist is creatively provocative. Defining a "womanist" as "[a] black feminist or feminist of color," Walker expresses the racial/ethnic politics of this identity within the varying skin-color tones of "the colored race." As a "universal[ist]," a womanist loves a body of different colors.

As an abstract artist, I purposely create a palette of color variation to exhibit the idea that all colors can make a difference. My interpretive aim is to *model* the life-enriched spirit of all colors, as I conceptualize their relatedness through African and indigenous patterns of shapes and designs. In this way, a canvas simply provides me an artistic landscape to envision a radical idea of global humanity. In sum, my artistic creativity—both visually and discursively—acts as a critical location to build a sanctuary where the Spirit of love for womanism may abide. As a model for art, behavior, Spirit, intellect, *and* activism, *Building Womanist Coalitions* is a visionary illustration of the life-transforming soul-work of body of *pro*-womanists. Its purpose promotes writings by women *and* men of *color* having come together in solidarity as models of activist-consciousness.

As Walker defines a womanist as "a black feminist or feminist of color," "love" functions as a fundamental aspect of her identity. She "Loves music. Loves dance. Loves the moon. *Loves* the Spirit. Loves love and food and roundness. Loves struggle. *Loves* the Folk. Loves herself. *Regardless*." So much of a womanist's character is personally interconnected artistically, naturally, spiritually, and politically. Interestingly, in all that a womanist cares for, particular emphasis is on the fact that she "*Loves* the Spirit" and "*Loves* the Folk." The passion she possesses for each of them is clearly emphasized (in italicization). It is, however, the lifesaving power of self-love that is personally liberating. In proclaiming love for herself, without needing validation from societal ideas of normativity, a womanist will not be bound.

Regardless of current U.S. government policies *re*-enforcing separatist ideology aimed to "make America great again," the contributors to this collection reclaim shades of difference(s) centered in womanist "universal[ism]." Communicating the self-liberatory value of its meaning in their writings, they counter forces upholding forms of racial/ethnic, cultural, and religious separatism. These writers seek to promote struggles that actively resist wall-building ideas of exclusionism. In the deadening wake of the *re*-currency of white supremacy supported by the Trump administration, the intersection of patriarchy, capitalism, sexism, *and* the sexual harassment of women has taken on a more *in your face* profile. A politics of "border"-building has become the new norm, also defining U.S. anti-immigration laws rooted in fear of the "other." As *the* single terrorist-identified threat to the "American Dream," this nation—founded upon the calculated erasure of this land's indigenous folk and the enslavement of Africans—created itself to be the "first-world." In its deadly, terroristic history of investment in white supremacy, people of color—especially those with dark-skin—can only exist as "third-world" citizens. Thus, the idea of wall-building becomes uplifting propaganda to protect this country's "dream" of global superiority. In its reinforcement of white privilege(s), patriarchy, sexism, and classism (focused on the protection of the wealthiest "Americans") it perpetuates an overt, loveless strategy of domination. Moreover, having normalized the sexual harassment of women, Donald Trump has publicly promoted an ideology of "locker-room," masculinist-based manhood.

In line with Trump's masculinist thinking, his resistance to more stringent, national gun-control laws sustains itself in an unwavering support of the NRA. Affirming the "stand your ground" law of self-protection, his ideas of hetero-masculine normativity is inextricably linked to his own misguided notions of phallic authority. In just two years across this nation, we have witnessed mass shootings perpetrated by men (white *and* of color). In fact, I live in the state of Florida where in Orlando, on June 2016, at the Pulse (a gay nightclub), 49 individuals were shot to death and 58 wounded by a man (of color). In October 2017 in Las Vegas, Nevada, a (white) male shot and killed 58 people at an outdoor concert. During the mass shooting, he wounded 546 people. In the same year, in the small town of Sutherland Springs, Texas, a (white) male killed 26 people during a Sunday morning church service. Under patriarchal dictatorship, gun-ownership legitimates the myth of male supremacy. However, when it becomes linked to white supremacy, it not only authorizes male violence it also reifies the systemic and institutionalized mythology of the black body as a living display of disorderly conduct that needs to be corrected (even if by death).

Building Womanist Coalitions includes works by teachers/professors, students, and creative artists (poets as well as actors/directors). They collectively embody an unwavering defense of human rights and social justice. Among feminist and womanist contributors in this book who are educators and represent themselves as social activists, I stand with them as a black male who professes womanism as a lifesaving idea. For more than two decades, I have challenged my students to explore the depth of self-fulfillment gained from an engagement in womanism as a liberatory strategy for creating activist alliance possibilities—in and outside the classroom. In the introduction to *Black Male Outsider* "When the Teacher Moves from Silence to Voice: 'Talking Back' to Patriarchy and White Supremacy," I begin by citing the self-empowering words of Audre Lorde from *Sister Outsider*. She proclaims: "The fact that we are here . . . is an attempt to break . . . silence and bridge some of [the] differences between us, for it is not difference which immobilizes us, but silence. . . . And there are so many silences to be broken."[2] Her activist stand in *Sister Outsider* became the inspiration for the title of my first book. As a memoir tracing the evolution of my work teaching African American literature from a black feminist-womanist point of view, in it I own my voice publicly declaring my stance as a traitor to patriarchy and white supremacist myths of black male identity.

In search of allies *of all colors* in struggle against white supremacy and patriarchy, I have spent most of my academic career writing about this journey. I have found it one filled with continued challenges climbing up the "ivory tower," having taught only in majority white institutions of higher learning. From my pedagogical labor engendered with students I have taught over time (who have become "professors" of pro-feminist and womanist pedagogy), to my mentorship of colleagues (with whom I have served in long-standing pedagogical camaraderie), I have produced a body of scholarship that demonstrates the lifesaving power of activist-centered, personal relationships. Student voice-empowerment is a critically important pedagogical strategy promoted by contributors in *Building Womanist Coalitions* who are (or have been) professors in colleges and universities in the United States. In womanist terminology, envisioning the classroom as a metaphoric garden to fertilize the minds of our students, we plant seeds of social activism. However, as mentioned earlier, as a black male professor having taught in the South for a decade, I have continuously confronted the "undertonality" of myth-laden stereotypes imposed upon the black male body. In light of stereotypical race, gender, and sexual ideologies linked to feminism, my identification to it is actually caught up in loads of historical sexist and homophobic baggage. Can/should a "black" man be a feminist? Why would he necessarily desire to be in the face of a history of white male supremacy invested in *effeminizing* black men? Deep within the phallic politics of white supremacist patriarchy—ideologically in this contemporary moment in U.S. police authority—as a black man, I am a living threat to its power.

One night in 2016, while I was driving on a street on the university campus where I teach, a police officer signaled me to pull over. Rolling down my window, looking at the officer, I immediately began to panic. Instantaneously, the race and gender of identity of the officer struck a deeply troublesome chord in me. The police officer was "white" and "male." When he told me I had driven over the speed limit and asked for my driver's license, I panicked again, wondering if reaching in my back packet for my wallet (to show him my license) would be misinterpreted as an attempt to pull for a weapon/gun. In that moment, my mind began to play repeated jumbled-up images of white male police officers' violent encounters with blacks—especially males. I sat there, frozen, not moving. The officer repeated what he had requested. I told him that my wallet was in my back pocket and asked if I he would allow me to reach for it. He said, "Yes." I slowly reached for my wallet, opened it, and showed him my license. He then requested to see proof of my car registration/insurance. As I reached out to open the car's compartment where this information was stored, again fear began to reign over me in the darkness of that night. Without a witness, I thought that my reaching for it would be misinterpreted as yet another attempt to cause more trouble.

As the police officer watched, I slowly opened the compartment, took out the information, and placed it in his hand. As he reviewed the material, I mentioned to him (in the most "professional," non-stereotypical black male voice I could muster) that I was a professor at the university. I quickly added a sincere apology, telling him that I was sorry for rushing on campus to pick up my wife (also a professor at the university); in that moment, the tone of his voice shifted dramatically to one more cordial. He actually told me he understood, and for that reason, he chose not to write me a speeding ticket. With all fear gone, I felt that I had passed the test. On the grounds of a majority white institution of "higher" education, I was a black man trained in the power of the "ivory tower." I knew in that moment it was not my blackness that the white officer observed in the darkness of the night, it was the whiteness of my "professorial" identity he saw that I had internalized for years. On that night, in my racially paranoid mind-set, it kept me alive—unlike so many of the other black folk in the "'hood" who had not reached my "A-class" status.

Teaching students about the life-transforming power of womanism is actualized in its politics of "universalist" inclusion. It means taking off the mask of "political correctness"—not only for students but for teachers as well. I am not always comfortable in sharing my personal struggles, especially dealing with the internalization of white supremacy. However, in open dialogue and writing for critical self-consciousness, we challenge the institutionalized and systemic manifestations of oppression in our daily lives. Sharing our experiences of, and/or encounters with, its life-threatening effects, together we redefine the classroom as a strategic space for radical self-transformation. Both Paul T. Corrigan and Atika Chaudhary are former graduate students who studied with me. In the "postscript" of his essay, "Nepantlera as Midwife of Empathy," Paul references his experience in my "Literature by Radical Women of Color" class. At the time, neither he nor I had any idea that his scholarship would have so much pedagogical influence on his work as a professor in the college classroom. He says, "In the time since that class, I've come to learn in my own teaching that what calls out to me so deeply [is] to truly hear and care about the lives and works of others who are different from me, particularly those whose voices have so often been marginalized."

Speaking out in support of historically marginalized individuals, among other activist-oriented writers in *Building Womanist Writing Coalitions*, Andrea Assaf promotes activism as a signifier of loving soul-work. She is a poet/spoken word artist, as well as a performer and director of plays. As the founding director of *Art2Action Inc.* (an artist/activist organization), Assaf conceptualized it to "support women artists, artists of color, queer or trans artists, and creative allies." Her inclusive vision of gender, race, and sexuality aligns with Walker's progressive definition of a womanist as "[a] woman who loves other women, sexually and/or nonsexually. . . . Sometimes loves individual men sexually and/or nonsexually." Integrally tied to this idea is the concept of a womanist being "committed to survival and wholeness of entire people, male *and* female" (and, perhaps, inclusive of those who do not ascribe to these categories—as *Art2Action Inc.* embraces). I bear witness to the coalitional labor Andrea Assaf promotes. I was a participant in a creative writing workshop she sponsored in 2017. The workshop compelled me to be even more creative in how I write from an autocritographical perspective. As creative performance artists, directors, and acting teachers, the activist viewpoints that Fanni Green and Dora Arreola represent in their essays provide indisputable evidence for the liberatory power of womanist alliance-building.

Together, the contributors in this collection cultivate lines of womanist thinking that thrive as the narrative and thematic heart of their work. Like so many of the scholarly paths I have taken over the years, editing this book called me to a deeper place of inner soulful reflection. I have learned from Walker and this book's contributors that to be womanist-identified, *love* would have to be an integral tool in what I profess to be and represent. "The womanist idea," as it relates to the life-transforming power of love, sets into play some very life-changing lessons about emancipatory ways of listening, seeing, and being with each other as human beings. Living in a culture of "white supremacist capitalist patriarchy," as bell hooks has rightly identified it, I have needed to challenge myself continuously to embrace the idea of *loving* as a political act.

Laboring in a Soul-Full Garden

Breaking Silence: Communing in Womanist "Folk" Work

In the Foreword to the first edition of *This Bridge Called My Back*, Toni Cade Bambara speaks to the unifying force that "break[ing] the silence" enacts against the wounding effects of oppression and "the diabolically erected barriers" that it creates.[3] She claims that our "listening to each other and learning each other's ways of seeing and being" begins the process of inner and outer healing. As the writers in this book attest, there remains much labor to be accomplished in our efforts to tear down walls of separation. From sun up to sun down, we are committed to tilling the ideological soil of this earthly plain to create a garden for soul-full transformation. Laboring together in the "Spirit" of love toward "building womanist coalitions," we have planted liberatory seeds of activist consciousness ultimately to produce a harvest of enriched principles of human rights. As the title of her essay, Fanni Green declares, "Now Is Not the Time for Silence." Speaking out against border-building acts of domination (literal and ideological) is precisely what I asked the writers to do in this book—especially for those among us not only experiencing life on the border of heteronormativity but also having to struggle continuously against homophobia. As a core of activists in womanist solidarity, we write—across genres and traditional disciplinary boundaries—and we break silence to open up new ground, determined not be silent. We dig to germinate hope in a plain injustice rooted in systemic oppression. Once again, imaginatively, I envision the contributors planting gardens of womanist coalitions laboring to sow seeds of radical self-transformation. Shovels in hand, we have determined to cultivate innovative ground together listening to each other sharing heartfelt stories of survival.

I am married to a black woman of Caribbean ancestry who possesses a passion and love for gardening. Among all the different kinds of plants (flowers, vegetables, herbs, and fruit-bearing ones), she has a sign situated that says, "Gardening is good for the Soul." In assisting her in varying ways to care for these plants, I work hard in sacrificing my time, strength, and energy to assist in their fruition. When I look out at the beautiful flowers her labor has produced, I behold the natural beauty and life-sustaining power her gardening skills have produced. It is, indeed, the same feeling I experience when reflecting upon the intensity of the joy a womanist owns as she voices *all* her "loves." Loving all that we personify in the garden of human being is precisely what this body of writings is *all* about.

Furthermore, I believe it is the Spirit of love that led us to a deeper comprehension of Walker's metaphoric garden of colorful related human beings: We "are . . . brown, pink, and yellow, and our cousins are white, beige, and black. . . . [Y]ou know the colored race is just like a flower garden, with every color flower represented." The skin color variations of the contributors in this book also epitomize our cultural differences. As world-citizens, we characterize the essence of a global community—South Asian, African

(American), Middle-Eastern, Canadian, Caribbean, Latina/Chicana, as well as European. In the womanist idea of "the colored race," no skin color is superior to another. Atika Chaudhary (a woman of Pakistani decent) calls into question a politics of skin color conceptualized in the myth of white supremacy in her essay, "A Deeper Shade of Consciousness: My Voice Is My Resistance." Chaudhary boldly claims herself as a "woman of color and a feminist/womanist." All folk identifying with her inclusive skin-color politics of womanism are set free from the racist myth of white supremacy. As members of "the colored race," we are one family in the human race.

On a fertile plain of social, political, *and* spiritual inclusion—owning our family membership—we have tilled the ideological soil of humanity as the groundwork for visionary coalitional possibility. Enlarging the interpretive landscape in which to view ourselves, we have produced a flower garden of human hope-fullness for liberatory global transformation. From this metaphoric perspective, the labor the contributors have offered in the production of this "work"-book has not been in vain. It will act as a guiding standpoint for all individuals "committed to survival and wholeness of entire people, male *and* female" to cultivate a level of unfestered critical consciousness. On this ground, they receive the tools to grasp a firm hold on the principles of womanism to weed out the infertility of silence.

Speaking in An("Other") Language

Womanism as a Radical Means of Survival

These days, language promoting "multiculturalism" and "global diversity" employed by state-supported institutions of higher learning *sound* progressively marketable. Certainly, as a recruitment strategy for attracting students and faculty of color—across differences of culture, sexuality, and religion—"inclusion" resonates with definitional openness. Yet, for many black/folk of color in the United States, who have experienced institutionalized ways that white privilege masks itself in terms of *political correctness*, it denotes a form of liberalistic "window-dressing. In a culture of white supremacy—where the current president of this nation believes that even white supremacists should be validated and affirmed as good people—black/people of color in (and outside the United States) are stigmatized as the "the other." Alice Walker not only personifies the wording of womanism in artistic ways that passionately enable black/women of color feminism to be themselves, she articulates a language of "love" exemplifying the heartfelt reality of an all-"Folk" inclusivity. Thus, Walker calls into question liberalist *marketability* of gender, racial, cultural, and sexual diversity. In pro-womanist, discursive communion with the contributors toward the production of this text, I found the language I needed to express my hope *and* faith in the Spirit of love. Symbolically, in the words of Toni Cade Bambara, "we [sat] down with trust and [broke] bread together." In the rigor of our listening, hearing, and becoming more perceptive to the complexity of our differences, we moved to a deeper place of human compassion for each other.

I link the writings of the contributors to this collection in three sections illustrating the inclusive politics of womanism. Part I, "Teaching in the "Universal[ist]" Spirit of Womanism," is composed of essays that address the transformative implications Walker's vision of global *oneness* is in the context of the college classroom. The writers of these essays address the liberatory agency linked to teaching literature by authors—across territorial and ideological borders. In her essay, "Spirituality in the Classroom: Some Womanist Reflections," Layli Maparyan writes about her experiences with spirituality in the classroom. For most of Maparyan's life, the classroom has not been a hospitable place for the expression of spirituality or even for the serious consideration of spirituality. She notes that it would be true until she completed her second book about womanism, *The Womanist Idea*, at the end of 2010. It was at that point that she decided to bring spirituality into the classroom—and into all of her academic, scholarly, intellectual, and political work—whether people liked it or not.

In "Coming into Being: Metta to Womanist Teachers," Kendra Nicole Bryant bears witness to the life-changing effects of the self-liberating theory and practice of women of color feminism. Honoring four womanist professors with whom she studied while a doctoral student, she writes in an epistolary format. In this way, Bryant narrates her experiences in each of these women's classrooms. Clearly, as she professes from a deeply heartfelt location, these "professors" of womanism made a life-changing impression on her. In line with Bryant's confessional mode of thought, in "Professing the Liberatory Power of Womanism," I discuss what it means for me as a *black* man to teach in a women's studies department at a university in the South. I maintain that for me personally, politically, *and* pedagogically, teaching "writings by radical [black] women of color" has been lifesaving both in *and* outside academia. Also in the confessional mode, as referenced in earlier writing, Ylce Irizarry, in her essay, "A Doctored Voice: Resistance, Reading, and Righting as Womanist Pedagogy," maps the evolution of her consciousness as a Latina professor of literary studies. She discourses about the politics of her ethnic identity and its relation to what and how she teaches. More concisely, Irizarry notes that she employs her voice to right wrongs: wrong information, wrong assumptions, and wrong conclusions about racism, sexism, and homophobia. Recalling her struggle to speak publicly about the complexity of color politics in her personal life, Irizarry notes that, like Cherríe Moraga, she has chosen to reflect publicly about her painful and joyous process of coming to voice.

Part II, "Womanist Alliances for Human Rights and Social Justice," not only underscores Walker's idea of self-recovery as a fundamental element in defining the womanist but also complements the notion of critical consciousness as a crucial aspect of self-liberation. M. Jacqui Alexander and Beverly Guy-Sheftall—having obtained a grant from the Arcus Foundation—conceptualized a radical project to advance the equality of black GLBT students. They titled the project "Facilitating Campus Climates of Pluralism, Inclusivity, and Progressive Change at HBCUs." Writing about their vision of it in "Breaking Silence," Alexander and Guy-Sheftall share the historically groundbreaking plan for the work they began together in 2006 to challenge historical black colleges and universities (HBCUs) in the United States to eradicate heteronormative and homophobic ideas of black identity. As an introduction to the aim and goals they sought to accomplish, these two esteemed black feminist scholars in women's studies connect their project to Walker's womanist concept of love for all LGBT black "Folk."

Both Alexander and Guy-Sheftall have made a deep impression on my evolution in the field of feminist/womanist studies. My long-standing comradeship with Jacqui began when we taught at the New School University years ago, as she recounts in her book *Pedagogies of Crossing*, I know well her commitment to social and political justice globally. Having organized a conference honoring the legacy of feminist women of color writers (during her time as chair of women's studies at Connecticut College), Jacqui introduced me to the radical writings in *This Bridge Called My Back*. My relationship with Beverly has been personally revolutionary. In her labor as the founding director of the Women's Research and Resource Center at Spelman College, she would make a transformative contribution to my evolution as a pro-feminist black. When she and Rudolph P. Byrd invited me to be a contributor to their edited volume, *Traps: African American Men on Gender and Sexuality*, published in 2001, I knew the Spirit had led me to a home where my commitment to womanism would take scholarly root. I titled my essay "'When and Where [We] Enter': In Search of a Feminist Forefather—Reclaiming the Womanist Legacy of W. E. B. Du Bois." It would be the foundation for my book *Womanist Forefathers: Frederick Douglass and W. E. B. Du Bois*. When Jacqui and Beverly asked me to write an essay in support of their project's goal as funded by the Arcus Foundation, I received their invitation as yet another *loving* affirmation of my having entered a personal, political, and spiritual space of "universal[ism]." In this space of radical inclusivity, I, too, could imagine myself as a womanist.

Following the inclusive vision of camaraderie conceptualized by Alexander and Guy-Sheftall, Susie Hoeller in her essay, "From Exile to Healing: I 'Too' Am a Womanist," writes about her identity as a Canadian-born white woman. In this essay, she documents her path as an immigrant-exile coming to voice about the liberatory power of womanism. Recalling her journey growing up in a lower working-class family in Canada, she writes about the disempowering effects of ruling-class nationality. Interrogating its separatist-based ideology, rather than allowing it to lead her to a place of outer bitterness, she discovered critical, self-transformative ways to deconstruct it personally, socially, and spiritually. Claiming the womanist idea of inner healing, Hoeller embraces Alice Walker's definition of a womanist, especially related to her "not [being] a separatist . . . [but] [t]raditionally universalist"—open to all humanity. As in the writings by Hoeller, Alexander, and Guy-Sheftall, the two essays that follow theirs, authored by Corrigan and Chaudhary address each writer's academic labor as graduate students in black/women of color literary studies.

Having referenced Corrigan and Chaudhary earlier, I underscore their reinforcement for the self-empowering dynamics of border-crossing for building womanist coalitions. Thematically linked, their essays exemplify thought-provoking strategies for liberatory pedagogical strategies that contest hegemonic marginalization of "otherness." In "Nepantlera as Midwife of Empathy," Corrigan contends that feminist women of color reveal the inspirited, loving value of what it means to be a *nepantlera*, a "midwife of empathy." As a pro-feminist–identified, white male professor, he positions Gloria Anzaldúa's conceptualization of nepantlera at the center of his discussion of empathy shown in *This Bridge Called My Back* and anthologies it has inspired such as *This Bridge We Call Home*. Acknowledging the personal life-changing dynamics of studying writings by blacks/women of color, in "A Deeper Shade of Consciousness: My Voice Is My Resistance," Chaudhary writes about having come to consciousness as a woman of "color." In the [r] evolution of her identity politics, she boldly articulates her "start [toward] identifying as 'woman of color' and a budding feminist." Radically, loving herself as a woman of color remains central to Chaudhary's struggle for voice and visibility. Coming to accept oneself as a person of color personified in color-"filled" words of self-declaration is a bold act of emancipation.

In Part III, "Speaking and Acting Out in Womanist Solidarity," activist educators, performers, and poets create integral connections between gender, sexual, and cultural/territorial differences. In their writings, they act out Alice Walker's opening definition of the womanist: "From *womanish* . . . [u]sually referring to outrageous, audacious, courageous or *willful* behavior. Wanting to know more and in greater depth than is considered 'good' for one . . . Responsible. In charge. *Serious*." As *women*—"Acting grown up. Being grown up"—they write about their activist calling from a standpoint representing uncompromised self-actualization. They lay "*Serious*" groundwork for building womanist coalitions in support of human rights and social justice for all people—in and outside the borders of the United States. In this way, as Gloria Anzaldúa declared in *This Bridge Called My Back* (2nd edition): "our struggles [are neither] separate nor autonomous but that we—white black straight queer female male—are connected and interdependent."[4]

Validating the practice of art for the empowerment of female identity contesting borders of gender and sexual identities, in "Transgenero Performance: Gender and Transformation in *Mujeres en Ritual*," Dora Arreola describes the collaborative process of Mujeres en Ritual Danza-Teatro, a cross-border, all-women dance-theatre company, which she founded in 1999 in Tijuana, México. Rooted in ritual and contemporary techniques of physical theatre, the work of Mujeres en Ritual explores the limits of gender, taboo sexuality, and culture in the border region. It examines the exploitation of women's bodies as an extension of U.S.-México relations and political economy. Through a community-based process with women on both sides of the border, the company experiments with gender transgression and transformation to arrive at *transgenero* ("transgender" and "trans-genre") performance. Further demonstrating the artistic, living power of empathetic imagining, "Soy Mujer Cuando . . . A Collective Poem" by Andrea Assaf is a poetic excerpt from the theatre work, *Fronteras Desviadas/Deviant Borders*. Bilingual in conception, Assaf wrote the poem in collaboration with Dora Arreola and Mujeres en Ritual Danza-Teatro. Created through a community-based process with women on both sides of the U.S.-Mexico border in 2005, conceptually, "Soy Mujer Cuando" comprises three parts as a recurrent thread through the larger work. The first two parts incorporate the multiple voices of women from the community and the ensemble of collaborating artists. Assaf and Arreola worked together to write the poem's final section.

In line with the transgressive, territorial politics of border-defiance Assaf and Arreola express in their creative connection together, Fanni Green reveals the personal, political, and performative implications of her most recent work as a womanist playwright, director, and acting professor. In "Now Is Not the Time for Silence: Writing and Directing *What the Heart Remembers*," Green writes about the conceptual process of the "choreo-poem" and her journey toward its production. As an artistic-activist educator, Green utilizes the play's thematic focus as her personal response to the gender politics of genocide and ongoing civil war between North and South Sudan, in Africa. She not only reflects upon her position as a black/woman of color, she also addresses the politics of race and gender border crossing involved in the play's production related to her collaboration with Jeanne Travis, a white female dance colleague and choreographer for the play. In 2012, Green and Travis premiered *What the Heart Remembers* in Scotland at the Edinburgh International Theatre Festival.

Erica Sutherlin's poem "I Come from a Dream Deferred" speaks unapologetically about the complex identity politics related to the herstory of "Third World" women in the United States. While the poem's theme resonates within the twists and turns of strategic movement for survival—not only in body but in mind and spirit as well—it lines up with the thematic concept of Fanni Green's *What the Heart Remembers.* Considering the genocidal (mis)treatment of the women (and children) in Darfur that Green exposes in her play, it is insightfully clear that the territorial background that Sutherlin's narrator finds herself tied down to is filled with a politics of race, gender, class, and sexual identities violated by institutionalized and systemic power dynamics perpetuating a politics of inhumanity toward the "Other"—especially connected to the subjugation of the *feminine.*

However, as Sutherlin concludes in the last line of her poem—in solidarity with the voice of Teresa and those women who Green represents in her play contesting female oppression—there is hope in the voice of the female speaking and acting out on her own behalf. "I Come from a Dream Deferred" ends with the line: "I come from the soul the source the spirit the one the god that is and gave birth to the feminine." In this one line, the narrator clearly comprehends what enabled her to survive that which she was not meant on earth to survive. According to her, it's a "soul" matter determined by "the source [known as] the spirit," the only "one, the god who possessed the power to [give] birth to the feminine." I suggest that the life-giver of the feminine that the narrator references here is the same inspirited one that Alice Walker references. As Sutherlin's poetic narrator honors the soul-source from which she emerged—birthed as a woman of color (from multiple cultural backgrounds)—so the womanist voices the same feelings of self-endearment.

In stories of black female survival against multiple forms of oppression and domestic violence, Rudolph P. Byrd and M. Thandabantu Iverson write about how womanist thinking possesses the power to enable *all* men to recover from the trauma of childhood domestic violence. Byrd's essay is groundbreaking. It stands as a testament to his legacy as a pro-feminist–identified black man. For men like Byrd and Iverson to be willing to share personal stories of childhood experiences of domestic violence in which they stood against paternal abuse is a radical gesture of self-transformation. In "On Becoming a Feminist," Byrd writes about his childhood experience of domestic violence and the impact his mother's life experiences would have upon him. He recalls one particular moment while witnessing his mother being physically abused by his father. Taking a bold stand of resistance, Byrd remembers that as an eleven-year-old boy "from that day to the last day of his [father's] life . . . [he] would be at war with [him]." Yet, as the son of an abusive parent, Byrd states that this event would mark the beginning of his "commitment to feminism," a stand against domestic violence. His mother became the first model of feminist identity in how she viewed herself, her independence, and ways she maintained her family's home. In sum, she taught him how to be a feminist. Additionally, as a college student, Byrd would come to read writings by noted pro-feminist female and male authors of varying races. Particularly, he would be influenced by the lives and works of Alice Walker, as well as Beverly Guy-Sheftall and bell hooks. Byrd identifies himself, as I do, as "a spiritual descendent of Frederick Douglass."

In "Compelled by the Spirit: My Journey to Become a Womanist Man," Iverson writes about his personal journey toward feminist *and* womanist manhood. Revisiting relationships with family members, he records his experience of "patriarchal masculinity and heterosexist battering abuse." He attributes his pro-feminist/womanist identity to his mother and what she taught him about her life as a black woman. Iverson states that she would be the first woman to introduce him to the meaning of feminism. As he continues his narrative toward self-transformation, he shares how his college education and his work as a professor and activist in Labor Studies would transport him to a deeper understanding of his mother's life and that of other black/women of color. He calls them his "other mothers and soul sisters." Ultimately, Iverson aims to "challenge males of all ages and (of all races and ethnicities) to open themselves up to the self-transforming power of feminism *and* womanism." Clearly, his purpose in reaching out to all men and boys is rooted in the Spirit of womanist love. In *The Will to Change*, hooks further talks about the invaluable place of love in male liberatory progression toward comradeship with women:

> As long as men dominate women, we cannot have love between us. That love and domination can coexist is one of the most powerful lies patriarchy tells us all. Most men and women continue to believe it, but in truth, love transforms domination. When men do the work of creating selves outside the patriarchal box, they create the emotional awareness needed for them to learn to love. Feminism makes it possible for women and men to know love. . . . The soul of feminist politics is the commitment to ending patriarchal domination of women and men, girls and boys.[5]

Standing in resistance to masculinist and misogynistic ideas of manhood, we show the "work [men need to do toward] creating [our]selves outside the patriarchal box" to begin to love ourselves and the womanist within us. As I have written in *Black Male Outsider* and in this introduction to this book, many men who are childhood survivors of domestic violence perpetrated by their fathers have weathered the storm of its physical, emotional, and psychological damage. Coming to accept "the soul of feminist politics [as] the commitment to ending patriarchal domination of women and men, girls and boys," we possess the power to build womanist coalitions for human rights and social justice for *all* people—across borders of difference.

In the Image of Zora Neale Hurston

Like a "Bag of Miscellany"—in Florida

Building Womanist Coalitions did not begin with a "call for papers." Rather, it started when I made personal calls to persons whom I had come to know a decade ago, when I began teaching at a large public university in Florida. It exists in a city less than an hour's drive from where esteemed writer and activist Zora Neale Hurston was born. Having been trained academically as an anthropologist, in her travels studying the folklore of blacks, in and outside the United States, she would creatively write her findings into fiction. Having taught her fictional *and* nonfictional writings in the college classroom for more than two decades, I have witnessed the healing effects of womanist regionality as Hurston conceived it. Interestingly, the majority of the contributors to this book are, on some level, regionally connected to Florida. In the inspirational enlightenment of Alice Walker's idea of a womanist, my visionary sense of her spirit rests at the thematic core of this volume. Furthermore, I believe that for Walker, Zora symbolizes the womanist Spirit of love. When Walker goes in "search" of Hurston, she writes in "Looking for Zora": "On August 15, 1973, I wake up just as the plane is lowering over Sanford, Florida, which means I am also looking down on Eatonville, Zora Neale Hurston's birthplace. . . . From the air Florida looks completely flat. . . . This is the first time I have seen the interior of the state, which Zora wrote about so well.[6]

As long as I have taught writings by Walker, I have positioned Hurston as a model of womanism in my courses on "writings by radical women of color." In her groundbreaking essay, "How It Feels to Be Colored Me," I believe the image Zora creates of herself—as not "tragically colored"—is radically self-liberatory. She boldly states: "There is no great sorrow damned up in my soul. . . . I have seen that the world is to the strong *regardless* of a little pigmentation more or less. No, I do not weep at the world—I am too busy sharpening my oyster knife (emphasis added)."[7] Like the womanist, Hurston loves who she is in all of her life experiences.

It is the creative description of how she feels about herself that reminds me of the inclusive principles a womanist embodies. Hurston says, "I feel like a brown bag of miscellany propped against a wall. Against a wall in company with other bags, white, red and yellow. Pour out the contents, and there is discovered a jumble of small things priceless and worthless. . . . [B]efore you is the jumble [they hold]. . . . Perhaps that is how the Great Stuffer of Bags filled [it] in the first place who knows?"[8] Personally, I do know that "the Great Stuffer of Bags" loaded *Building Womanist Coalitions* with writings by folks courageously willing to cross borders to create *new* bridges for visionary alliances. Thus, our contributions to this activist project symbolically represent colorful "bags of miscellany." Many of the writers in this collection I first came to know as professors, artists, and students in Florida. Together in the creation of this book, they deepened my faith in the Spirit of love for human rights and social justice for all people—"*Regardless*." I close this introduction in my own poetic rendering of our inspirited coalitional labor:

"IN THE NAME OF A WOMANIST"

In the Spirit of love,
we must *re*-possess—
our power to plant new seeds
to nurture them and grow a new vision of liberation,
living as survivors—together always struggling to see,
in the Spirit of love,
our vulnerability when we know we must be

(for the greater good),
sweet for no reason but to give joy,
in the Spirit of love,
soft as in pliable
(meaning that who we are as human beings)
does not reside in power to oppress,
but to lift up,
in the Spirit of love,
to call and respond with our hearts,
to give what we have of ourselves
(our time, labor, comradeship
in the time of creative need),
in the Spirit of love
to be always becoming
without fear of what we will
be—
envisioning new bridge-work,
for naming our deepest desires
(without harm to another),
to feel ourselves free in the embrace
of the arms of another—
in the Spirit of love,
receiving the fullness of life and living,
once and for all—to be whole again!
In terms we have called into being for ourselves.
This will be the moment of our great revolution!
In the Spirit of love.
Let us prepare to begin again.
Let us hear the voices of the womanist warriors,
for they call us to serve the people with them—
(without regard to the level of the task).
"Come, come, come," ever so gently they beckon us.
"Stand beside us—serve the people."
"Stand beside us, like this—arm in arm"
(ever so gentle they guide us).
"We will show you how"—
(and we will trust them fearlessly).
Let us prepare to serve the people
with the womanist warriors,

in the Spirit of love;
the people await our hands.
They are hungry for love—"*Regardless*"

Notes

1. Alice Walker, *In Search of Our Mothers' Gardens: Womanist Prose* (New York: Harcourt Brace Jovanovich, 1983), 4.

2. Gary L. Lemons, *Black Male Outsider, a Memoir: Teaching as a Pro-Feminist Man,* (Albany: State University of New York Press, 2008), 1–2.

3. Toni Cade Bambara, Foreword, Cherríe Moraga and Gloria Anzaldúa, eds. *This Bridge Called My Back: Writings by Radical Women of Color*, 2nd Edition (New York: Kitchen Table: Women of Color Press, 1983), vi.

4. Gloria Anzaldúa, "Foreword to the Second Edition," *This Bridge Called My Back.*

5. bell hooks, *The Will to Change: Men, Masculinity, and Love* (New York: Atria Books, 2004), 123.

6. Walker, *In Search of Our Mothers' Gardens*, 94.

7. Zora Neale Hurston, "How It Feels to Be Colored Me," in *The Norton Anthology of African American Literature*, eds. Henry Louis Gates Jr. and Nellie Y. McKay (New York: W. W. Norton and Company, Inc., 2004), 1031.

8. Ibid., 1032–1033.

PART I

Teaching in the "Universal[ist]" Spirit of Womanism

1

Spirituality in the Classroom

Some Womanist Reflections

LAYLI MAPARYAN

I want to write about my experiences with spirituality in the classroom. For most of my life, the classroom has not been a hospitable place for the expression of spirituality, or even for the serious consideration of spirituality. This was true when I was growing up as a Baha'í kid in the Deep South in the 1970s and '80s, it was true when I was in graduate school in psychology in Pennsylvania in the late 1980s and early 1990s, and it was true from the time I became a professor (first in psychology and African American Studies, later women's studies and African American studies, both times in Georgia) in the mid-1990s and beyond. In fact, it was true until I finished my second book about womanism, *The Womanist Idea*, at the very end of 2010.[1] That was when I decided that I was going to bring spirituality into the classroom—and into all of my academic, scholarly, intellectual, and political work—whether people liked it or not.

I have always been a deeply spiritual person—sometimes also deeply religious, but not always—and one of the first things I learned as a schoolchild was that I needed to hide that. Not that I always did. But being spiritual in the classroom was never without consequences: being ridiculed, being viewed as anti-intellectual or intellectually inferior, being silenced, being sidelined, being ignored. The message was only reinforced when I became the professor: *Don't express (or expose) your personal beliefs in the classroom. If you can't measure it, then it's not scientific, and thus outside the realm of what we do. Religion is the opiate of the masses, the biggest cause of the oppression of women, a former justification for slavery—bad, bad, bad.* And on and on. Not only was spirituality always equated with religion in these conversations (and, generally, the worst possible version of religion), but all the messages about spirituality were also negative. I was caught between a rock and a hard place, which eventually led to a constant double consciousness and a feeling that I was leading a double life. These feelings meant that I could not "be all of who I was in one place."[2]

There were some interesting exceptions—college, for example. My alma mater, Spelman College, a prominent historically black college (HBCU) for women, is a place where religiosity has always run strong. Spelman's motto is "Our Whole School for Christ." When I entered as a deeply religious Baha'í youth in the fall of 1982, I was happy with this "official" orientation toward the Divine (especially since Baha'ís accept and uphold all of the world's major religions, including Christianity), but I was plagued by the awkwardness of being the only Baha'í in a school full of Christians who did not share my enthusiasm for other religions. The fact that we often prayed at school functions and that prayer even cropped up in the classroom on occasion actually made me feel comfortable. I also felt very comfortable at this school because it was very affirming of Black heritage and culture—something I never experienced at any other school to such a degree. It was there that I "discovered" my "Afrikanity," Black intellectualism, and Black spirituality per se. These were important formative and inoculating experiences for me. So, I do not rate my time at Spelman as a time of discomfort with spirituality in the classroom, but rather as a time of comfort, even though I know there were others who did not share my sense of comfort about Spelman's religiosity.

I left Spelman for the Great Northeast, the supposed mecca of intellectualism, and a place where the culture was decidedly not overtly expressive in terms of spirituality or religion. I found it hard to find my bearings there, although my ongoing involvement in Baha'í activities certainly provided my life with a thread of continuity for a while. Over time, though, my own religiosity declined and I became more involved in political movements and identities—Afrocentrism, Black feminism, Hip Hop, ACT-UP and Queer Nation, anti-neoliberalism, the green movement—pretty much anything transgressive, counter-establishment, or Afri-cultural. This was my 1990s. For the first half, I was in the classroom as a student or student-teacher in the Northeast; for the second half, I was in the classroom as a professor, back in the South. Somewhere in there—I think it was 1993—I spent a year as an intentional agnostic. But, for the rest of the time, with or without any religiosity, I was a deeply spiritual person, a deep believer in God, an explorer of the spiritual realms, and someone always in awe of the magnificence of the Cosmos. During this period, I did not push the envelope on spirituality in the classroom; rather, it pushed me.

A second exception, that is, a place where I did not experience dissonance with regard to talking about spirituality in the classroom, was while teaching African American Studies or Africana Studies courses. Generally speaking, when the subject matter was "Black" or the vast majority of the students in the class were of African descent, I felt quite comfortable making references to spirituality and discussing spiritual topics, because they felt endemic to African American and African culture. My students tended to respond with naturalness when these topics were raised, and we had great breadth in terms of being able to talk about traditional doctrinal religions (Christianity, Islam), nontraditional doctrinal religions (Rastafarianism, the Hebrew Israelites, and so forth), African-based religions (Ifa, Yoruba, Voudoun, Santería, Candomblé, and so forth), and metaphysical wisdom traditions (MDW NTR, Dogon, and so forth). The Black Studies classroom felt like a safe space to me with regard to spirituality and its expressions, both personal and academic.

My first exposure to womanism was somewhere between 1990 and 1993. A friend of mine who had majored in women's studies suggested that I take a look at some Black feminist writings. I headed straight to the public library and checked out *Home Girls: A Black Feminist Anthology*, where I encountered Alice Walker's rudimentary, pre–*In Search of Our Mothers' Gardens* definition of womanism, in Barbara Smith's introduction to the volume. It reads:

> WOMANIST: (According to Walker) From womanish (Opp. Of "girlish," i.e. frivolous, irresponsible, not serious.) A black feminist or feminist of color. From the colloquial expression of mothers to daughters, "You're acting womanish," i.e., like a woman. Usually referring to outrageous, audacious, courageous or *willful* behavior. Wanting to know more and in greater depth than is considered "good" for one. Interested in grown-up doings. Acting grown up. Being grown-up. Interchangeable with other colloquial expression: "You're trying to be grown." Responsible. In charge. Serious . . .
>
> 2. Also: Herstorically capable, as in "Mama, I'm walking to Canada and I'm taking you and a bunch of other slaves with me." Reply: "It wouldn't be the first time."[3]

It stuck with me, and on a subsequent trip home to Florida, I pulled *In Search of Our Mothers' Gardens*[4] from my own mother's bookshelf, where she had placed it as one of her Book-of-the-Month Club selections. I took it back North and added it to a collection that now included *All the Women Are White, All the Blacks Are Men, but Some of Us Are Brave: Black Women's Studies*,[5] *Sister Outsider*,[6] and *ZAMI: A New Spelling of My Name*[7]—books that felt (and still feel) like bibles to me. I quietly noted the spiritual texture of womanism and parked that awareness in the part of my brain (or was it my soul?) that was still trying to get my spiritual bearings, post–political awakening, and in the (literally and figuratively) cold Northeast. When I arrived at my first job down in Georgia, I decided to "follow up on that womanist thing," and I launched a womanist "newsletter" with my colleague Barbara McCaskill in 1994. This became *The Womanist: A Newsletter for Afrocentric Feminists* and later *Womanist Theory and Research*. It was because womanism seemed a kind of sacred vessel in which my metamorphosing spirituality could grow and expand that I think I embraced it so passionately from that point forward. It was an intellectually suitable "holder" for my submerged spirituality—in the classroom and in my academic work—and it was a place where I could work out the growing merger between my spirituality and my politics.

Like two vines growing around and around each other, my work in womanism and my spiritual development grew and expanded in relationship. Explorations of African spirituality as well as indigenous spiritual traditions from around the world commenced, adding to all that I had learned about the Abrahamic and major Eastern religions through the Baha'í Faith from childhood onward. My interest and expertise in divinatory traditions and practices deepened, providing an entrée into mysticism that spanned many years and many traditions, including a variety of forms of contemplative practice. Eventually, all that I was learning was having too great an impact on me and my understandings of life, the world, and people to keep it out of the classroom and my writing, so I just started bringing it in, without permission, at first tentatively and, eventually, boldly.

Two Stories of Spirituality in the College Classroom

In 2009, I was awarded a Contemplative Practice Fellowship from the Center for Contemplative Mind in Society, an organization that exists to facilitate the development of contemplative pedagogy, primarily on college and university campuses. This award allowed me to visit Plum Village in France, where I lived, worked, and learned among the monks and nuns of the Buddhist Order of Interbeing (Tiep Hien), including cofounders Thich Nhat Hanh and Sister Chan Khong, for a brief but transformative period. In preparation for this visit, I read Chan Khong's memoir, *Learning True Love: Practicing Buddhism in a Time of War*,[8] a moving narrative of spiritual activism that eventually anchored the course I would design under the fellowship, "Womanist Perspectives on Spiritual Activism."

This course was designed to expose students to a variety of types of contemplative practice and the traditions from which they emerge, while also bringing consideration to how various women activists from around the world have used these and other methods in their social and ecological change work. We studied "womanist spiritual activism memoirs" by Chan Khong, Immaculée Ilibagiza, Kiran Bedi, Pregs Govender, and Wangari Maathai, and we tried a different form of contemplative practice at the beginning of each class session, 22 in all. We also watched films, had guest lecturers, and read other supporting texts to get a sense of how the metaphysical and mystical dimensions of life might add a unique dimension to our social movement theorizing and activism.

The students in this class came from multiple religious traditions—North, South, East, and West. Some were atheists and agnostics. Our class was like a microcosm of the world. And, because we were in the Deep South, the room included a couple fundamentalist Christians. Although curious about womanism, they were deeply skeptical about the contemplative practice component of the course, because they associated meditation with "heathen" Eastern religious traditions. They were worried that it might go against their religious proscriptions to participate, and that they might forfeit their place in heaven if they engaged in the practices. This was on the first day of class, and it was a complex moment for so many reasons.

First, I was glad that the students felt that they could share their concerns with me. This was a small victory for spirituality in the classroom. Even in the deeply religious Deep South, it is not always easy to speak so openly about one's faith, particularly in a highly secularized state university context. Second, I was worried that the students' classmates, particularly the nonreligious "radical" students and the students who were adherents of the so-called "heathen" religions, might judge these students negatively because of their concerns. Third, I was worried that the students who espoused Eastern religious traditions or who were already meditators might feel insulted and maligned by the fundamentalist Christian students' characterization of their religions or practices, because this would undermine their experience or expression of spirituality in the classroom. Fourth, I wanted badly for the students to learn that contemplative practice spans religions and traditions, and that even Christianity has its own contemplative practice traditions. I wanted to convince the students to give it time and explore the subject before withdrawing their interest or their participation. Fifth, I wanted to keep us united as a classroom. Having been in highly polarized classroom situations before, where students had formed oppositional "camps" and the mood of the class had deteriorated, leading to bad behavior and even course withdrawals, I definitely wanted to avoid this outcome. And, sixth, I was on display as a womanist teacher when the students expressed their concerns in front of the whole room, so I needed to be able to respond as a womanist. Just how would a womanist respond?

I turned to an example set by Kiran Bedi when she first visited Tihar Jail as the first female Inspector General of Prisons in India—an anecdote relayed in her spiritual activist memoir, *It's Always Possible*.[9] Faced with a group of edgy male prisoners who didn't know what to expect, and a group of billy-club-wielding prison wardens, prepared to strike if any of the men got out of line in the presence of the new Inspector General, she broke the ice with an unexpected question: "Do you pray?" At first the men were stunned; it was so unusual to discuss this topic at the prison, and most likely they felt vulnerable being asked about such a private yet common activity in the presence of those who surveilled them, but then they answered: "Yes." From there, Kiran Bedi said, "Would it be better if we say a prayer together?" and she selected a well-known Hindi prayer song from a popular movie. Everyone prayed, and the rest is history.

In my case, I simply asked the students, "Do you pray?" They responded, expressing obviousness, "Yes, of course." "Do you ever pray silently in your heart?" I asked. Again, "Yes." "Well, then," I said, "you have already participated in Christian contemplative practice." I explained, repeating what I already knew them to understand, that prayer was communication with an invisible realm, a divine realm, the realm of God and/or the Angels, Christ, and so on, and that all other forms of contemplative practice were basically the same thing, adapted for different religions, cultures, and understandings about spirituality. Although they still remained a bit reluctant, I could see an "Aha!" moment come to pass, and from that point forward, they eagerly participated in all of our class's contemplative practices, even though I emphasized from the very beginning that all were voluntary, the purpose was exploratory, and anyone could opt out if they decided to. But I had averted a boycott and created a welcoming space for spirituality in my classroom.

That classroom became an important space wherein students could ask questions they had never dared to ask in a classroom—to me or to their fellow students—about religions with which they were unfamiliar, about beliefs they had always found baffling or troubling, about metaphysical mysteries, and even, at times, the "meaning of life" and the "nature of existence." Everyone stayed friendly and, seemingly, relatively nonjudgmental. I consider it one of the peak teaching experiences of my career. By the end of it, we had experienced what happens when you run toward spirituality, religion, and metaphysics rather than away from them, and what happens when you believe that such encounters and discussions enhance rather than threaten good human relations. Very womanist, in my estimation!

My second story about spirituality in the classroom involves a women's studies graduate capstone course called "New Directions in Women's Studies" that I was teaching concurrently with "Womanist Perspectives on Spiritual Activism." Our topic was our own power to *influence* and *shape* the new directions in women's studies and not just to *note* and *locate* them. There was a particular student who didn't talk much in class and whom the other students viewed as conservative, both because of the part of the country she was from and because of her "conventional" self-presentation in a department where many of the students displayed a "radical" or "transgressive" self-presentation.

One day, I launched a discussion about how, despite the focus identities and intersectionality in women's studies, religious and spiritual identities and belief systems are often left outside of the theorizing and, consequently, verboten in the women's studies classroom. I mentioned how this particular institutionalized invalidation of religion and spirituality—which are, for a large segment of humanity, quite central to their experiences of self, daily life, and the creation of meaning—creates a form of exclusion—intellectual and social—that leaves many people, including many women, and including myself, on the sidelines. I asked the students whether women's studies intended such an exclusion, and what would happen if we allowed religion and spirituality into the women's studies classroom, without automatically bracketing it as "the opiate of the masses" or "the chief historical cause of women's oppression." What if we took religion and spirituality on their own terms?

I could tell that the students did not expect this line of questioning and that they were, in fact, scratching their heads. All except for one: my "conservative" student. She actually spoke up and said that this was the first time she felt her own experience validated in the women's studies classroom, because she was a very religious person in an arguably conservative Christian denomination, even though she cared deeply about women's issues and had entered a women's studies graduate program in order to work on issues related to gender equality and women's empowerment—especially the empowerment of girls. From this point forward, this student participated much more—not only in my class, but in other classes as well. She told me later that being "authorized" to speak about her religious identity and its importance to her was liberating, and helped her make a connection to feminism and other feminists that had previously been lacking. She also appreciated very much that she saw womanism as a perspective that was inclusive of people who are religious or spiritual, and she asked whether white women (of which she was one) could be womanists. I let her know that, while opinions varied, one prominent womanist who happens to be very Afrocentric, namely Clenora Hudson-Weems, had argued that anyone could be womanist as long as they acknowledged their own culture as foundational for their womanism.

Not every student in the class shared my enthusiasm for what religion and spirituality could contribute to feminism and activism. I'll mention two, with very different outcomes. The first was a student who fought me tooth and nail for the first few sessions of class about the relevance, indeed the reality, of spirituality. She wasn't sure that she wanted to continue with the course or that she would be able to take the content seriously. This student argued vigorously for the sufficiency of pure reason and the invalidity of people's "spiritual" experiences and insights. Then, one day, she came to class and reported that she had had a dream in which a luminous figure had come to her and revealed the spiritual dimension to her. This student proclaimed, "Now I know it's real. I can't deny that I had that experience or that I saw what I saw. And I also can no longer deny what other people have seen." She described a feeling that she had had in the dream that she had never experienced at any other time in her life, which had left quite an impression on her. She was surprised that a dream had opened her eyes, but she could not deny that it had radically altered her perspective, creating more openness to thinking about what spirituality might offer our more intellectual or political concerns. From this point forward, the student's skepticism turned more into curiosity.

The second student relates to one of the more disheartening events in my experience during that period of time. He was considered a "star" student in our department. I had thought he was a reasonably engaged student during the course, although it was clear he retained some skepticism about the spiritual and metaphysical content. Yet, a short time later, he failed to mention any significant content from my course in his response to a preliminary exam question that was built to capture learning from my course. Instead, he focused on other more popular theorists and theories in his response, linking his answers to content from my colleagues' courses, but not from mine. Even though I graded the student's response as low for this question due to this deficiency of sources, citations, and arguments, my grade was overridden by my colleagues who did not want to see this student fail. I felt dismissed and invalidated by this response from my colleagues, and while I do not know their full reasons for overriding my grade on this exam, it only cemented a feeling that had already accumulated that I was the "square peg" in my department due to my approach to womanism and my increasing focus on the relevance of spirituality, intellectually and psychologically, to our field of study and our constituency.

It was actually during this period of time that I was working on my manuscript for *The Womanist Idea*, the writing of which was not only highly therapeutic given this state of affairs, but which also empowered me to decisively stop apologizing for my intellectual/spiritual/cultural "difference." I finished the book and left the department shortly after it was published. I also discovered, in the process of teaching and lecturing about the book after it was published, that there were many, many people who had been waiting for such a book—one that acknowledged and embraced spirituality "out loud," that incorporated not only traditional religion(s), but also indigenous spirituality, wisdom traditions, mysticism, and metaphysics, into discourses on gender, sexuality, and activism—and felt liberated by its appearance. "Write it, and they will come" was my feeling. And I had only done what so many had done before me, namely, write the book I had always needed to read, the book that allowed me to speak truthfully about the way spirituality had informed and shaped my intellectual and activist pursuits.

The Foremothers of My Bravery

In the process of my connecting spirituality with critical studies scholarship, activism, and social movements, there were certain foremothers and "friends along the journey" who gave me the inspiration and courage to push through barriers, obstacles, and moments of doubt or discouragement. For example, Gloria Anzaldúa's incredible bravery in connecting the spiritual to the political, her unapologetic acknowledgment of a very lively and heterogeneous invisible realm, her refusal to be boxed in by others' notions of her identity or politics along with her willingness to claim, define, and expand the labels that had been ascribed to her, set an example. Gloria's willingness to discuss everything from the occult and divination to aliens and out-of-body experiences and her contributions of psychospiritual terms like *la facultad*, *coatlicue* state, *nepantla*, and *conocimiento* that simply have no equivalent in English, all contributed materially to my own understandings, language, and ability to communicate what I felt I needed to communicate.[10] From the early "La Prieta"[11] with its "El Mundo Zurdo" to her final "now let us shift . . . the path of conocimiento . . . inner work, public acts," she was a guide star.

AnaLouise Keating, the foremost scholar on Gloria Anzaldúa, was the one who introduced "spiritual activism" into my lexicon when she gave a very memorable talk at my university in 2000. That talk was a turning point in my womanist work and in my intellectual-spiritual self-articulation, inside and outside the classroom. It was also AnaLouise Keating who, with Gloria Anzaldúa, published *Interviews/Entrevistas*, a compilation of the latter's interviews, in which some of her most unorthodox spiritual ideas and experiences are revealed. Although perplexing to many—even those who love Anzaldúa for her contributions Chicana feminist theory, lesbian/queer studies, and border studies—this book has been central to my thinking because Anzaldúa's (and Keating's) spiritual eclecticism is similar to my own. Additionally, AnaLouise's own work on non/post-oppositional politics and "threshold theories" in both *Teaching Transformation: Transcultural Classroom Dialogues*[12] and *Transformation Now! Toward a Post-Oppositional Politics of Change*[13] has both informed and supported my own work on the politics of invitation, spiritual movement, and LUXOCRACY. Both of us have been committed to putting language and possibility around a way of radical social and ecological transformation that need not rely on prevalent oppositional models and logics. Both of us have also been committed to bringing these strategies into the classroom.

Beverly Guy-Sheftall's *Words of Fire: An Anthology of African-American Feminist Thought*, which compiles over 150 years' worth of original source material, offered the moral support of some ancestral figures whose own passionate spirituality and religiosity seamlessly fed their activism for racial and gender equality.[14] Figures like Mariah Stewart, Anna Julia Cooper, and Julia Foote, were foremothers of the womanist train of thought, demonstrating that womanism as spiritualized political and intellectual praxis existed as a way of being in the world long before it was given a name by Alice Walker in 1979. Alice Walker's writing about a 19th century contemporary, Rebecca Jackson, in "Gifts of Power," reinforced this feeling.[15] I could relate to these women, and I could summon them up in my heart and mind when I felt the need for companions.

Alice Walker's life as a spiritually curious person was also inspiring to me. Her engagements with meditation, ecospirituality, and Buddhism have been a text all their own. Her praxis has interwoven spirituality, politics, and art in a way that feels holistic and right. Similarly, Akasha Gloria Hull's spiritual eclecticism, recorded in her breakout text, *Soul Talk: The New Spirituality of African-American Women*,[16] gave voice to a journey that many have chosen to keep quiet and gave validation to my experiences. Her text reassured me that it was not only all right, but it was also timely, to speak out on the subject of Black women's spirituality-politics nexus and its dynamic integration of religious, spiritual, and cultural influences. She showed how she and many other women had, like Anzaldúa and Walker, interwoven insights gained from many sources into a meaningful, intelligible, holistic way of making—and talking about—change. Along these same lines, M. Jacqui Alexander's essay, "Pedagogies of the Sacred: Making the Invisible Tangible," was a watershed for me because of her acknowledgment and validation of the invisible realm and our ability to access it in very specific and palpable ways—even to help our research.[17] Her essay was the most concrete example I had seen in print, and I considered her extremely brave and honest to publish about her experiences with Thisbe/Kitsimba, a historical figure she was researching who came to speak directly to her from the realm of the spiritual. I'd also like to mention theologian Barbara E. Holmes, whose book *Race and the Cosmos* gave me a whole new perspective, linking religion, race, and quantum science.[18] It reminded me that out-of-the box thinking and moving beyond the confines defined by conventional academic discourse is okay.

There are many other people, some far less famous, who have influenced me deeply and supported my ability to bring spirituality into the classroom in a womanist way. Not only have these people supported me, they have supported the many students who have felt supported in my classroom by this invitational, womanist approach to spirituality and pedagogy. All of us are truly, as I once spoke in a dream about womanism, "a neighborhood, with everybody coming together for a common purpose." That purpose is the liberation of students, and, by extension, society, from all of the forces that strive to restrain, obstruct, or deform our humanity and the validity and wealth of our diverse cultures, as well as the recognition of our limitless capabilities and goodness.

Conclusion

Womanism is a spiritualized perspective on human life and social and ecological change. Moving beyond mere social movement, womanism activates spiritual movement, the movement of energy, the transformation of heart, minds, and consciousness. Womanist pedagogy brings this spirit into the classroom. Classroom environments that allow students to acknowledge their full dimensionality, including those aspects related to their spirituality and the spiritually infused nature of all creation, are part of womanist pedagogical praxis. They are part of what many womanist pedagogues have uniquely to offer. Such womanist pedagogy does not overwrite other valuable forms of pedagogy, but it should not be excluded just because the academy decided so many decades or centuries ago that it was not a good idea to talk about religion or spirituality in the classroom, specifically, outside religious studies disciplines. Spirituality is part of what makes humans whole beings and, particularly for those who believe or want to question these things, having opportunities in the classroom for unfettered self-expression is essential to their intellectual, emotional, and political development.

By sharing stories from my own journey, I hope to have opened doors for others that were once closed to me and my students. In this essay, I have discussed my own experiences with spirituality in the classroom as a student and a professor, illuminating how womanism has given me the platform to make spiritual space for myself and others in the face of various forms of spiritual exclusion. By sharing my experiences, I hope to have made it easier for others to blaze along this same path in ways that are empowering to individuals and facilitative of better relations between and among groups, particularly different religious and spiritual groups, as well as between religious/spiritual folk and secular, atheist, and agnostic people. My experience is that it is possible for us to become less divided if we incorporate explicit discussion of religious and spiritual material in the classroom, acknowledging that the world has diverse spiritual and religious cultures and traditions, and insisting that we learn about them and engage them, on their own terms and from our places of criticality. In today's world, we can no longer pretend that the spiritual and religious dimensions of people's lives and politics are unimportant or ignorable. We must engage, connect, and learn, and womanism provides a welcoming platform for doing so.

Notes

1. Layli Maparyan, *The Womanist Idea* (New York: Routledge, 2012).

2. Duchess Harris, "'All of Who I Am in the Same Place': The Combahee River Collective," *Womanist Theory and Research* 2 (1999): 9–20.

3. Barbara Smith, Introduction to *Home Girls: A Black Feminist Anthology*, edited by Barbara Smith (New York: Kitchen Table: Women of Color Press, 1983), xxiv–xxv. Barbara Smith's own reference citation for this definition of womanism (op. cit., liv) reads as follows: "Walker, Alice. *In Search of Our Mothers' Gardens*, (Forthcoming, 1983). Cited from manuscript, n.p." Scholars of womanism will note the differences between this version of Walker's definition of "womanist" and the one that actually appeared in the published version of *In Search of Our Mothers' Gardens*, demonstrating the evolution and expansion of Walker's thought on womanists. Smith's citation

from Walker's prepublication manuscript also hints at the close degree of social and intellectual connection between these two women, both signally important to the unfolding intellectual and social movement by women of colors during the late 1970s, early 1980s, and beyond.

4. Alice Walker, *In Search of Our Mothers' Gardens: Womanist Prose* (New York: Harcourt Brace Jovanovich, 1983).

5. Gloria T. Hull, Patricia Bell Scott, and Barbara Smith, eds., *All the Women Are White, All the Blacks Are Men, but Some of Us Are Brave: Black Women's Studies* (New York: Feminist Press, 1982).

6. Audre Lorde, *Sister Outsider: Essays and Speeches* (Freedom, Calif.: Crossing Press, 1984).

7. Audre Lorde, *ZAMI: A New Spelling of My Name* (Freedom, Calif.: Crossing Press, 1982).

8. Sister Chan Khong, *Learning True Love: Practicing Buddhism in a Time of War* (Berkeley: Parallax Press, 2008).

9. Kiran Bedi, *It's Always Possible: One Woman's Transformation of India's Prison System* (Honesdale, Pa.: Himalayan Institute Press, 1998), 8–10.

10. Gloria E. Anzaldúa, *Borderlands/La Frontera: The New Mestiza, Second Edition* (San Francisco: Aunt Lute Books), 60–61 (for *la facultad*) and 63–64 (for *coatlicue* state). See also AnaLouise Keating, ed., *Interviews/Entrevistas: Gloria E. Anzaldúa* (New York: Routledge, 2000), 225–226 (for *nepantla*); and Gloria E. Anzaldúa, "now let us shift . . . the path of conocimiento . . . inner work, public acts," in Gloria E. Anzaldúa and AnaLouise Keating, eds., *This Bridge We Call Home: Radical Visions for Transformation* (New York: Routledge, 2002), 540–578 (541 for *conocimiento*).

11. Cherríe Moraga and Gloria E. Anzaldúa, eds., *This Bridge Called My Back: Writings by Radical Women of Color* (New York: Kitchen Table: Women of Color Press, 1983). See pp. 208–209 for "El Mundo Zurdo."

12. AnaLouise Keating, *Teaching Transformation: Transcultural Classroom Dialogues* (New York: Palgrave Macmillan, 2007).

13. AnaLouise Keating, *Transformation Now! Toward a Post-Oppositional Politics of Change* (Urbana: University of Illinois Press, 2013).

14. Beverly Guy-Sheftall, ed., *Words of Fire: An Anthology of African-American Feminist Thought* (New York: New Press, 1995).

15. Walker, *In Search of Our Mothers' Gardens*, 71–82.

16. Akasha Gloria Hull, *Soul Talk: The New Spirituality of African American Women* (Rochester, Vt.: Inner Traditions).

17. M. Jacqui Alexander, *Pedagogies of Crossing: Meditations on Feminism, Sexual Politics, Memory, and the Sacred* (Durham: Duke University Press), 287–332.

18. Barbara E. Holmes, *Race and the Cosmos: An Invitation to View the World Differently* (Harrisburg, Pa.: Trinity Press International, 2002).

2

Coming into Being

Metta to Womanist Teachers

KENDRA N. BRYANT

That teachers are so often poorly paid and little appreciated is a crime against humanity.
—Alice Walker

As an African American lesbian graduate student enrolled in a historically white English Department in the predominantly white University of South Florida (USF), Tampa, I met four women of color who first affirmed the necessity of my being in a doctoral program, but most importantly, whose classroom instruction transformed my way of being a Christian, an African American, a woman, a lesbian—a human being. Dr. Shirley Toland-Dix's *20th Century African American Literature*, Dr. Gurleen Grewal's *Toni Morrison* and *Women's Spiritual Memoirs*, Dr. Mozella Mitchell's *Mysticism*, and Dr. Deborah G. Plant's *Spirituality in Africana Cultures* classes were—as Joan Tollifson's subtitle to her *Bare Bones Meditation* states—my "waking up from the story of my life."

Each of these women validated my humanity and made me realize that love is all there is, and that, as Alice Walker notes, "It's just the way to be in the world" (Hull 97). They also helped me to understand the creative genius of one's spirit and the significance of using that genius to sustain Mother Earth. In the Introduction to her 2006 *We Are the Ones We Have Been Waiting For*, Alice Walker says,

> To begin our long journey toward balance as a planet, we have only to study the world and its peoples, to see they are *so like ourselves! To trust that this is so.* That different clothes and religions do not create people who can escape

> from humanity. When we face the people of the world with open hands, and in honesty and fearlessness speak what is in our memories and our hearts, the dots connect themselves. [author's emphasis] (10)

Certainly, we are more alike than we are unalike, and as classroom teachers, it seems that Drs. Toland-Dix, Grewal, Mitchell, and Plant understood that their being stewards of the earth required that they share themselves—"to be the opening, the channel, the site of connection to transpersonal, transcendent, metaphysical ideas and energies"—with their students (Hull 230). Their generosity has encouraged my wholeness, or my holiness.

By way of my teachers' offerings I have come to understand and receive education as a possible place for transformation. Walker says that although the world is facing "the worst of times," we still have libraries, bookstores, and books. "*There are still teachers*," she says [author's emphasis] (Walker, 2006, 10). And so it seems, my classroom spaces have mimicked sanghas; my teachers have been my gurus and their meditative offerings have been suggested contemplative readings that encourage *lectio divina*[1] practice. Undoubtedly, I was receiving a communion in each of those classroom spaces, and those woman teachers were an amazing grace.

While I have not left a stone unturned as it relates to professing my gratitude to those teachers who have assisted me in my transformation, I have just come to realize that each of them initiated our togetherness by way of their literary interests. Parker Palmer claims that "[t]eaching emerges from one's inwardness," which explains the compassion, forgiveness, patience, and love I have developed as a result of my relationships with classroom teachers who embody the aforementioned characteristics (Palmer 2). And so, as Walker suggests in her essay "Metta to Muriel and Other Marvels: A Poet's Experience of Meditation," I am sending *metta*—"loving-kindness"—to each of the four "special" teachers who have done more than teach me the required curriculum "but also how to live and to think and to relate to others with compassion" (2006, 162). It is this loving relationship between student and teacher that I have carried into the classrooms where I teach—with the purpose of reminding my students of their own humanity—and thereby, making more possible the peace the world imagines.

* * *

Womanist 1. From *womanish*. (opp. of "girlish," i.e., frivolous, irresponsible, not serious) A black feminist or feminist of color. From the black folk expression of mothers to female children, "You acting womanish," i.e., like a woman.

Usually referring to outrageous, audacious, courageous or *willful* behavior. Wanting to know more and in greater depth than is considered "good" for one. Interested in grown-up doings. Acting grown up. Being grown up. Interchangeable with another black folk expression: "You trying to be grown." Responsible. In charge. *Serious*. (Walker, 1983, xi)

Dear Dr. Toland-Dix,

You know how you know something, but you don't understand what you know? It's like how Alice Walker explained her experience with meditation to Akasha Gloria Hull. In *Soul Talk: The New Spirituality of African American Women* (2001), Hull asked Walker if meditation made her aware of her connection to other people. Walker replied, "[I]t didn't come first through meditation. That was what I understood *after* I learned meditation" [emphasis mine] (99). Well, after you introduced me to Barbara Christian's "A Race for Theory" (1987), I understood theory in two ways in particular: 1. Black folks been theorizing before the term "theory" was coined, for African Americans had to recreate themselves in order to survive the New World. Their creative genius manifested itself in the African American ethos—how we walk, talk, dress, do church . . . pimp our rides; and 2. Creative writing is just as theoretical as the esoterically formalized academic writing that often keeps people of color out of major discourses. bell hooks leads that particular discussion quite often, particularly in her 1990 "Postmodern Blackness."

I wrote a poem titled "We Be Theorizin" after reading Christian's piece. Dr. Plant liked it so much that she actually included it in her book, "*The Inside Light": New Critical Essays on Zora Neale Hurston* (2010). The poem opens with these lines:

> They thought we was over there
> shuckin and jivin
> when all the while we been theorizin
> How else you think black folks survivin

I used to sit in white classrooms listening to white professors go on about Derrida, Marx, Leo Tolstoy, and Nietzsche and wondered why Phyllis Wheatley, W. E. B. Du Bois, Frederick Douglas, hip hop, and my grandmother never entered the conversation. I've known how theoretical blacks have been since I was a little girl watching *Good Times* and *The Jeffersons*. And Michael Jackson definitely put the "post" in postmodernism. Do you think white folks will ever look at our blackness and see how colorfully brilliant we are?

You know I thought I was the best thing since slice bread when I entered your classroom, right? I was the only black student taking your *African American Literature* course, and I had all the answers—at least my white classmates thought I did. But that "C" I earned on my mid-term paper about Zora Neale Hurston's Janie knocked me down a peg or two. I had never cried about a grade before, but I cried about that one, because I felt like you didn't have my back. I obviously thought that our blackness would automatically be my ticket toward your favor—an ethnocentric attitude that you quickly helped me to dispel.

You asked that I come see you in your office to discuss my paper, despite my ignoring you during the following class meeting by failing to participate in the class discussion. I was so angry with you, and I carried my anger into your office. But you didn't mind my anger, and instead, proceeded to guide me through my theoretical entanglements. You also assured me that that "C" was not a reflection of my personhood and that you were well aware of my intelligence—and *that* was the biggest lesson; that "C" did not define me.

I had lost sight of the practice—of the *doing* student—and got caught up in the judgment. I was ego tripping, and I totally appreciate you for calling me out on it, for you reminded me of how attached the ego can get to judgments and how that attachment can cause both false feelings of entitlement and inferiority.

Thank you, Dr. Toland-Dix, for holding me accountable to myself and for sharing your life with me. I am a better human being because of your being.

Love & Light,
Kendra Nicole

* * *

Womanist 2. A Woman who loves other women, sexually and/or nonsexually. Appreciates and prefers women's culture, women's emotional flexibility (values tears as natural counterbalance of laughter), and women's strength. Sometimes loves individual men, sexually and/or nonsexually. Committed to survival and wholeness of entire people, male and female. Not a separatist, except periodically, for health. Traditionally universalist, as in: "Mama, why are we brown, pink, and yellow, and our cousins are white, beige, and black?" Ans.: "Well, you know the colored race is just like a flower garden, with every color flower represented." Traditionally capable, as in: "Mama, I'm walking to Canada and I'm taking you and a bunch of other slaves with me." Reply: "It wouldn't be the first time." (Walker, 1983, xi)

Dear Dr. Grewal,

Do you remember when I was a student in your *Toni Morrison* class and during a discussion about reparations I emphatically claimed that the Native Americans have already received their 40 acres and a mule via the many casinos that line their reservations? You neither laughed at me nor shunned me for my ignorance—but you thoughtfully and compassionately explained to me and my classmates how hatred and greed could annihilate an entire group of people. Your explanation, which included long moments of silence, brought an awareness regarding people's inhumanity that so few students realize. There were no Native Americans sitting in our classroom, there are none in governmental positions, and none in popular culture. Besides at the margins, where are the Native Americans who shared the land with European visitors because the Natives understood that the land did not belong to them, but they belonged to it? At the end of your unplanned lesson, you named Native American writers, including Sherman Alexie and Leslie Marmon Silko, and when you saw how few of us knew those popular authors, you said that you would consider creating and teaching a course in Native American literature.

And do you remember the next semester when I was a student in your *Women's Spiritual Memoirs* class? You began each class period with five-ten minutes of guided meditation, because you believed—like Mary Rose O'Reilley, Arthur Zajonc, Tobin Hart, and other contemplative educators—that silent spaces create a serenity that makes possible creativity, patience, and present awareness. You also required that each student sit in a circle facing one another, and that after each novel we read, that we write our responses to it and share them with each other out loud. This mindful approach to classroom teaching was my first experience with a contemplative education—which inspired both my dissertation and my own mindful practices both in and outside of the classroom. But in addition to teaching me how to contemplate via mindful exercises, you uncovered a bigotry that I carried with me regarding white people.

We read Dorothy Allison's *Two or Three Things I Know for Sure* (1995), which exposed me to the relationship among racism, classism, and sexism. Prior to reading Allison's text, I was under the grave false impression that only black women had experienced the—isms that Allison shares have been her experiences. I use[d] to believe that America always benefitted white people, and thus, never considered that more than race matters. Even though I had a poster of Malcolm X hanging in my office that quoted him having said, "I believe that there will be a clash between those who want freedom, justice and equality for everyone and those who want to continue the system of exploitation . . . but I don't think it will be based on the color of the skin" (Barnard College, NY, 1965), I apparently didn't understand his message. I was so unaware of how oppressive American capitalism is. African Americans seemed to be the only face of oppression. I know better now.

And then you required that our class read other texts by white women, including Sue Monk Kidd's *Dance of the Dissident Daughter* (1996), which made me aware of the effects of gender bias and uncovered the depth of women's vitality; Mary Rose O'Reilley's *The Barn at the End of the World* (2000), which validated for me the interrelationship of diverse religions; and Annie Dillard's *Pilgrim at Tinker Creek* (1974) which reconnected me—although I went grudgingly—to nature. I am so thankful for your offerings.

Thank you for your compassion for and patience with me and all other beings—human and nonhuman. You reawakened me to my higher self—with the person who is innately compassionate, patient, forgiving, and loving, and you have acquainted me with a contemplative approach to teaching and writing which makes transformation possible.

I wrote the poem below after reading Kidd's piece. Although it is titled after her work, it definitely summates what I have learned from and think of you as a woman teacher who deserves praise.

IN RESPONSE TO SUE MONK KIDD'S *THE DANCE OF THE DISSIDENT DAUGHTER*

And so it is
I give praise to woman
The woman in she
The woman in her
The woman in girl
The grandmother woman
The mother woman
The daughter woman
The refuge
The earth
The peace of mind woman
Woman whose womb is a labyrinth
Her umbilical cord / the thread that threads me home
Her kinky coiled hair
Each strand snaking her wisdom her power / her regeneration
Her breasts hanging and dangling unlike strange fruit
Offering themselves for the edification of those who take her in
She / El Shaddai
She / Holy Spirit
She / Mother God
She / Sophia
And her woman makes me holy ghost
Her woman makes me whole
I am her light
The embodiment of enlightenment

I / her crescent moon
I shine
Goddess of the Dark
Earth, wind, and fire
She is my blessing
And so it is
As'e
That I speak her name
Hoping to define and re-shape reality
She / Maya Angelou
She / Alice Walker
She / Zora Neale Hurston
She / Toni Morrison
Her paradise is in her bosom
And she prefers the hazards of freedom than the safety of cages
And when I look at her, my eyes are watching God
She / Goddess
She / Great Mother
Oshun
Yemaya
Mungu
Mary
Hokhmah
She / Shirley Chisolm
She / Phyllis Wheatley
She / Nefertiti
She / Harriet Tubman
She / Woman
Her back is a turtle's shell
Supporting and balancing the universe
Her lap holds its burdens
And I stand on her shoulders / reaching for her genius
A'se
She / Nina Simone
She / Nikki Giovanni
She / Gwendolyn Brooks
She / bell hooks
She / Assata Shakur
A'se
She / Angela Davis
She / Elaine Brown

She / Queen of Sheba
She / Joan of Arc
A'se
Sacred Feminine
Goddess of Crete
Artemis
Nike
Ariadne
Persephone
Athena
Her buffalo skin is sacred and powerful
Her feminine center / a unicorn uniqueness that centers me
And I stand balanced in her virginity
A'se
She / Coretta Scott King
She / Betty Shabazz
She / Audre Lorde
She / Mahalia Jackson
She / Fannie Lou Hammer
She / Ruth, Naomi, and Esther—caryatids
A'se
She / Rosa Parks
She / Billie Holiday
She / Shug Avery
She / Sojourner Truth
A'se
She / June Jordan
She / Toni Cade
She / Barbara Christian
She / Lucille Clifton
A'se
And like Sappho I speak these truths through my poetry
Because if I don't tell her story, who will?
A'se
So like dust, I rise
Like volcanoes, I erupt
Like a glitzy black sequins shawl wrapped around me in a horizon of stars, I shimmy
My rage is outrageous
And I am a woman on the loose who cannot stay silent
Because silence will not save me

A'se
And I refuse to be a victim
Because she / her / woman / has given me her traveling shoes
And so I dance, I swirl, I sashay
In her femininity
In her divinity
In her womb
And I celebrate her in all of her beauty
Because she is beautiful
Beautiful in her menstruation
Beautiful in her pregnancy
Beautiful in her menopause
And she is one-in-herself
She is Jesus
She is Love
And her heart is a seed planted in the world
Like a tree that's planted by the waters
And because she is not moved
She keeps the movement moving
A'se
She is woman
A'se
And she's got the whole world in her hands
A'se
And so I praise her name
A'se
Because she is worthy to be praised
A'se
A'se
A'se.

Thank you, Dr. Grewal, for sharing yourself with me. I am a better human being because of your being.

Love & Light,
k

* * *

Womanist 3. Loves music. Loves dance. Loves the moon. *Loves* the Spirit. Loves love and food and roundness. Loves struggle. *Loves* the Folk. Loves herself. *Regardless.* (Walker, 1983, xii)

Dear Dr. Mozella Mitchell,

I had not experienced a teacher in my English graduate program who allowed me to express my knowing through my creative works until I encountered you. As a Rhetoric & Composition student in a 21st century that has transcended the ideas of postmodernism so much that the theory is now termed "post-postmodernism," I would have imagined that writing students would be allowed the creative space to defend their own theories and knowings by way of both formal written communications and the creative arts; that they would be encouraged to engage in the *mestiza rhetoric*—a "rich mixture of genres" that allows a writer to find her voice in the multiplicity of artistic voices—that Gloria Anzaldúa proposed in 2004 (Lunsford, 35). Alas, too many academic institutions are still in the business of indirectly extinguishing students' creative genius. Perhaps because of the separation of church and state, more public academies than not are under the false impression that spirituality has little to do with genius. But you know better—and you showed me better by way of Martin Luther King, Mahatma Gandhi, Howard Thurman, Thomas Merton, Hildegard of Bingen, and Saint Teresa of Ávila. You acquainted me with mysticism and helped me to understand the untethered spirit's creative desire to maintain peace, love, patience, and understanding among all beings, despite crisis situations.

Thank you for allowing me to submit a revised rendition of Salvador Dalí's (1954) "The Crucifixion" in order to explicate my understanding of Howard Thurman's philosophies. Thank you for allowing me to write an essay that invited readers to see Michael Jackson as a mystic that he was—despite the *Journal of Popular Culture*'s rejection of my notions; editors there actually thought my ideas absurd. But you didn't. I appreciate your allowing me to explore my response to his passing while under your direction. I also wrote what I think is one of my better poems after reading Beverly J. Lanzetta's *The Other Side of Nothingness: Toward a Theology of Radical Openness* (2001), which was the final text you required me to read:

THE OTHER SIDE OF NOTHINGNESS, WITH REGARDS TO BEVERLY J. LANZETTA

I need to commit suicide.
I need to commit suicide because all that I know is that I know nothing
  at all
and in order to know God I must be in that nothingness.
I must be in that nothingness between here and nowhere
where nothing makes sense and
everything is such as it is, not such as it is
both such as it is and not such as it is

and neither such as it is nor such as it is not.
I need to empty myself of myself and void myself of ego.
Lord have mercy.
I need to commit suicide.

I need to commit suicide because I want to grasp the aspect of divinity that is ungraspable.
I want to touch the hem of Its garment
go to the mountain top
and be the change I want to see in the world.
I need to commit suicide because I want to uphold the perception of a universal letting-be.
I want to release gods and mortals, earth and sky
male and female
Greek and Jew
East and West
weak and strong
healthy and sick
animal and human
young and old
black and white
gay and straight
rich and poor
and invite them to join a symphony wherein the whole created world
world of humanity and divinity
world of body and soul
is united in the praise of God.
Lord have mercy.
I need to commit suicide.

I need to commit suicide because I want to give birth to and liberate my consciousness.
I want to walk over the threshold into unaccessed revelatory experience
and move beyond theology,
breaking through and undoing all theologizing,
freeing my mind from the illusions of this world so that I might find salvation.
I need to commit suicide because I am seeking truth where it is bare and unconcealed.
I am seeking truth that is free from images and signs

truth that can stand by itself
truth without the why
truth that lies in nature and begins with blasphemies.
I am seeking truth that is simply truth.
O Lord have mercy.
I need to commit suicide.

I need to commit suicide because although silence will not protect me
neither will my words,
for speech and linguistic sources can do no justice for the comprehension of God
and although language might affirm the way and celebrate divine fullness and rejoice in the beauty of creation, holding a privilege place, speaking prose and poetry,
it is a language of nothing that is the higher mode of contemplation
the *via negativa*
where God is obscure, hidden, and silent.
I need to commit suicide.
To push myself into *anatta* and *sunyata*;
to go alone to the alone
to be transformed from *yesh* to *ayin*
to crash into an encounter that radicalizes my understanding of life
so that the eye with which I see God is the eye with which God sees me
and I can let God be God
Thy will be done
and I be saved because saving no longer matters.

Lord have mercy.
I need to commit suicide.

Thank you, Dr. Mitchell, for allowing me to submit this poem for my final paper. Your giving me the creative space to accomplish academic tasks that are usually devoid of one's creative voice, was both healing and freeing; it is a testament to good teaching. You essentially enabled me to embody Hildegard who believed that one's creative expression is one's expression of spirit, and is, therefore, all knowing.

Thank you, Dr. Mitchell, for sharing yourself with me. I am a better human being because of your being.

Love & Light,
Kendra N. Bryant

* * *

Womanist 4. Womanist is to feminist as purple is to lavender. (Walker, 1983, xii)

Dear Dr. Deborah Plant,

Do you remember when you invited me to write an essay for your latest Zora Neale Hurston text, and I asked you why you love Hurston so much? You told me that Hurston pointed you toward God. I smiled big—like Celie when Shug Avery kisses her on the lips—because Alice Walker pointed me. Although Walker calls Zora Neale Hurston "a Genius of the South,"[2] Walker is undoubtedly this century's southern genius. As a matter of fact, I think she is very much the "grandmother spirit" she says Mother Earth sends to teach us wisdom. And then I asked you—because I had no idea what to say about Hurston when it seems the critics have already said it all—how do you come up with so many different approaches to writing about Hurston? And you answered my question with a question: "How do so many people find so many different ways to talk about love?" And I smiled big again. Clearly, Dr. Plant, if womanist is to feminist as purple is to lavender, then Walker is to Hurston as *Their Eyes Were Watching God* is to *The Color Purple*.

I have loved you before you realized I was here. I enrolled in your *Africana Spirituality* class because while I watched you in the hallways walking and talking with other students, I wanted to become more familiar with your energy—which I think was the love that you see in Hurston and I in Walker. And I am so thankful that I did, for I understood very little about Africana Spirituality before taking your class, and so understood very little about the genius of African American people whose ethos allowed them to survive slavery. Your discussions about African Americans' spirituality, complemented by Harold Bloom's *Genius: A Mosaic of One Hundred Exemplary Creative Minds* (2003), Akasha Gloria Hull's *Soul Talk: The New Spirituality of African American Women* (2001), Dona Marimba Ani's *Let the Circle Be Unbroken: The Implications of African American Spirituality* (1992), and Jarvis Masters' *Finding Freedom: Writings from Death Row* (1997) affirmed my own creative genius and substantiated my relentless appreciation for black people. Our spirit, says Ani—that creative energy that allowed us to maintain our humanity despite the Europeans' efforts to dehumanize us—is what helped us "get ovuh." *That* is our genius.

Other texts you required me to read such as Malidoma Patrice Somé's *Of Water and the Spirit* (1994) challenged me to consider how my African American traditions are indoctrinated by European ideologies, while Randall Robinson's *Defending the Spirit* (1999) encouraged me by his example to remain humane in the face of inhumane conditions, and Alice Walker's *We Are the Ones We Have Been Waiting For* (2006) dared me to become an active participant in sustaining Mother Earth. After reading and discussing those texts in class, I loved myself and other sentient beings so much more; my heart got wider. I borrow from those texts quite often, especially Walker's, to reawaken me to my spirit.

Dr. Plant, in addition to the community you provided in class, I appreciate your being available to me for an entire year after the semester ended. Coming to sit with you in your office for hours to talk about everything was my absolute pleasure. I used to take notes when I'd visit you in your office, because to me, everything that fell off of your lips was profound—at least to the development of my personhood. I think it no mistake that our paths crossed when they did, for I experienced many sad and lonely days while at USF. However, you reminded me often that I am not separate from the world, and that at the very least, I do not have to feel lonely as long as you were here. You also told me once that the universe will always take care of me and that nothing external of me is greater than me. I feel like my knowing you during my tenure at USF was the universe's taking care of me; you were a friend and a confidant.

I wrote a poem for you while I sat in your living room. You were working on an article about Alice Walker and there was a text lying on the floor about *The Color Purple* being banned from public schools. I sat in your living room reading that text and occasionally staring at everything that created your meditation altar, and I happened upon a poem:

FOR DEBORAH PLANT, WITH REGARDS TO ALICE WALKER

She is sitting cross-legged on an oversized pillow that faces an alabaster
  stoned Buddha.
It surrounded by water and wine by books and crystals
by candles and incense
frankincense and myrrh—
whose smoke summons her ancestors to join her,
for she must give thanks to the Grandmother Spirit because Her being
  has made her possible.

And there are flowers there—blue daisies.
Substitutes for the Egyptian Lotussymbols of her wisdom
a proclamation for pure speech.
She calls each one Sophia,
and with a knowing so deep, she acknowledges that each blossom—
like the river and the tree
the stone and the mountain
the fowl and the beast—

is a life form that deserves her gratitude.
So she thanks them because they are so beautiful.

And she is sitting there.
Still.
And with eyes closed, head bowed, heart opened, hands clasped
in prayer
she chants—seven times—

One earth. One people. One love.
One earth. One people. One love.
One earth. One people. One love.
One earth. One people. One love.
One earth. One people. One love.
One earth. One people. One love.
One earth. One people. One love.

Re-minding herself that love *is* all there is.

Thank you, Dr. Plant, for sharing yourself with me—for being my "sometime."[3] I am a better human being because of your being.

Love & Light,
kn

* * *

Drs. Toland-Dix, Grewal, Mitchell, and Plant invited me to reflect on the concepts that I believe have defined me all my life. Their assigned authors—ranging from spiritually-minded African male to poor white female—affirm that the human spirit is a divine energy that connects all human beings and makes possible the peace and freedom we literally die for. However, because so many human beings are products of a consumerist culture that has conditioned us to believe that peace and freedom are equivalent to wealth, materialism, and power—a belief that structures the current patriarchal system that has pushed many people of color to the end of the margins, that has reinforced patriarchal tendencies, and that has pitted many religious institutions against others—human beings search for peace and freedom in every*thing* but themselves. My teachers and their suggested readings initiated my quest of self beyond the preconceived concepts of myself.

Engaging with the aforementioned works of literature, while also practicing theories associated with expressivism[4] and critical thinking, disrupted my fixed ideas regarding race, gender, class, and religion/spirituality; contemplative inquiry disrupted my perception of my very self. I was being unattached from my black skin, my sexual preference, and my gender, while letting go of all the judgments and expectations that came with being an African American lesbian woman. I was literally in a matrix of dis-identification. And although these profound inquiries made me unsure of the self I had known for the past 30 years, unsure if God was God, and unsure of any future I had planned for myself, I felt more alive. How can the letting go of everything you lived for, that defined you, make you feel so alive? So purposeful? I think this aliveness is the freedom that Walker expresses in her poem "Lost," wherein she affirms that freedom is a love that allows one to possess herself.

This aliveness I was experiencing in my graduate classes, I had known before; it's a return to the love that I came into the world as—"the paradise that's lost, that feeling of being at one with everyone and everything" (Hull, 99). However, after taking classes with Drs. Shirley Toland-Dix, Gurleen Grewal, Mozella Mitchell, and Deborah G. Plant, I came to understand and wholeheartedly want to be present to the love that I am.

Notes

1. Historically, *lectio divina*, or divine reading, is a 6th-century monastic practice in contemplative reading; it is one's thoughtful deliberation and musing over a reading passage with the intention of seeking wisdom.

2. See Walker's "Looking for Zora." *In Search of Our Mothers' Gardens*, 93–116.

3. "Sometimes" (1981) is a song by the all-woman's singing group Sweet Honey in the Rock.

4. *Expressivism* is a term associated with the theories of "expressivist" writing, which invites compositionists to write in their authentic voices and to focus their attention on the writing process versus the finished product.

Bibliography

Allison, Dorothy. *Two or Three Things I Know for Sure*. New York: Plume, 1995.

Ani, Dona Marimba. *Let the Circle Be Unbroken: The Implications of Africana Spirituality in the Diaspora*. New Jersey: Red Sea Press, 1992.

Bloom, Harold. Introduction. *Genius: A Mosaic of One Hundred Exemplary Creative Minds*. New York: Warner Books, 2002. 1–12.

Christian, Barbara. "A Race for Theory." *Cultural Critique: The Nature and Context of Minority Discourse* 6 (1987): 51–63.

Dillard, Annie. *Pilgrim at Tinker Creek*. New York: Harper Magazine Press, 1974.

hooks, bell. "Postmodern Blackness." *Postmodern Culture* 1.1 (1990).

Hull, Akasha Gloria. *Soul Talk: The New Spirituality of African American Women.* Rochester: Inner Traditions, 2001.
Hurston, Zora Neale. *Their Eyes Were Watching God.* Philadelphia: J. B. Lippincott Co., 1937.
Kidd, Sue Monk. *Dance of the Dissident Daughter: A Woman's Journey from Christian Tradition to the Sacred Feminine.* New York: HarperCollins, 1996.
Lanzetta, Beverly J. *The Other Side of Nothingness: Toward a Theology of Radical Openness.* New York: State University of New York Press, 2001.
Lunsford, A. "Toward A Mestiza Rhetoric: Gloria Anzaldúa on Composition and Postcoloniality." *Crossing Borderlands: Composition and Postcoloniality Studies.* A. Lunsford and L. Ouzgane's, eds. Pittsburgh: University of Pittsburgh Press, 2004. 33–66.
Master, Jarvis Jay. *Finding Freedom: Writings from Death Row.* California: Padma Publications, 1997.
O'Reilley, Mary Rose. *The Barn at the End of the World: The Apprenticeship of a Quaker, Buddhist, Shepard.* Minnesota: Milkweed Editions, 2000.
Palmer, Parker. *To Know As We Are Known: Education As a Spiritual Journey.* New York: HarperCollins, 1993.
Robinson, Randall. *Defending the Spirit: A Black Life in America.* New York: Plume, 1998.
Somé, Malidoma Patrice. *Of Water and the Spirit: Ritual, Magic, and Initiation in the Life of an African Shaman.* New York: Penguin Books, 1994.
Tollifson, Jean. *Bare Bones Meditation: Waking Up from the Story of My Life.* New York: Bell Tower, 1996.
"The Inside Light": New Critical Essays on Zora Neale Hurston. Dr. Deborah G. Plant, ed. California: Praeger, 2010.
Walker, Alice. *The Color Purple.* New York: Washington Square Press, 1982.
———. *Hard Times Requires Furious Dancing: New Poems by Alice Walker.* California: New World Library, 2010.
———. *In Search of Our Mothers' Gardens: Womanist Prose by Alice Walker.* Harcourt Brace Jovanovich: New York, 1983.
———. *We Are the Ones We Have Been Waiting For: Inner Light in the Time of Darkness.* New York: The New Press, 2006.

3

Professing the Liberatory Power of Womanism

GARY L. LEMONS

It is, in the end, the saving of lives that we writers are about. Whether we are "minority" writers or "majority." It is simply in our power to do this. We do it because we care. . . . We care because we know this: *the life we save is our own.*

—Alice Walker, 1976, from *In Search of Our Mothers' Gardens: Womanist Prose* (1983)

For me, when Walker conceived the term "womanist" to distinguish a black/feminist of color, she opened up a strategic space full of possibility for *black male* pro-feminists. With its emphasis on the humanity of all people—across gender difference—I found in womanist thinking an ideological and political space to identify myself as a black man supporting feminism.

—Gary L. Lemons, *Black Male Outsider, a Memoir: Teaching as a Pro-Feminist Man* (2008)

In teaching courses in black/women of color literature in and outside "Women's Studies" at the University of South Florida, I have more fully come to understand the intersectional, *life-saving* power that Alice Walker conceived in her definition of a *womanist*—as "[a] black feminist or feminist of color." In my pedagogical practice (both undergraduate and graduate level), I make a critical link between writings by black feminists and feminists of color. Not only have I found in Walker's "universal[ist]" concept of womanism a place to perform what I teach, but I have also employed it as an inclusive idea for alliance-building with students in my courses. Even as it functions in my pedagogical practice to bring people together—across differences of race, gender, class, sexuality, *and* culture—it acts to ground the coalitional politics of the writings represented in *Building Womanist Coalitions.*

In this essay, while mainly focused on my pedagogical experience teaching a graduate course on "writings by radical [black] women of color" in 2012 (as an "English" professor), it also includes a discussion of my work with undergraduate students when I taught the course (originally) as a visiting professor in the Department of Women's Studies at USF in 2009. In recalling my labor in both courses, I aim to illustrate the coalitional power of womanist thought—within an academic context. As I first conceptualized the course in women's studies, my desire focused on enabling students to form intellectual "bridges" between the "borders" of their identities and varying academic pursuits. I sought to foreground the activist positionality that Walker espouses in her definition of the womanist—particularly related to her "commit[ment] to survival and wholeness of entire people, male *and* female." Even as this essay concentrates on how I navigated the complex race and gender dynamics of the graduate version of the course, I document my lifesaving visitation as a black man teaching in *women's studies.*

My First Work as a "Visiting" Black Male Professor in Women's Studies

As stated above, while teaching "writings by radical women of color" as a graduate class in USF's English department was, indeed, personally and pedagogically engaging, I must acknowledge the lasting impact undergraduate students in women's studies had on my commitment to womanist pedagogy. The course I taught in the Women's Studies Department was officially titled "Literature by Women of Color in the Diaspora." I was invited to teach it by Kim Vaz, the department chair at that time. As the first black woman to head the Women's Studies Department at USF, Kim inviting me to teach the course provided me a pedagogical and scholarly "home." Having come to USF as a faculty member appointed to teach in the English department, I wholeheartedly welcomed the idea of a "joint" appointment.

In *Feminist Solidarity at the Crossroads: Intersectional Women's Studies for Transracial Alliance* (which Kim and I coedited in 2012), I write about my commitment to the continuation of the "departmental" status of Women's Studies at USF. In this book, I also document my experience teaching courses in the Department when Kim acted as its chair. I titled the chapter, "'Women's

Studies Is Not My Home?' When Personal and Political Professions Become Acts of Emancipatory Confession" In it I state:

> I can remember no other time as a professor in feminist studies more self-empowering than teaching in women studies under Kim's direction. She gave me an office, "a room of my own." She assigned me courses to teach that stretched my pedagogical vision. She made me feel like I belonged, not only as a black male professor of feminism but one who possessed the credentials and passion to teach in a department of women's studies.[1]

Of the courses she asked me to teach, it was "Literature by Women of Color in the Diaspora" (a senior-level class) that set me up to teach the graduate version of it later in the English department. Along with requiring the WST students to read *This Bridge Called My Back*, I also had them read *The Woman That I Am: the Literature and Culture of Contemporary Women of Color* (1994), edited by D. Soyini Madison. While both texts provoked deeply engaging class discussions, it would be this book that activated an unforgettable moment of creative power in the course. Connected to the heartfelt responses students wrote to readings I assigned from the book, during one of the last class meetings of the semester, I asked students (29 of them, all women) to write for five minutes in self-reflection about the meaning of womanhood related to the writings in *The Woman I Am*. The students were a bit surprised by my having suddenly shifted the focus of the discussion. However, each woman began to write.

Adding credibility to this writing exercise, in preparation for the next class, I asked each woman to type out her five-minute reflection and to share it verbally during the session. Before the course ended, I collected each woman's reflection. As a parting "gift" to the class members, I printed out their self-reflections as a single body of writings and gave each woman a copy in remembrance of our work together in the course. I titled the collection of writings "A Woman(ist)-Authored Chapbook." On its cover page, I wrote the following:

> I take this opportunity to thank each woman who followed through with the impromptu, unplanned, and unanticipated nature of the assignment. You clearly stood the test of my request. For having embraced the vision of it, I receive your poems as a gift to our course of study. They give light to the emancipatory path of justice we create for all who dare to tread. As each of your voices have given me a deeper realization and understanding of what it means to be a woman, self-possessed, autonomous in her sense of self, owning

> her freedom to be to the woman that she *IS* and in continual process toward becoming the woman she aims *TO BE*, I say thank you! Finally, in gratitude for her faith in my work as a pro-feminist male professor in women's studies, I dedicate this chapbook to Dr. Kim Vaz, former chair of the Department of Women's Studies at the University of South Florida. It was she who first gave me the gift of this course to teach. [This Chapbook] is a small gift to [you] in return as the fruit of my labor in WST. (Fall, 2009)

In hindsight, as stated earlier, remembering my labor with students in the undergraduate women's studies course would prepare me to meet the challenge of having graduate students write in a mode of self-reflection, interconnected to the texts I would require them to read in the "Literature by Women of Color."

Teaching Teachers "Literature by Women of Color"

Many of the students I would teach in the graduate course were already serving in various teaching capacities. Most of them planned to teach in a college or university setting once they completed their graduate studies. In configuring the course, my hope was that while studying writings by black/ women of color feminists with me, these students would come to claim the bridge-building activism set forth by radical feminist and womanist writers they would study in the course.

In her Foreword to the first edition of *This Bridge Called My Back*, Toni Cade Bambara underscores the necessity for alliance-building in support for social justice. It begins in our listening and learning from each other: "This Bridge can get us there. Can coax us into the habit of listening to each other and learning each other's ways of seeing and being."[2] Teaching feminist literature by black/women of color, I not only claim the transformative power of womanist thought, but I also seek to pass on the legacy of womanist activism to my students. I see them as the next generation of teachers and scholars standing together in solidarity against all forms of domination and oppression. In the 4th edition preface to *This Bridge Called My Back*, Moraga clearly articulates the legacy of cross-generational movement that constituted the politics of the writings in the 1981 first edition. Speaking directly to the "next generation," Moraga asserts:

> Ultimately, as all people of progressive politic do, we wrote this book for you—the next generation, *and the next one*. Your lives are so vast before you—you whom the popular culture has impassively termed "Millennials."

> But I think the women of *Bridge* would've simply called you, "familia"—our progeny, entrusting you with the legacy of our thoughts and activisms, in order to better grow them into a flourishing planet and a just world. . . . It is also promised in the spirit of those young people who may first pick up this collection of poems, protests, and prayers and suddenly, without warning feel their own consciousness catch fire.[3]

Acknowledging the powerful influence of *This Bridge Called My Back*, I taught the graduate course as a model of feminism in the lives of "young women of color." As one of the primary texts for it, I included Daisy Hernández and Bushra Rehman's *Colonize This! Young Women of Color on Today's Feminism* in which Cherríe Moraga wrote the Foreword, "The War Path of Greater Empowerment." In it she writes,

> *Colonize This!* is a collection of writings by young women of color that testifies to the movement—political and physical—of a new generation of global citizens, activists and artists. . . . As immigrant, native-born, and survivor-of-slavery daughters, these women are the female children of those "refugees from a world on fire," described in the 1983 edition of *This Bridge Called My Back*.. . . . They are young sisters (our daughters) who didn't "grow up to be statistics" . . . who have read and been schooled by the feminist writings and works of the women of color who preceded them, and as such are free to ask questions of feminism more deeply than we could have imagined twenty years ago.[4]

First of all, I believe it far from accidental that *Colonize This!* and *This Bridge We Call Home* were published in the same year (2002). Secondly, the fact that they are so closely interrelated to the liberatory politics of voice empowerment found in *This Bridge Call my Back* is evidence of their carrying forward its legacy of what I would call womanist "familia." As "sister" texts, *Colonize This!* and *This Bridge We Call Home*, were caught up in the visionary, groundbreaking Spirit of their "mother" text. As I have stated, my task related to this legacy has been simple. My assignment in the college classroom—from the first time I taught "Womanist Thought" at the New School in New York City to the year when I first taught the graduate class at the University of South Florida—has been to follow my own "course-work." From a womanist positionality in my study and teaching of black women and women of color feminist writers, I have not wavered in my attempts to make sure that their voices continue to be *heard* and that their works remain *visibly* accessible to all students who desire to take on the authorial struggle of these women for voice, visibility, and self-recovery.

First and foremost, my long-standing goal has been to teach the dynamic interplay among the autobiographical, the personal, the political, and the spiritual in texts by black women and women of color feminists. Secondly, I have been led to employ their writings as discursive models for students to explore the self-transforming implications of what it means to be a womanist—writing from an autocritographical point of view. The descriptor as I employ it here is derived from the term "autocritography." According to Michael Awkward in *Scenes of Instruction, a Memoir* (1999), the term originated with Henry Louis Gates Jr. He defines it as a discursive strategy based upon "an autobiography of a critical concept."[5] For Awkward, a well-known, black male feminist scholar and literary critic, the term takes on a different shade of meaning in the context of how he represents it and employs it in his own writings:

> [Autocritography] is a self-reflexive, self-consciously academic act that foregrounds aspects of the genre typically dissolved into authors' always strategic self-portraits. Autocritography, in other words, is an account of individual, social, and institutional conditions that help to produce a scholar and, hence, his or her professional concerns. Although the intensity of investigation of any of these conditions may vary widely, their self-consciously interactive presence distinguishes autocritography from other forms of autobiographical recall.[6]

Over the years, having adapted Awkward's concept to describe the rhetorical strategy appearing in so much memoir writing by feminist black women and women of color feminists, I have employed it as a core strategy for teaching writing for student voice empowerment and self-transformation. For years it has fueled my passion for teaching writings by black women and women of color. In particular, they have utilized memoir as a genre for personal, political, and spiritual self-actualization.

Calling Out the Invisible "to Raise Our Voices"

When I wrote the syllabus for the "Literature by [Black] Women of Color" course, the one thing I was sure of—beyond the requirements listed in the syllabus when the course initially began—was that at the end of it each student would submit her/his "final" paper for publication consideration in a feminist or women's studies journal. Coming to the end of the term, after having closely read and evaluated eight of the weekly autocritographical papers students had written (once each week during the semester), I felt a collective groundswell had occurred. As I perceived, it had to do with a marked display of two things that had clearly emerged for me in the students' writings: a pronounced power and depth in their command of voice and an insightful display of critical consciousness connected to their textual analyses of the course readings. Across differences of race, ethnicity, class, and sexual identity, collectively my students exhibited the possibilities of autocritography centered on liberatory subject-hood and womanist coalition.

As a response to the body of writings students produced toward the end of the course (far beyond my original expectations), I proposed to them that the last paper they would write should be a retrospective re-engagement in their own struggle to "come to voice" during the semester. I asked them to recount ways they had been challenged by the writers they read. In what ways did their own gender, race, class, and/or sexual identities get called into question? Each week as they were writing and openly reading from their papers in class, I heard from them what it cost them to speak publicly personal stories of hurt, shame, fear, victimization. For me, every class posed the same two challenges for each student. First, could (would) s/he rise to the challenge of comprehending the standpoint/position of the writer(s) under consideration? It called for the student to embrace the idea of "empathetic imagination" derived from Chinua Achebe's concept of "imaginative identification." It has to do with "our capacity to understand and feel the suffering of others even though we have never experienced that particular suffering ourselves."[7] Secondly, would each student be willing, without my prompting, to share openly her/his writing in the form of class participation?

It was precisely the students' willing openness to write about and then disclose in class personal life narratives inspired by those in the *Bridge* texts and *Colonize This!*. The courageousness of their voices reminded me of that reflected in the students' writings from a course I had taught at the New School so many years before, which focused on bell hooks's autocritographical writings in *Talking Back: Thinking Feminist, Thinking Black* (1989). Over the years, her commitment to the transformative power of voice has remained at the core of my passion for teaching student voice empowerment through feminism conceptualized by black women and women of color. Affirming the life-sustaining power of voice and the emancipatory sense of self derived from it, beyond desire for acceptance in the college classroom—hooks asserts:

> When we dare to speak in a liberatory voice, we threaten even those who may initially claim to want our words. In the act of overcoming our fear of speech, of being seen as threatening, in the process of learning to speak as subjects, we participate in the global struggle to end domination. *When we end our*

> *silence, when we speak in a liberated voice, our words connect us with anyone, anywhere who lives in silence* (emphasis added).[8]

What I clearly understood in hooks's words in this passage when reciting it in the first feminist class I taught on her writings in 1993, is that the "liberated voice" enables our words to "connect us with anyone, anywhere who lives in silence." Toward the end of the graduate course, I remembered the liberating message hooks delivered in these words. They fueled my desire to continue the work that students and I had begun in the class.

In retrospect, as I have stated, I recall being unabated by the fact that when I taught the course, in 2012, *This Bridge Called My Back* was still out of print years. Hoping that my students would be able to find copies of it before the course ended, I began with *Colonize This!*. Considering the fact that its editors conceived this book as a testament to the transformative influence *This Bridge Called My Back* had in their personal lives and the lives of their volume's contributors, I determined that beginning the course with the voices of this younger generation of women of color feminists would set a radical tone for the class until students acquired its "mother" text.

For the editors of *Colonize This!*, Moraga notes in her Foreword: "*The feminism portrayed in* Colonize This! *reflects what in the 1980s we understood as 'theory in the flesh,' a strategy for women's liberation, which is wrought from the living example of female labor and woman acts of loving*" (emphasis added).[9] At the same time, in the book's introduction, its editors Daisy Hernandez and Bushra Rehman quote Angela Davis about the lifesaving possibility to be found in womanist coalition "despite" our differences:

> 'We are living in a world for which old forms of activism are not enough and today's activism is about creating coalitions between communities.' *This is exactly our hope for this book. Despite differences of language, skin color and class, we have a long, shared history of oppression and resistance. For us, this book is activism, a way to continue the conversations among young women of color found in earlier books like* This Bridge Called My Back *and* Making Face, Making Soul [by Gloria Anzaldúa] (emphasis added).[10]

During the first weeks of the course, after having evaluated students' autocritographical responses to writings in *Colonize This!*, several things became clear to me (offsetting my frustration of having not opened the course with *This Bridge Called My Back*): 1) The overall depth of critical analysis and self-reflection the papers displayed told me I had made the right choice in not only having selected *Colonize This!* as a required course text, but also in having decided to start with it. 2) The book's contributors had so clearly set into motion ideas, issues, and questions about radical feminism conceptualized by "young women of color" that supplied the underpinning for a level of intense self-reflective engagement in students' writings. Moreover, it acted as a catalyst for compelling class dialogue that would continue for the remainder of the term. 3) Most importantly, together the readings in *Colonize This!* reinforced Hernandez and Rehman's vision of the book itself as a critical piece of activism for (in Angela Davis's words) "creating coalitions between communities."

In my mind, the autocritographies students wrote in the class, even at this early point in the semester, bore proof of my conviction about the power of memoir writing for critical self-reflection linked to social and spiritual agency. Such writing represents a merger of the head and heart as a means to bring people together in heartfelt dialogue. First and foremost, the challenge confronting students at the beginning of the semester had to do with students' willingness to engage in a politics of difference, as represented in the course texts and in the personal differences that would inform the varying individual perspectives students would present in their own writings.

What had been clear in teaching *Colonize This!* is that notions of "difference" remained centered on the identity politics of young *women* of color. Hernandez and Rehman stayed true to the woman-centered vision Moraga and Anzaldúa had conceived for *This Bridge Called My Back*. However, Anzaldúa and Keating would venture beyond its visionary scope. Writing the preface to *This Bridge We Call Home* in 2001, Anzaldúa states that the "categories of race and gender are more permeable and flexible than they were for those of us growing up prior to the 1980s."[11] Pushing the boundaries of identity in this book, she (with AnaLouise Keating) asserts a radically "new" bridge politics with an invitation prompting us

> to move beyond separate and easy identifications, creating bridges that cross race and other classifications among different groups via intergenerational dialogue. . . . In our efforts to rethink the border of race, gender, and identity we must guard against creating new binaries. . . . *Expanding* This Bridge Called My Back *we incorporate additional underrepresented voices such as those of transgendered people, and Arab and South Asian/Indian Americans.*[12]

While the editors of *Colonize This!* remained committed to a focus on an emancipatory politics of gender for women of color, like Anzaldúa and Keating, they cross borders of ethnicity and nationality within this framework. However, *This Bridge We Call Home* not only crosses borders of gender difference, it transcends them. Even as it has makes space for men, it *expands* the concept of bridge-building to include the voices of "transgendered people."

And like *Colonize This!*, this book devoted itself to the voices of "Arab and South Asian/Indian Americans." In their vision of "home," the editors of *This Bridge We Call Home* reopened U.S. borders beyond the reactionary politics of exclusion that followed 911.

Crossing Borders Thirty Years Later

Toward a Multicultural Feminist Approach

What really distinguishes *This Bridge We Call Home* from the original *Bridge* text (related to the scope of its vision of "voice" inclusivity) is its "multicultural" approach to feminism. According to Anzaldúa,

> We attempt to break the impasse between women of color and other groups. *By including women and men of different "races," nationalities, classes, sexualities, genders, and ages we complicate the debates within feminist theory both inside and outside the academy and inside and outside the United States* (emphasis added).[13]

In this text, it is precisely the bringing together of multiple voices within an *all*-inclusive framework that would in theory open up the writing and dialogic space in the graduate class I taught, particularly connected to differences of gender, race, and sexuality that my students represented. Of the twelve students enrolled in the course, there were nine who identified as female (five "women of color," four African Americans, and one South Asian); three white males (two of whom identified as heterosexual). Related to the sexual politics of the women students, most on various levels were questioning traditional categories of sexuality as socially constructed.

Furthermore, Anzaldúa and Keating's inclusive approach to feminist identity validated my own position and place within the classroom as a profeminist and womanist-identified, black male professor. As I have written before, having taught courses on feminist writings by black/women of color for a number of years, my own personal struggle has centered on the politics, power, and position of the "male" voice in a feminist/womanist classroom. In continuing to navigate lines of authority and privilege(s) that come with being male in a patriarchal, male-supremacist, and heterosexist culture. It not enough to "say" that I am pro-feminist, I must act out my commitment to the struggle against systemic and institutionalized oppression.

In teaching *This Bridge We Call Home*, I (as well as the other males in the graduate course I taught) received further validation of male support in struggles against sexism. Additionally, the book allowed me to promote a global, multicultural approach to the study of writings by individuals across nation-state territorial borders. As its editors envisioned:

> Gathering people from many geographies in a multicultural approach is a mark of inclusivity, increased consciousness, and dialogue. This inclusivity reflects the hybrid quality of our lives and identities—todas somos nos/otras. *Living in multicultural communities and the complexities of our age demand that we develop a perspective that takes into account the whole planet* (emphasis added).[14]

Considering "the complexities of our age" as still bound up in racist, sexist, capitalist, and homophobic ideas of identity, *This Bridge We Call Home* offered my students a critically inclusive opportunity to explore d*ifference.* In this way, I compelled them to bring their whole selves to the study of writings by individuals in and beyond U.S. borders.

During the weeks students wrote responses to the readings from *This Bridge We Call Home*, however, the apparent differences between them threatened to close down dialogue rather than create a space of openness to listen and learn from each other. During one class session in particular, a woman of color student called into question what she believed to be a display of white male privilege in the presentation of writing by one of the white men in the course. At this point in the semester (midway through the course), I felt led to call for an individual conference with each student to determine how we might work against the gender and racial fallout that had occurred. Meeting with each student the following week, I listened carefully while taking notes for later reflection. As we revisited the race and gender tensions that arose in the prior class session, it became clear to me some of the students' feelings of frustrations had to do with other conflicting issues—in addition to the critique of white male privilege.

Students' concerns included the following: problems associated with feelings of being silenced by voices that dominated class discussions; experiences of moments where voice empowerment was undermined by language that attacked difference; hearing different perspectives without negative judgment; racial segregation between white and women of color students in class; knowing when not to speak; and a general lack of awareness among white students concerning the complexity of race and ethnic differences between women of color and black women's identity politics. While students voiced feelings of exasperation, at the same time, they spoke about that which needed to be further challenged: the level of critical consciousness related to myths and stereotypes of white female innocence; the degree of "empathetic imagination"; self-critical awareness; engagement in open dialogue about sexual difference(s); and dialogue linked to the place of activism related to autocritographical writing. For those students working as teachers—on and below the college level—the need for more discussion about the relationship between theory and practice became clearer.

Through some of the frustrations students shared during their individual conference time with me, I concluded that my task was clear for the remainder of the term. Rather than perform as an agent of conflict resolution—mediating or shifting class dialogue away from confrontation—I would continue to advocate for the power of voice as represented in the authors' personal, political, and spiritual pronouncements we were reading. Furthermore, I would move on to affirm the students' levels of critical consciousness that had emerged midway through the course. The overall impression I would gain from writings students produced emerged from the overtly pronounced ways they reflected upon their personal struggles to come to voice. The majority of them had moved beyond the superficial limitations of "political correctness." The content and tone of their autocritographies suggested movement away from fixed categories of identities toward the exploration of their fluidity and interconnection.

Thirty years after the publication of *This Bridge Called My Back*, the representation of a multicultural approach to feminism stood on solid pedagogical ground in *This Bridge We Call Home*. Ten years after its publication, in a graduate class I would teach on literature by black/women of color, this book prepared my students to test the radical politics of difference it represented. While defending the emancipatory benefits that come with it, Anzaldúa does not shy away from confrontational elements embedded in it:

> Our goal is not to use differences to separate us from others, but neither is it to gloss over those differences. . . . Though most of us live entremundos, between and among worlds, we are frustrated by those who step over the line, by hybridities and ambiguities, and by what does not fit our expectations of "race" and sex.
>
> I fear that many mujeres de color will not want whites or males to be contributors in our book. We risk their displeasure. It would have been easier for AnaLouise and me to limit the dialogue to women of color. Many women of color are possessive of *This Bridge Called My Back* and view it as a safe space, as "home." *But there are no safe spaces* (emphasis added).[15]

Making space(s) for difference defines and characterizes the border-crossing positionality Anzaldúa and Keating advance despite the possibility of criticism from within women of color feminist communities invested in a form of separatism advocating the exclusion of "whites or males [as] contributors in our book." Alice Walker clearly defines a womanist as "not a separatist, except periodically, for health."

Once again, what strikes me about the transgressive race and gender editorial politics of Anzaldúa and Keating exhibited in *This Bridge We Call Home* is its contestation of "home" as a "safe space." I certainly understand the reticence that women of color continue to display toward some whites (men *and* women) and black/men of color who possess a desire for cross-racial feminist alliance. Many black/women of color perceive this desire to be couched in internalized racist guilt, political correctness, and just plain old disingenuousness. Nevertheless, to hold out against the possibility of identity transformation through an engagement in literature by radical women of color would go against everything it stands for. As bell hooks argued in her first book, *Ain't I a Woman: Black Women and Feminism*, published in 1981 (the same year *This Bridge Called My Back* was released), struggles against racism and sexism will not be won by black women alone. The same applies to the battle against these oppressions faced by *all* women of color. This is precisely the case hooks makes in *Feminist Theory: From Margin to Center* (1984). In "Men as Comrades" (chapter five), she states,

> Separatist ideology encourages us to believe that women alone can make feminist revolution—we cannot. . . . [M]ore than ever before non-white people are currently calling attention to the primary role white people must play in anti-racist struggle. The same is true of the struggle to eradicate sexism—men have a primary role to play.[16]

Even in 1984, hooks cast a vision of feminist solidarity that strategically included whites (women *and* men) and black/men of color. As I write in *Black Male Outsider*, it prepared the groundwork for my vision of anti-racist feminism in the college classroom.

Anzaldúa and Keating cast a visionary net that captures us all—across our differences. I held onto the strength of their insightfulness when thinking about my approach to the "Literature by Black/Women of Color" course and the texts that guided it. I knew they would challenge students reading and writing about them. Anzaldúa and Keating pushed me to come to voice about the ways I had been made to feel as an "outsider" in my own black community, particularly because I did not fit the hetero-normative ideas of black masculinity. These texts I taught in the course helped me to flip the script of black manhood.

A Vision of a New "Home": From Classroom to "Living" Room

As I have shown, the "Literature by [Black] Women of Color" course was not a traditionally "safe space"—not because of any ill intention on my part but *because*. As Anzaldúa boldly declares: "There are no safe spaces. 'Home' can be unsafe and dangerous because it bears the likelihood of intimacy and thus thinner boundaries. Staying 'home' and not venturing out from our own groups comes from woundedness, and stagnates our growth."[17] It was this idea that students in the class had to grapple with for most of the term. As Toni Cade Bambara stated in her Foreword to *This Bridge Called My Back*, this form of open-thinking—requiring attributes of careful "hearing" and "seeing," critical consciousness, heartfelt self-reflection, and imaginative identification—would ultimately determine the substantive value of students writing their personal experiences into the analytical interpretations of the texts they read in the course.

Teaching *This Bridge Called My Back* during the final weeks of the semester was not only personally empowering for me, it also set our study "back on course" as I had originally planned. Just as contributors to *This Bridge We Call Home* and *Colonize This!* speak about the influence of the "mother text" in their personal, political, and spiritual evolution; so my students in the class reveled in their writings about the transformative experience that the original *Bridge* text afforded them. Rereading the "writings by radical women of color" *This Bridge Called My Back* volume contains, I recall Moraga and Anzaldúa's pedagogical vision for it:

> We envision the book being used as a *required* text in most women's studies course. And we don't mean just "special" courses on Third World Women or Racism, but also courses dealing with sexual politics, feminist thought, women's spirituality, etc. Similarly, we want to see this book on the shelf of, and used in the classroom by, every ethnic studies teacher in this country, male and female alike.[18]

For nearly two decades teaching this book, I have followed the vision of Moraga and Anzaldúa.

Perhaps, over the years, had more professors in women's studies and those teaching in ethnic studies ("male and female alike") taught and "required" *This Bridge Called My Back* in their courses, it would never have gone out of print (more than once). As I have stated, even when *This Bridge Called My Back* was out of print, I still *required* my students to read it. Every time I have taught this book, my students have taken up intellectual and emotional residence in it. There—as many of them have shared with me *and* each other—it offers a liberatory home space. Free to speak and write themselves into whole beings, they represent the "Millennials" as Cherríe Moraga would conceptualize them in "Catching Fire: Preface to the Fourth Edition" of *This Bridge Called My Back.*

Moreover, the passage of their editorial labor, promoting human rights and social justice for all people across territorial and cultural borders, embodies itself in the conceptual ideas of both *This Bridge We Call Home* and *Colonize This!* Students in my "Literature by Black/Women of Color" class were clearly inspired by the radical voices in these texts. They compelled my students to write out boldly their own process of coming to voice, not only for self-liberation but for all people cast on the margins of humanity.

Collectively, the *Bridge* texts moved the students to raise their voices aligned with the Spirit of all women of color feminists and womanists, bridging periods of time and generational struggles. For me, these *Bridge* works furnished the inspiration I needed to formulate a life-transformative pedagogy in the college classroom that would model, in the words of bell hooks, "education as the practice of freedom" (*Teaching to Transgress*). In this place, I labor to be in solidarity with women of color feminist writers to make their voices heard and their presence felt, as a lifesaving experience for my students. Teaching the *Bridge* texts and *Colonize This!*, I have functioned as a "home"-place for me, as a "black male outsider." According to Moraga and Anzaldúa in *This Bridge Called My Back*: "The revolution begins at home."[19] In the residency I have taken up in feminist and womanist studies, the *bridge works* I teach stand as an emancipatory location where I feel free to teach my students ways to live whole lives in mind, body, and spirit—as imagined in the radical writings of women of color feminists—across all shades of their differences.

Writing from the Inside Out

And the Lifesaving Power of Womanism

In her Foreword to the 1983 second edition of *This Bridge Called My Back*, Gloria Anzaldúa calls into preeminence a politics of resistance built upon a coalition anchored in a solidarity of *difference*: "We have come to realize that we are not alone in our struggles nor separate nor autonomous but that we—white black straight queer female male—are connected and interdependent."[20] In what has become one of her most often quoted essays,

"The Transformation of Silence into Language and Action" (1977) in *Sister Outsider*, Audre Lorde speaks about the fact that "It is necessary to teach by living and speaking those truths which we believe and know beyond understanding."[21]

I have come to understand that the truths that Lorde references but leaves unnamed are meaningfully articulated in the conceptual spaces Alice Walker would define in her innovative work in *In Search of Our Mothers' Gardens*. In my personal struggle to bring to fruition pedagogy rooted in the loving Spirit of Walker's creative vision, I have sought to live, teach, and speak in solidarity with womanism. Purposely positioning myself outside prescriptive, hetero-patriarchal myths of black manhood and masculinity is as an act of personal survival. Teaching feminist black/women of color texts over the years, I have learned from them that men can be feminists.

However, in my studies of foundational writings by black/women of color feminists and womanists, particularly from the 1980s, I would comprehend that building political alliances to end domination must be grounded in the Spirit of love. In "Love as the Practice of Freedom," from *Outlaw Culture: Resisting Representations* (1994), bell hooks connects community-building with the process of decolonization. In it the power of love acts as a critical agent moving one toward "the practice of love." For hooks, that "awareness is central to the process of life as the practice of freedom." She claims this is what "folks want to know."[22] This is what I wanted to know when I began teaching "Literature by Women of Color." Through it, I came to understand that teaching from a womanist standpoint has been about mapping my own personal course of pedagogical freedom. In the rigor of our listening, hearing, and becoming more perceptive to ways of seeing and being with each other in the course, during the semester we would render a sustained idea of solidarity that moved us to a place of deeper human compassion, personal reflection, and spiritual enrichment.

Notes

1. Kim Marie Vaz and Gary L. Lemons, eds., *Feminist Solidarity at the Crossroads: Intersectional Women's Studies for Transracial Alliance* (New York: Routledge, 2012), 166.

2. Toni Cade Bambara, Foreword, *This Bridge Called My Back*, Cherríe Moraga and Gloria Anzaldúa, eds. (New York: Kitchen Table: Women of Color Press, 1981), vi–vii.

3. Cherríe Moraga, "Catching Fire: Preface to the Fourth Edition," *This Bridge Called My Back: Writings by Radical Women of Color*, Moraga and The Gloria E.

Anzaldúa Literary Trust, eds. (New York: State University of New York Press, 2015), vii.

4. Daisy Hernandez and Bushra Rehman, eds., *Colonize This! Young Women of Color on Today's Feminism* (New York: Seal Press, 2002), xi.

5. Michael Awkward, *Scenes of Instruction, A Memoir* (Durham: Duke University Press, 1999), 7.

6. Ibid.

7. Jane Lazarre, *Beyond the Whiteness of Whiteness: Memoir of a White Mother of Black Sons* (Durham: Duke University Press, 1996), 4.

8. bell hooks, *Talking Back: Thinking Feminist, Thinking Black* (Boston: South End Press, 1989), 18.

9. Cherríe Moraga, Foreword, *Colonize This!* xi–xii.

10. Quote by Angela Davis in *Colonize This!* xxi.

11. Gloria Anzaldúa and AnaLouise Keating, eds., *This Bridge We Call Home: Radical Visions for Transformation* (New York: Routledge, 2002), 2.

12. Ibid., 3.

13. Ibid.

14. Ibid.

15. Ibid.

16. bell hooks, *Feminist Theory: From Margin to Center* (Boston: South End Press, 1984), 81.

17. Anzaldúa, *This Bridge We Call Home*, 1983, 3.

18. Moraga, Foreword, *This Bridge Called My Back*, 1981, xxvi.

19. Ibid.

20. This quote appears in the Appendix of Moraga, *This Bridge Called My Back*, 253.

21. Audre Lorde, *Sister Outsider* (Freedom, Calif.: The Crossing Press, 1984), 43.

22. bell hooks, *Outlaw Culture: Resisting Representations* (New York: Routledge, 1994), 248.

4

A Doctored Voice

Resistance, Reading, and Righting as Womanist Pedagogy

YLCE IRIZARRY

The murder of Florida teenager Trayvon Martin captured and held national attention due to the obvious racial and juridical elements of the case.[1] Beyond the tragic reality of the violence Black men face daily that his murder reflects, what disconcerts me about the media treatment of the case is the manner in which voice—both literal and figurative—became fundamental to the criminal case's development and resolution. From the dispute about whose voice is screaming for help on the 911 call, to the revelation that NBC editors doctored the audio on the call to make it appear that George Zimmerman used racist slurs when describing Martin, I have been reminded how dangerous and how easy it is to alter voice. Trayvon Martin's death made me think about how my parents, like Martin's, wanted their children to be identified through their actions not their racial appearances. Like the voices of so many other people of color, my voice was doctored. Institutions—familial, social, and educational—have all relied on altering and silencing our voices to obscure the realities of their discrimination and oppression.[2]

I was Chicana before I was Latina. Chicana literature and feminist theory taught me much of what I learned about oppression and empowerment. I first came to an understanding of how my parents had actively constructed my sisters and I as "white" when I read Cherríe Moraga's essay "La Güera" in the urgently important volume, *This Bridge Called My Back: Writings by Radical Women of Color* (1981). My older sister, Bernadette, had taken Women's Studies classes in college; after graduation, she was cleaning out her books. She picked the anthology up, gently rubbed the cover, handed it to me, and said, "you need to read this." She did not say, "You'll like this" or "This is a good book." She was right. I needed *This Bridge* to find and use my voice as a working-class Latina. Over the years, *This Bridge* developed my *mestiza* consciousness, through which I understand both my oppression and my privilege. The writers of *This Bridge* gave me the first words with which to articulate my ethnic feminist identity; their work still empowers my own.

In "*La Güera*," Moraga discusses being "bleached and beached." Her parents strove to have her consider herself white so that she could enter the white world: the world of social mobility. This essay articulated things I had felt for a long time but simply did not have the words to speak. I would love to say that once I read Moraga, I sought out every opportunity to use my voice, to make my non-whiteness visible, but I could not immediately enact the revolutionary practices Moraga performs and advocates. My feminist pedagogy takes various forms in my research and teaching and it has taken many experiences to cohere. As I reflect on these experiences and reread writing I have not looked at in over two decades, I realize how I continue to develop my feminist pedagogy: in the classroom and in my scholarship, I use my voice to right wrongs: wrong assumptions, wrong information, and wrong conclusions about the perpetuation of racism, ableism, heterosexism, and ageism.

Before I really started to use my voice, I had to cross many of my own bridges. Moraga writes, "We women have a similar nightmare, for each of us in some way has been both oppressed and the oppressor" ("La Güera" 32). I had to recognize those moments when I did not challenge someone's construction of me either as only white or as Latina or even understand that the racial identifier "white Latina" was a social construction eliding the historical reality of racial mixing, especially within the Hispanic Caribbean. I had to recognize those moments when I did not stand up for someone when I had the ability to do so, the moments when "silence is like starvation" (29). This essay is structured to mirror my relationship with feminist and womanist pedagogy: sometimes the narrative is progressive; sometimes I return to memories that help me understand an experience; sometimes I narrate the present as I think about the future. By rereading my "miseducation" and considering my efforts to help students resist similar doctored identities, I hope to show what feminist and womanist pedagogies mean for this doctored woman of color.[3]

The Voices of My Youth

Growing up, my sisters and I heard two starkly different voices about our family's identity as Hispanic.[4] For my father, whose parents came to New York in the early 1940s, the United States was a place where education lifted you out of poverty. His favorite motto is "If you can read, you can do anything." Yet, my father has been the victim of discrimination throughout his life. Some of his childhood experiences were so painful that it was only when my sisters and I became adults that he even recounted them. One story I particularly recall was about his prom. He went to pick up his date; the girl's father threw him out of the house because he was Puerto Rican. As a blue-eyed, light-skinned, non-accented "Hispanic" living in the Bronx in the 1950s, my father experienced discrimination from white communities because of his ethnicity, which while not visible, was still not white. In the dialects of racism, Puerto Rican translates to "not American."[5]

My mother told a different story about ethnicity, once nuanced by nationalism. She came here involuntarily in 1961, after the assassination of Dominican dictator Rafael Leónidas Trujillo Molina. My grandfather felt that she and my aunt would be in danger; they were. My uncle, Ángel Salvador Corneille, had been a high-ranking officer during the Trujillato; in 1969, he was murdered in New York. Tragically, he was assassinated because he chose not to use his voice. His "strategic silence," refusing to endorse or participate in a new military coup, cost him his life.[6] Like my father, my mother did not tell us many stories about her youth; but her reasons were different. We knew little about her life in the Dominican Republic. She became a citizen and lived in the United States for over 30 years. Yet, this was not her country.

A generation later, my life echoes some of the stories of my parents. Many Anglo-Americans[7] have tried to make me feel that I do not belong in this country. It would be years before I came to understand how insidious nationalism can be; while children, though, our sense of being American was the blanket my parents used to keep us warm against the cold reality of racism. We were painfully aware of the racism in our neighborhood. The neighbors on both sides of us and across the street chose "white flight"; they moved out shortly after we moved in. When I was six years old, my neighbor friend Patty told me that her father said she could not play with "the daughters of a Puerto Rican." We could not ignore occasions such as when our second oldest sister, Simone, the toughest of all of us, came home crying: someone had called her "chink." My father refused to ignore this racism any longer when his oldest daughter, Nicole, came home with cigarettes burning in the hood of her coat. She had become the object of bullying during desegregation because neither group—White nor Black—perceived her as belonging. Eventually, all of us entered private Catholic school. My parents really could not afford to send us there, but our lives literally depended on getting out of public school.

Yet, even Catholic school could be a field of racial and nationalist landmines. When I was in high school, the new Spanish teacher asked if I was "Vasca," meaning Basque, from Spain. I had a vague idea that my paternal great grandparents were, but I said, "no, I'm Puerto Rican and Dominican." She said "oh," with a disappointed sigh. I was Hispanic; so what? Everybody was something. Our neighbors were Italian, German, Irish, and Polish. My parents protected us from those slurs by positioning us above those who would belittle us. Whenever we came home upset about a new incident, my mother would say, "consider the source," meaning that the person was low-class and uneducated and therefore, his or her words should not matter. I often wonder: if my parents had not experienced such racism, would class have become so critical for them? Until graduate school, I did not understand that the triangle of race, class, and gender had *always* shaped my life. Just as some of my peers began to find intersectionality vogue and desired to incorporate it in their work, I realized the painful difference between embodying intersectionality and dissecting it from a supposed critical distance. Recognizing that I was a woman of color was the first step in becoming a feminist and, later, a womanist who recognizes the urgency of the equal and humane treatment of all people.

These racialized and class-inflected experiences determined how my parents raised us. We were not allowed to speak Spanish in our home for fear we would be "left-back" or put into remedial classes. This is what the school district attempted to do to my two eldest sisters when they entered school as Spanish speakers. My social activities were limited to girlfriends who lived across the street and while in public school, I was discouraged from associating with the other Latina/o children. Our family rarely discussed "being" Hispanic. My father created a distinction between ethnicity and identity: "You are not Hispanic, you are educated." For my father, the two were mutually exclusive for many years; this was his survival strategy in a workplace and town that did not acknowledge the significant portion of Latinas/os within its boundaries until the 1990s. Likewise, my mother's experiences as an immigrant led her to return to the Dominican Republic when she and my father divorced. Despite working and living in the United States for decades, she would always be a second-class citizen in this country.

Perhaps the most troubling experience, one that led me back to these memories of discrimination in my youth, occurred in my first week of university at Le Moyne College. This incident made me aware of my precarious ethnic identity; in particular, I realized not everyone recognized my "authenticity" as a Hispanic. Hanging out with other new students, some were joking in Spanish. Understanding the joke, I laughed, only to be silenced by the following conversation:

her: "You speak Spanish?"
me: "I understand more than I speak."
her: "Are you Spanish?"
me: "Well, yeah, but my parents didn't speak it at home; I learned in school."
her: "No wonder I couldn't tell you were Spanish. You talk like a white girl. You dress like a white girl. You are WHITE."
me: " . . ."

This conversation—if I can even call it that—took place with an African American girl, another first-year student. Having been the victim of racism, I assumed I would fit into the group because I was not white and that she and the other students would acknowledge our shared experience of not being white. This assumption was an epic failure and perhaps the hardest thing I have to teach my students: shared oppression does not guarantee shared allegiance or alliance.

Unfortunately, my silence was not strategic; it was the product of shock. I cannot even remember what the joke was and I was not conscious of the many battles I would face as I developed my voice. In college, I started to scratch the surface of understanding of racism and sexism, but it was not until graduate school, when I read Chicana authors such as Cherríe Moraga and Gloria Anzaldúa, that I began to fit the pieces of my simultaneous comfort and discomfort in "white" and "colored" worlds. Over the years, as I studied and taught Anzaldúa's *Borderlands/ La Frontera*, in particular, I developed a way to understand my own life: I had developed a "tolerance for ambiguity" because it was the only way I could survive the barrage of racism and classism I routinely faced then and now.[8]

These experiences, perhaps best described as micro aggressions, start literally almost every time I meet someone. Having a first name that is not immediately recognizable as Latina/o separates me from Anglos and Latinos alike. If I pronounce it correctly, it is recognizable as a Spanish language name to a Spanish speaker; however, if the Spanish speaker is also a U.S. Latina/o, then I am often asked if I am Puerto Rican or Cuban or Dominican, as if these are the only kinds of Latinas/os that exist. Sometimes if the person asking is Puerto Rican, he or she will joke, "oh, you are really *boriqua*"; similarly, when the other person has been Dominican, he or she has joked, "oh, you are really *dominicana*." These comments reveal the intra-Caribbean racism and nationalism so painfully reinscribed in this country. My last name is a little more recognizable, thanks to soap opera star Vincent Irizarry. It is Basque; if I pronounce it correctly to a non-Spanish speaker, I am plummeted into the box of super exotic other and asked, "*where* are you *from*?"

My sisters and I call this the "where are you from game." Even when I pronounce my name in an Anglicized way and am asked, "where are you from?" I respond: "New York." I am asked again, "no, I mean where are you from originally?" I respond: Long Island. If that does not dispel the belief that I cannot possibly be American because of my name, I ask the other person, "where do you think I am from"? That forces people to acknowledge their assumptions and ignorance, to voice their very conscious belief that I am not from "here." Like so many of my experiences of racism, it was not until graduate school that I could discern the particular form of belonging in question at the time: citizenship. As I advanced in my studies, I came to understand something only a "natural born" citizen could take for granted: citizenship is not equal for all. Regardless of where or how one obtains citizenship, one's body, language, class, and gender all enhance or diminish the actual functionality of citizenship. The U.S.-based human rights group Black Lives Matter and human rights groups worldwide illustrate this daily.

Of Miseducations and Missed Educations

Obviously, I did not blend in well with these students at college. Most of them were students of color who, like the woman quoted above, felt that I was not "ethnic" enough. For some, I did not speak Spanish well enough. For others, I lacked the Manhattan/urban styles of dress and attitude they possessed. For others, the fact that I lived in a racially mixed area but had attended a predominantly white, private high school signaled my non-belonging. Perhaps worst of all, I came to college on academic scholarships, not federally funded programs such as HEOP.[9] When I tried to connect with the students on a class level because I was paying for college myself, my words were ignored. Eventually, I decided to ignore them; for some time, I was also silent. Moraga's words encapsulate my undergraduate experiences: "I experience, daily, a huge disparity between what I was born into and what I was to grow up to become" (Moraga 28). In the spring of my junior year, though, I took the course, "U.S. Ethnic Literature." This course introduced me to the idea of feminist pedagogy and changed my life in ways I am still coming to understand.

On the first day of class, the professor Dr. Julie Olin-Ammentorp made us sit in a circle and explained this was part of her "feminist pedagogy." I am not sure I even knew what a feminist was at that point, but I liked the idea that she wanted to hear what we had to say. This modeling of feminist pedagogy is one I use to this day; and to this day, I am amazed at how uncomfortable my students are using their voices and facing one another in an intellectual space. We read a variety of authors in the class, but Sandra Cisneros and Anzia Yezierska particularly affected me. Beyond the other texts, which moved me to think of issues of communities and the development of identity through ethnic, gender, and political self/positioning, oppression, and marginalization, these two women wrote about experiences I felt I shared. I cried when I read Cisneros because I could laugh at her jokes. Yezierska's struggles as an immigrant were versions of stories I had heard in my house, told by aunts, uncles, and cousins. For the first time, I felt that it was ok that my Spanish was not so good; there was more to being Latina than being bilingual. Back then, I measured my external *Latinidad* in my abilities to dance, cook, and be sexy: the stereotypes of Latin women that remain glibly accepted and reinscribed by Anglos and Latinos alike. Yet, internally, I felt my *Latinidad* in the often unspoken understanding of the continual rage other Latinos or people of color I met outside Le Moyne seemed to share. These books helped me address how my family and my schools constructed my identity. The books provoked many questions for me: Why were there no courses specifically on Latina/o, African, or any other ethnic writing? Why was there one course on Ethnic Literature when there were multiple courses on Shakespeare? My ethnic voice began to gurgle.

Julie Olin-Ammentorp was a wonderful mentor. When I needed academic or personal help, she was there. She offered me learning opportunities, such as participation in a feminist theory-reading group that she began. When an incident occurred in my campus townhouse that made it unsafe to stay there, she took me to her home. She became my surrogate mother; at the time, that was feminism to me. The first of several important feminist professors I had, Julie taught me something I now understand through Walker's concept of *womanism*: being a feminist is about equality for everyone in all contexts. To be a womanist is to move beyond feminism; it is to be concerned not only with your specific community but also with everyone's community. To practice womanism is to question and not be complacent with knowledge we receive at home, in school, or at work. Walker's theorization of *womanist* as encompassing humanity strikes me as especially urgent. To practice womanism is to be "committed to survival and wholeness of entire people, male *and* female" (xi). In today's world, human rights are violated daily in heinous proportion with the full recognition and documentation of these violations. If the U.S. presidential election of 2016 demonstrated anything, it showed that hate for anything not privileged, white, male, and heterosexual is operative. Yet, I am hopeful. As I drafted this, hundreds of thousands of women and men marched nationwide to resist the clear and present threats against the survival of humanity this administration has already begun to advance. As I revised this in 2018, similar marches are occurring in resistance to the separation of asylum-seeking families and the detention of thousands of minor children.

After this first course in ethnic literatures, I became even angrier, but now, at my college. Why did it take three years before I read anything written by a person of color? I may have read authors of color in previous classes but none that I can recall and certainly none whose authorship was contextualized through their intersections of race and or gender. I was living what cultural critics such as bell hooks have decried: reading *about* people of color but not reading their work. How did I end up at a college that seemed uninterested in ongoing multicultural movements? That, I realized, was the product of the single guidance session I had in high school. My counselor slid a group of college brochures across the desk and said, "These are good schools for you;" it did not occur to me to ask why they would be good for me. I applied to schools just like Le Moyne: Siena, Marist, Seton Hall, Scranton: small, predominately Anglo-American schools, some with religious affiliations. In the 1980s, such schools were just starting to consider how to make students of color feel at home and valued on campus; they relied on their pronouncements of being "in a liberal tradition" to recruit students but, as many schools still do today, utterly failed to make those campuses accessible and welcoming.

Ironically, the seeds of this essay were sown in a workshop on multiculturalism I attended after I graduated from Le Moyne in 1993. I now recognize that Le Moyne College began dealing with multiculturalism even though it had seemed to neglect to do so during my years there. My postgraduate education helped me reconcile those years of exclusion and rage. Because I was paying for my own education, I worked too much and I could not participate in activities that may have facilitated my sociopolitical awareness. When not in class or working, I spent time with my Anglo-American professors. Their mentoring and the various jobs they provided so I could pay for school made it possible for me to graduate; however, my professors also failed me in some critical ways. In my last year of school, I started the process of applying to graduate school. This was the most critical time for my educational career and it was a disaster of epic proportion.

My well-intentioned mentors advised me to go "where you can get money as a minority." This, I realized later, was bad advice. At the graduate level, one has to go where the faculty members in your area of interest are performing leading research. I had a dream—I do not know why—not to go Harvard, but to go to Brown. When I mentioned this to a mentor, she said, "Aiming kind of high, huh?" I was devastated because I assumed she had to be right and I had to be foolish to even think an Ivy League school was within my personal reach. Perhaps she had a better view of institutional constraints that would make it hard for a Le Moyne graduate to make it to Brown. Whatever my professor's thinking, my own lack of thinking was the problem. I failed to realize it was not too high for me to aim. On paper at least, my grades, test scores, and community service made Brown a reasonable aim. And, if Affirmative Action ever held its magical sway, I should have been precisely the kind of student of color Brown would want.

But this was my continuing, tragic mistake: I was not equipped to ask questions or choose something other than what I was being directed toward. I followed the money and the disaster followed me. In my first semester at Purdue University, it became clear that the program did not have courses in my area of interest—Multiethnic Poetry. Just as many of the scholars of the previous and my own generation of Chicana/o and Latina/o scholars-in-training did, I ended up taking courses in multiple departments, just to get some exposure to the kinds of writing I wanted to study: English, Spanish, Women's Studies, and Comparative Literature. When I realized I needed to be in an Ethnic Studies program, it was almost too late. I applied to these types of doctoral programs but got in nowhere except Purdue. I decided a PhD was better than no PhD and began the doctoral program at Purdue. Through the CIC Minority Predoctoral Fellowship I had, though, I had met a remarkable group of aspiring scholars who changed my understanding of my options.[10] At the end of the first year in the doctoral program, I left for the Pennsylvania State University (Penn State). In recent years, the horrific revelations of sexual assault by an athletic staff member damaged the entire university. My years there were not perfect, but I would not have become the scholar I am had Penn State and my doctoral advisor, Professor Kathryn (Kit) Hume, not ended my miseducation.

Dismantling the Master's House

Through my educational experiences, I have come sometimes willingly, more often unwillingly, to the task of embodying feminism, especially feminism informed by the intersections of race and class, woman of color feminism, and womanism.[11] There is a wealth of scholarship on underrepresented people continually educating others. I get tired of it; my like-minded friends and colleagues get tired of it. One of the other critical pieces for me in *This Bridge* is Audre Lorde's essay, "The Master's Tools Will Never Dismantle the Master's House." Originally delivered as a set of comments for "The Personal and the Political" at the Second Sex Conference, this essay has rightly become the cornerstone of much woman of color feminist theory and pedagogy. Lorde describes this imposition of teaching others so well: "Women of today are still being called upon to stretch across the gap of male ignorance, and to educate men as to our existence and our needs. This is an old and primary tool of all oppressors to keep the oppressed occupied with the master's concerns" (100). How I learn, how I teach, and how I position myself within communities has become a conscious endeavor to get others to assume responsibility for their own knowledge.

While I understood the basic premise that Lorde found the conference's lack of address of difference a central aspect of discrimination, it would be a long time before I really grasped what the Master's Tools were. When I first read her essay, I was in graduate school and was feeling more and more comfortable as a Latina. I had never felt inadequate as a woman; my parents, particularly my father, raised my sisters and me to understand there was nothing we could not do because we were "girls." My friends wanted to *be* Barbie because she was beautiful, but I wanted what Barbie *had*: her *own* house and her *own* muscle car (the purple Corvette). This sense of distance from the American Dream recurred as a graduate student. My peers were the second or third generation to earn a PhD in their families. While we were all "equal" as graduate students, I was often reminded that I was *less* equal and ostracized for having been awarded diversity-based academic merit fellowships. My exclusion from this elite scholars' club occurred in academic and social spaces.

Lorde's essay, though, made me think that I had something to bring to the table. In particular, my experiences as a woman of color had lessons in them. This passage addresses issues I was still facing: "Those of us who stand outside the circle of this society's definition of acceptable women; those of us who have been forged in the crucibles of difference; those of us who are poor, who are lesbians, who are black, who are older, know that *survival is not an academic skill*" (99). I had focused on the danger of not developing academic skills I perceived necessary: mastery of the "language" everyone seemed to know, comprised of words such as *reification*, *epistemological*, *hegemonic*, *reinscribed*. At the same time, I was stunned at the assumptions some of my professors, scholars in possession of great knowledge and this language, voiced publicly. In one seminar at Purdue, we were discussing a poem. We had just talked about a reference to *bok choi* when my professor turned to me and said, "Oh, Ylce, you must have great recipes for tacos!" I cannot relate the simultaneous rage at her ignorant assumption about my ethno-national identity and my disappointment with myself for this utterly ineffectual response: "I am not Mexican." In thinking about Lorde's essay, I realize I failed in this: "It is learning how to take our differences and make them strengths. *For the master's tools will never dismantle the master's house*" (ibid.). Rather, I had done precisely this: "as women, we have been taught to either ignore our differences or to view them as causes for separation and suspicion rather than forces for change" (ibid.).

How much was I to blame? In my early twenties, in a graduate program with others supposedly like me—those who loved to read—I felt utterly alone. I was so grateful to be in graduate school that I did not realize I had put myself in an intellectually foreign place: as Lorde notes, "Without community, there is no liberation, only the most vulnerable and temporary armistice between an individual and her oppression" (99). It was not until I met other students truly like myself, students of color who were the first to complete college and graduate degrees in their families, that I could articulate my rage. I could turn it outward, look at it, and think about ways to deal with it. My understanding of social construction was instrumental in this. Realizing that things were not "just the way they were" because of history, but because individuals, communities, and nations actively shaped them made me understand that this "master narrative" my peers kept referring to *really did exist*. Worse, its long shadow wanted to make me a footnote if it could not erase me entirely.

The End of My Doctored Ethnicity: A PhD in Latina/o Literary Studies

The other critical piece in my development of a womanist voice was being a CIC graduate minority fellowship recipient. I felt an immense responsibility to be authentically ethnic, because this was the first scholarship I had garnered due to my ethnicity (my college scholarships were academic merit/grade-based). It was at the first conference, though, that generous scholars and peers dismantled my problematic concepts of ethnic authenticity. Dr. Neil Foley, a CIC alumnus, talked about his experiences as a Mexican and Irish man, one who was never "brown" enough for Mexicans and never "white" enough for Anglos. He was recounting experiences that resonated my own and, clearly, those of others because the room let out spontaneous affirmations like a huge Amen Corner. When talking in groups, I felt people actually listening to me and realized my experiences were not unique; we were continuing the fight of our scholar predecessors. Nancy Cardona, another student I met at the conference, modeled being a womanist. A doctoral candidate in Chicana/o Studies at another institution, she was several years ahead of me. As we talked, she realized there were simply a lot of books no one ever told me about while I was an MA student. When we returned home to Indiana, she invited me to her home and piled up my arms with just about every Chicana theory book she had. This generous, empowering act of offering me access to knowledge literally helped me survive personally and academically. This act is one I try to replicate; I am constantly giving my students books hoping they will help them locate the silences in their lives and eventually, help them rupture those silences.

At both Purdue and Penn State, I took a number of feminist theory classes. These courses were both productive and oppressive; I learned that some feminists have an inflexible way of thinking, so inflexible as to be a replication of patriarchal oppression. One of these courses required journals that I saved, because I save everything. In rereading them, I am surprised at how consistent my voice has been. When answering the question, "how have I become a feminist?" I answered that it "wasn't a larger identity crisis that triggered my feminism; I'd say it was a smaller series of experiences that spontaneously got me to call myself a feminist. Most of my conscious agreement with feminism comes from what comes most naturally to me: reading."

Words are powerful. The voice of a character moves people to act, to speak, or to silence. I have already described my first experiences of reading ethnic women writers. Those writers replaced the blanket my parents had used to shield me from much of the racism I now experienced in graduate school. At times, others used those writers to silence me. One particular experience occurred when I presented at a conference in my second year of graduate school, in 1994. A Chicano professor saw my paper title in the program; the night before I was scheduled to present, he sexually harassed me. It took me years to even put a name to his behavior. Initially, I was mad at myself because I had let him make me feel stupid. His actions, first making comments about my age, then taking issue with my paper topic, and finally, making derisive comments about the Chicana feminist theory I was using, were designed to make me feel inferior and incompetent. His design was temporarily effective. I tried to defend my literary and critical heroines but did not do it to my own satisfaction. My friend who was also presenting, Denise Galarza Sepúlveda, comforted me and helped me unravel his harassing techniques. We wondered if he resented the fact that I was not Chicana and thought about the sexism that Chicana feminism evolved to address. I remember most that she showed me how he used a lofty, academic Spanish to make me feel incompetent, while he joked with the male graduate students in familiar, accessible Spanglish. My rage crystalized when I realized he was trying to push me back to the intellectual margins we were supposed to be deconstructing together as scholars of color. His ageist, sexist, ethnonational, and linguistic harassment compelled me to use my woman of color feminist voice.

When I gave my talk, my harasser came in and sat in the first row. I did not want to give him the chance to silence me again, so I shortened my talk and ended by pointing out the criticisms he made. Noting they were "questions" in the field, I undid the arguments behind them, one by one. He left the room without a single comment or question. To experience this sexism from an educated person, one who should have been a welcoming mentor, was a harsh lesson. This man made it clear that there were divisions among scholars of color; I could no longer assume we were all invested in the same liberatory work. The following semester, I took the course I wrote these journal entries for; it was taught by Dr. Jacqueline (Jackie) Martinez, a phenomenal Chicana academic who was the welcoming mentor I desperately needed. She assuaged some of that rage, replacing it with better understanding of the intersections of race, gender, and class. Jackie's experiences and willingness to answer my questions were life altering. She prompted me to think about the impossibility of representation: no one can represent a whole culture. The best we can do is to represent ourselves: our histories, values, and concerns. Though I have struggled with the agents of racism, classism, and sexism, I see now that my voice has been consistent. My voice constantly questions.

In Martinez's class, I revisited some of the feminist readings I had read as a college student. I had read Elaine Showalter, Susan Gilbert, and Sandra Gubar and I noted this in my journal: "I always felt there was something missing. I just could not buy some of the arguments they presented, there were extremes to the point that I felt literary criticism was useless. It didn't do anything except look for new ways to talk about the literature, but this in itself didn't make the world better." If I was going to go out and change minds, this was not the way to do it. Reading Norma Alarcón against Elaine Showalter helped me flesh out the differences in the criticisms—most literary analysis I was familiar with applied to the confines of the text in question. Critics such as Alarcón, Alzaldúa, hooks, Lorde, and Moraga seemed to extend criticism to the real world.

Then there was *phenomenology*. While I could appreciate the ideology that says actual experience and awareness of one's role in others' life experiences can strengthen theory, I think that has serious implications for those who wish to write outside their experiences. The 1990s were fraught with debates around ethnic authenticity and identity politics. Lived experience is important but it cannot replace one's ability to synthesize and write based on observation, interaction, and reading. If we only interpret the lives of those who no longer have a voice, how do we connect to others and whom do we actually serve in the present? How can we enact womanism if we only interpret our own experiences? Certainly, shifts in fields such as Anthropology were interrogating the relationship between researcher and the object of research. The developments of autoethnography and autocritography are an extension of both the resistance to being silenced by being written about and the rejection of becoming a silencer by writing about others without self-reflection in that process.[12]

My own experiences with silence and story draw me to literature and criticism exploring these discourses. Perhaps this is why *testimonio*, a global narrative form that functions precisely through the tensions of silence and story, is so important to me. I have published two essays on it, both of which originate in my mother's untold stories of the Dominican Republic. While other scholars may be concerned about veracity or authorship of *testimonios*, I remain interested in the genre's construction of voice. That is, I argue for a reconsideration of how voice—the narrator of often unverifiable narrative—functions within the form.[13] In thinking about those essays in the context of feminist and womanist pedagogy, I realize that the lack of voice others have is what ultimately inspires me to use mine.

In another journal entry, I noted that the gap between feminist theory and practice seemed to be growing as I read more theory. Perhaps that was because at the time, I was volunteering at a local literacy program. The center served a wide variety of student/clients, including undocumented workers seeking to learn English as a Second Language. Helping these students made me painfully aware of my privilege. More importantly, working with the center's Anglo-American population challenged my understanding of the relationship between citizenship and privilege. Had I been working with undocumented students only, I might have felt their oppression was "greater" than the other students'. Tutoring illiterate white students ranging in age and gender opened my eyes to the realities of poverty and social inequity. In a very literal sense, illiteracy prevented these people from using their voices and the effects manifested in measurable lacks: lack of access to education, lack of employment opportunity, lack of adequate housing, food, and healthcare.

Thinking about Anglo-American experiences of oppression makes me recall my acquisition of critical language. Just the other day, one of my undergraduate students reminded me that I began our Latina/o Literature class with a discussion of various terms for Latinas/os, such as Hispanic, Latina/o, Boriqua, and Chicana/o. She felt this was so important that she is including it in a piece of her creative writing. I was thinking about why I do this; sometimes our teaching practices become so repetitive we forget why we teach the way we do. I found another journal entry that illustrates the development of my ethno-feminist literacy. Yolanda Lopez, a Chicana artist, opened a lecture she was giving with a breakdown of the historical origins of ethnic identity terms. As an early graduate student, I did not use the word Latina/o; it was not quite fashionable yet because the real world had not caught up with the theory. I realized I had just accepted the term *Hispanic*, a product of institutional naming. After that lecture and reading Moraga, in particular, I knew I had to call myself Latina because I was politicized. My culture was integral to my experiences, concerns, and goals in life.[14]

Jackie Martinez's women's studies class ended with me realizing more acutely how many ways I had been silenced. When recalling the "where are you from" game my sisters and I used to resist categorization, I realized we had been fighting racism all our lives. I also noted I was interested in narrative theory and the critical penalties women writers faced for crossing generic borders through experimentation while their male colleagues garnered praise and more publication. My final project, fittingly, was an interrogation of my ethnic identity and the narratives that constructed it. Entitled, "Ylctory: A Self-reflexive Perspective of a Hispanic in the Un-Making," this final project actually began each of its sections with the name, date of birth, and italicized voice of one of my family members. As so much of the Chicana and Latina literature I was reading taught me, my story was not my own: my story was a strand in the stories of all of my family and my ancestors. At the end, I attached a poem I had written inspired by Moraga's phrase, "Bleached and Beached." Looking at these journal entries and creative narratives, the echoes of my sisters' voices are especially humbling. Our stories remind me how hard some literacies are to obtain.

A different Feminist Theory class I enrolled in, however, went very badly. Initially, I was very excited about the professor's approach through genre. Women of color were on the reading list, including Anzaldúa; however, the professor discussed *Borderlands/La Frontera* as a Chicana "version" of feminism, not the distinct feminism it is. We focused on the generic experimentation of the text without addressing the politics behind the experimentation. The way I came to know Anzaldúa was very different. I felt that the professor might as well have not taught the text; by categorizing it in a narrow way, rather than on its own terms, she silenced it. Initially, I spoke up in the class but both the students and the professor silenced those of us who did not acquiesce to the professor's intellectual approach. This professor was not invested in Chicana feminism in the same way I was and as a student, I was vulnerable. I knew that I needed to keep my mouth shut or I would not get a good grade, which would jeopardize my career. For the first time ever in school I worked just to pass. My silence was strategic but not productive.

lo que nunca pasó por sus labios: Coming to Voice

The first half of my subhead is taken from Moraga's text, *Loving in the War Years*. The subtitle loosely translates to "what never passed through your lips." In Moraga's text, this is a double entendre, referring to her development of Chicana feminism and her reconciliation of her lesbian identity. The second half comes from Angela Davis's expression, theorized and made fundamental to feminist and womanist thought by bell hooks in her volume, *Talking Back, Thinking Feminist, Thinking Black*. In 1996, I took a huge risk; I changed doctoral programs. Just about everyone thought I was crazy. I was headed closer to my sociocultural home (the East Coast) to begin studying at Penn State.

Two things thrilled me. First, I was recruited; the program actually wanted me. Second, I had the chance to study with a specialist in Latina/o Studies. The first semester was blur of feeling as if I was playing with even bigger kids and that I needed to step up my game. I read voraciously, took notes from an obscene numbers of books, and handled every aspect of my new life with immense energy. I was feeling great until the untenured professor I came to work with told me she was leaving at the end of the year. Nonetheless, in that year, this professor introduced me to some wonderful texts and films. I was able to hear scholars, artists, writers, and filmmakers such as Pepón Osorio, Ela Troyano, and to my thrill, Cherríe Moraga herself! Moraga gave a general lecture and ran a workshop exploring the themes she discussed in the lecture. Since starting this essay, I have been scouring my house for notes of her visit. I could not find any notes but I found some sketches I made; I suspect I could not take academic notes because her lectures and workshop were so powerful that I chose to listen deeply to what she was saying, to embrace what was passing through her lips, rather than trying to dissect it.

What I recall most from that visit are Moraga's questions. When she opened the lecture, she asked something like, "what does a Chicano look like?" She answered the question something like this: "An upside down 'U.' Most Anglos see Chicanos only working in the fields, bending over, sweating horseshoes in the sun." She proceeded to outline the United Farm Workers' Movement, the development of *El Teatro Campesino*, and how her work evolved from the merger of the political and artistic traditions of Mexican American culture. During the course of her visit, I got to eat dinner with her and participate in the workshop she offered. This workshop was devastating and empowering. In one of the activities used as an icebreaker, Moraga asked us to draw all of the negative, ignorant things we had been called or experienced. We were not allowed to use words; when we were done, we had to explain our drawings. I cannot remember anyone who did not have a breakdown and cry, including me. My drawing included the racial slurs I had experienced; the experience of being invisible among many people, and my mouth covered with something. I think I made it look like stitches but I cannot remember exactly.

What I do recall is this: Moraga taught us that one cannot really empathize or engage with another person over complex social issues until you have done so with yourself. Before we left that day, I shyly got out my copy of Moraga's then most recent book, *The Last Generation*, and asked her to sign it. The inscription touched me for several reasons; Moraga spelled my name correctly, it was in Spanish, and I realized that despite all of the silencing in my life, I still had wanted to share my voice: "Ylce-gracias por tu corazón abierto." To this day, the description challenges me to make myself emotionally available, in my reading and writing, so that I can teach my students not just "how to think critically" but to use critical thought to become agents of resistance and righting in their everyday lives. For various reasons, I did not participate in the Women's March; however, several former students of mine, in multiple parts of the country, did march. I do not claim responsibility for their actions, but over the years, they have shared how my courses influenced their agency. I am simultaneously humbled and proud that something I said, read, or wrote empowers them beyond our classroom.

Inside the classroom, my feminist pedagogy requires something I have wrestled with throughout my education: "strategic silence." Strategic silence can be productive when it creates space for student voice. The creation of this space for my intellectual development is a debt I truly cannot repay to my doctoral advisor, Kit Hume. A specialist primarily in Contemporary American Fiction, she has published widely, and initially I thought there would be nothing I could possibly write about that she had not already written. Kit often proved me wrong in the most productive sense. She gave me all the room I needed to become a scholar in my own right. In many ways, Kit was the opposite of my first mentor, Julie Olin-Ammentorp. Kit did not foster an emotional relationship with me; this was sometimes difficult as I navigated racially charged intellectual spaces at Penn State. She was one of few professors who treated students as emerging scholars rather than students. Kit models rigorous thinking; she asked me seemingly endless questions and provided few answers. Though this was sometimes frustrating, I know she was helping me figure out what I wanted to say and prioritizing not telling me what to say. As I have done with the most useful and empowering aspects of feminism and womanism, I practice this aspect of Kit's pedagogy. By the time they write their evaluations, many of my students say this pedagogy was the best aspect of their course with me even if they were frustrated initially that I did not offer them "the" interpretation of a text.

At Penn State, I had the opportunity to teach courses in English/Literature and Women's Studies; these experiences were invaluable because I could draw my research areas into my teaching and develop my teaching voice. Because I experienced using my voice both negatively and positively as a student, I am mindful that my own students may equate having divergent ideas with getting a bad grade. Silencing does not foster multicultural critique or model womanist practice. I am not naive enough to think most students leave my courses as newly evolved feminists or womanists, but I do see a consistent result: students start to consider oppressions within their academic, social, and ethnic communities. It is my hope that such introspection will lead to consideration of such issues between their communities and those they consider to be "other"—that they will choose to be humane before any other allegiance they may value.

Diversity courses are not always enrolled with the willing. When I first finished my PhD, I was teaching an American Studies course entitled "Cultural Diversity: The Hispanic Experience in the U.S." for a small, private liberal arts college. The course was a requirement for teachers seeking K-12 state licensure, was comprised of nontraditional students only, and met at a regional site in rural Massachusetts. Most of the students were older than I was and when I first entered the room, they thought I was one of their cohorts, not the professor. When I introduced myself, the class members confessed they were worried because they could not guess what country I was from by reading my name.

This was the moment I face over and over again. But, this was my first teaching experience as a PhD and I wanted it to go well. I chose to joke about their worry, rather than criticize their obvious nationalist and racist assumptions. I said that where I was from might be a strange place, but technically, Long Island is part of the United States. My humor made the students feel more at ease and I was delighted that the first weekend went well.

The second weekend, disaster threatened. A student opened the 5 p.m. Friday session with this question: "If you Puerto Ricans or Mexicans don't like it here, why don't you go back?" I was stunned but realized this was a make it or break it moment. Instead of being the student shocked by the request for a taco recipe, I was the professor and I was going to exercise the power of my position. I said, "fabulous question!" wrote the word "Neo-colonialism" on the board, and began to explain how Chicana/o and Latina/o literatures examine conditions shaping Hispanic immigration. The next few sessions, the teachers kept asserting they were appalled that the material was entirely new. As the course progressed, I was appalled at my new understanding of diversity: geographic. Even though I had moved into a "blue" state, I had not escaped rural conservatism. Though I did not use the taxonomy of autocritography at the time, asking the students about their own educations and responsibilities as teachers helped them redirect their frustration with their own ignorance to the institutions that had failed them instead of projecting their frustrations onto me and "those Puerto Ricans or Mexicans." A beautiful thing happened: the students vowed they would bring these ideas back to their schools. I hoped some would, but I was thrilled when months later, the student who asked that angry question sent me a great present: a children's book about Mexican immigration, which she was using in her teaching. The power of such moments sustains me even as racist policies and incidences of fatal white supremacist violence replicate like a virus.

Bridging Silence and Voice

When my colleague and womanist forefather, Gary Lemons, asked me to contribute to this volume, I was not sure what I could write that would be faithful to the transformative work of our predecessors. As I climbed from adjunct to tenure track, I got farther and farther away from my journals, my heroines, and my reflections on pedagogy. Professors decry the corporatization of the university with good cause. Student evaluations make or break annual evaluations, tenure, and promotion. Faculty members are often asked to talk about pedagogy in quantitative ways including how our assessments of students help them meet explicit objectives the course description stated, Yes, these things matter, especially in states where, increasingly, student funding depends on faculty "cost effectiveness," however that is measured. The qualitative matters more. For those of us who work in cultural fields, the classroom is always a potentially negatively charged space. Attacks on our research and teaching by conservative, "alt-right" aligned organizations, including but not limited to Turning Point USA and its "The Professor's Watchlist," undermine our classrooms and facilitate the devolution of the university as a space of inquiry.

If we are to teach courses that address existing social reality, we must be hired, tenured, and promoted under standards that recognize and address the ideological challenges framing our classrooms. Our work is vital to the purported mission of nearly every institution of higher education: "to develop students into critical thinkers who will become leaders in the futures of their communities." One would think, then, that our voices would be welcome. This is not always the case, so my womanist pedagogy is invested in righting as many wrongs as I can. Sometimes it takes the form of mentoring excellent students who have not been encouraged to pursue honors programs, graduate school, or law school. Sometimes this takes the form of very focused literary discussion on the significance of the construction and evolution of the American literary canon. Mostly, it takes the form of unraveling dangerous narratives, of helping students understand the power that racial, gender, and class narratives have in shaping their lives. By taking time to teach students the narratives that poems, stories, books, and films respond to, I hope to connect them to the world. My womanist pedagogy demands I show students the dangers of altered voices and teach them to make their voices audible, unalterable, and most importantly, communal.

Dedication

This essay is un homenaje a Cherríe Moraga y Gloria Anzaldúa, two Chicanas who taught me how to be Latina.

Notes

1. Trayvon Martin was murdered on February 26, 2012. George Zimmerman was found not guilty of second-degree murder on July 13, 2014.

2. Resistance to police brutality against African Americans escalated to the riots in Ferguson, Missouri, following the death of Michael Brown. For a review of high-cases of murder of African American men by law enforcement, see Hafner, "Police Killings of Black Men."

3. I use this term to be in dialogue with Norma Alarcón's important critique of the exceptionalism and internalized racism in the essay, "Tropology of Hunger." I also find the word's use by singer Lauryn Hill provocative. Her first solo album, *The MisEducation of Lauryn Hill*, explores the complex intersections of love, spirituality, and political activism for Black women.

4. For clarity and consistency, I use the term *Latina/o*, with its gender inclusive and regional connotation: Latin America, to denote the literature of and/or the people originating from Mexico, the Caribbean, and South America. *Hispanic* is a term instituted by the U.S. government for census purposes. I use specific terms to denote the ethnic or political identity of authors I discuss: Chicana/o, Puerto Rican, Cuban, or Dominican American.

5. Puerto Ricans have been U.S. citizens since the passage of the Jones Act (1917). Nonetheless, as political debate during the 2016 U.S. Presidential elections showed, many Americans are ignorant of Puerto Rico's history and the citizenship status of its people. This ignorance was visible again in the aftermath of 2017's Hurricane Maria, when mainland Americans questioned why the U.S. government should provide relief to people who were not "Americans."

6. Sommer, "Resisting the Heat," especially page 416, in Kaplan and Pease.

7. The term *Anglo-American* is problematic in the sense that Americans have origins in other European nations since the first colonists arrived. To be consistent with usage within Chicana/o and Latina/o Studies, however, I will retain Anglo-American.

8. See Chapter 7, "la consciencia de la mestiza/Towards a New Consciousness," of Anzaldúa, *Borderlands/La Frontera*.

9. HEOP is the acronym for the federally funded Higher Education Opportunity Program, which was designed to recruit and retain underprepared and/or economically disadvantaged students of color in college.

10. CIC is the acronym for the Committee on Institutional Cooperation. This particular program, which supported underrepresented highly achieving students of color pursuing graduate and professional degrees, was very successful in recruiting, retaining, and graduating students of color. Unfortunately, its major funder, Eli Lilly, chose not to renew its funding after its initial twenty-year endowment ended.

11. I am retaining the early scholarly distinction between feminism and woman of color feminism made by the women of the Combahee River Collective in "A Black Feminist Statement" (*This Bridge* 210–218) and by Chela Sandoval's "Feminism and Racism."

12. I refer here to autocritography as developed by Michael Awkward in *Scenes of Instruction:* "Autocritography is, in other words, an account of individual, social, and institutional conditions that help to produce a scholar, and hence, his or her professional concerns" (7).

13. See the Bibliography for the full citations of these essays.

14. Readers may wonder why I retain "Latina/o" and do not used "Latinx," as is becoming more popular. I fully respect gender orientation diversity; if an author I

discuss uses Latinx as a descriptor, I will do so. I choose to respect individuals' self-definition, including my own gendered identity as Latina.

Bibliography

Alarcón, Norma. "Tropology of Hunger: The 'Miseducation' of Richard Rodríguez." In Palumbo-Liu, David, ed. *The Ethnic Canon: Histories, Institutions, and Interventions.* Minneapolis: University of Minnesota Press, 1995. 140–152.

Anzaldúa, Gloria. *Borderlands/La Frontera: The New Mestiza.* San Francisco: Aunt Lute Books, 1987.

Awkward, Michael. *Scenes of Instruction: A Memoir.* Durham: Duke University Press, 1999.

Combahee River Collective. "A Black Feminist Statement." In Moraga, Cherríe, and Gloria Anzaldúa, eds. *This Bridge Called My Back: Writings by Radical Women of Color.* New York: Kitchen Table Press, 1981. 210–218.

Hafner, Josh. "Police killings of black men in the U.S. and what happened to the officers." *USA Today*, March 30, 2018. https://www.usatoday.com/story/news/nation-now/2018/03/29/police-killings-black-men-us-and-what-happened-officers/469467002 (accessed August 27, 2018).

hooks, bell. *Talking Back: Thinking Feminist, Thinking Black.* Boston: South End Press, 1989.

Irizarry, Ylce. "The Ethics of Writing the Caribbean: U.S. Latina Narrative as *Testimonio.*" *LIT: Literature, Interpretation, Theory* 16. 3 (2005): 263–284.

———. "When Art Remembers: Museum Exhibits as *Testimonio* del Trujillato." *Antípodas: Journal of Hispanic and Galician Studies* XX (2009): 235–251.

Lorde, Audre. "The Master's Tools Will Never Dismantle the Master's House." In Moraga and Anzaldúa, *This Bridge Called My Back: Writings by Radical Women of Color.* New York: Kitchen Table Press, 1981.98–101.

Moraga, Cherríe. "*La Güera.*" In Moraga and Anzaldúa, *This Bridge Called My Back: Writings by Radical Women of Color*, New York: Kitchen Table Press, 1981, 27–34.

Moraga, Cherríe, and Gloria Anzaldúa, eds. *This Bridge Called My Back: Writings by Radical Women of Color.* New York: Kitchen Table Press, 1981.

Rodriguez, Richard. *Hunger of Memory: The Education of Richard Rodriguez.* New York: Godine, 1982.

Sandoval, Chela. "Feminism and Racism: A Report on the 1981 National Women's Studies Association Conference." In *Making Face, Making Soul: Hacienda Caras: Creative and Critical Perspectives by Feminists of Color.* Anzaldúa, Gloria, ed. San Francisco: Aunt Lute Foundation, 1990. 55–71.

Sommer, Doris. "Resisting the Heat: Menchú, Morrison, and Incompetent Readers." In *Cultures of United States Imperialism.* Amy Kaplan and Donald E. Pease, eds. Durham: Duke University, 1993. 407–432.

Walker, Alice. *In Search of Our Mother's Gardens.* Orlando: Mariner Books, 1983.

PART II

Womanist Alliances for Human Rights and Social Justice

5

Breaking Silence

M. JACQUI ALEXANDER AND
BEVERLY GUY-SHEFTALL

In solidarity with feminist/womanist comrades in *Building Womanist Coalitions*, we foreground the important work of eradicating all forms of oppression, including those within our own communities. While historically Black colleges and universities have been necessary bread for our survival since the 19th century, issues of difference around sexuality and heteronormativity have been particularly difficult to navigate. Audre Lorde's prophetic, now vintage, charge serves as a poignant response to the crisis we now face: "It is better to speak knowing we were never meant to survive." Now more than ever as old divisions are being reignited in the dismal service of political expediency, we cannot choose silence, nor can we afford to live in silos, cordoned off from one another. Commitment to a survival of wholeness is Alice Walker's elegant framing of the imperative we must embrace at this perilous moment, within and across communities . . . wholeness, of an entire people. This commitment requires us to bring the full dimensions of our being to this project we call life as we continually, consistently reimagine Martin Luther King Jr.'s dynamic vision of building "beloved" community on our campuses—indeed, wherever the stubborn traces of injustice reside. Let us not be afraid to say unequivocally: *All* Black lives matter.

Background: Section One

In 2006, the Spelman College Women's Research & Resource Center (Women's Center) received a one-year grant from the Arcus Foundation to launch *Breaking the Silence: The Audre Lorde Black Lesbian Feminist Project*. The project was named in honor of Audre Lorde, the most productive and influential Black, lesbian feminist/writer/activist/educator of the 20th century. This important project, the first of its kind on a historically Black college campus, is part of a larger effort to establish a Lesbian, Gay, Bisexual and Transgender (LGBT) program within the Women's Center at Spelman College. From the outset, we also conceptualized the project to be Phase I of a larger project surrounding LGBT issues at historically Black colleges and universities, and were pleased to attract major funding from the Arcus Foundation for a three-year project beginning July 1, 2008—*The Audre Lorde Project Phase II, Facilitating HBCU Campus Climates of Pluralism, Inclusivity and Progressive Change.*

The overall objectives of the Audre Lorde Project (Phases I and II) were to increase public awareness and understanding about African American gay and lesbian experiences as well as sexuality issues in the African diaspora; to increase awareness about the marginalization of racial issues in the LGBT movement and Gay and Lesbian Studies or Queer Studies; and to facilitate a climate of institutional change at HBCUs that acknowledges, values, and respects difference.

During Phase I of the Project, we inaugurated the Zami Salon, a series of student-driven activities designed to raise awareness, combat homophobia/heterosexism, and promote a more inclusive environment among students, faculty, and staff of the Atlanta University Center (AUC). This student-led Zami Salon brought LGBT scholars and activists to campus who discussed a variety of issues about their experiences both inside and outside Black communities. For example, Thomas Glave, now professor of English at SUNY, Binghamton, New York, and an award-winning writer, discussed the necessity of interrogating heteronormativity in African Diaspora cultural contexts, particularly Jamaica. Cara Page, National Director of the Committee on Women, Population and the Environment, presented a workshop entitled "Designer Genes: Queer Conversations on Genetic Technologies." Dr. Layli Phillips, Professor of Women's Studies at Georgia State University (Spelman alumna, Class of '86), announced a gift of $1,000 at the 25th anniversary celebration (2006) of the Women's Center to fund a LGBT student scholarship. In the spring of 2008, the Women's Center arranged for Dr. Phillips to offer a course on "Black Queer Studies," which was an elective for our comparative women's studies major/minor. Based on our survey of gay and lesbian studies curricula at Black colleges and universities, we believe this is the first time that a semester-long, dedicated queer theory course has been offered at one of our institutions. Prominent transgender activist, Leslie Feinberg, donated her honorarium from the 25th anniversary conference to the scholarship as well. Under the auspices of the Zami Salon, the Women's Center also sponsored the first Spelman faculty "Coming Out Day."

In September 2008, we held a major symposium on the life and work of Audre Lorde, in connection with our launching of an endowment campaign for the Women's Center, which was made possible by a major leadership gift of $1 million from the Ford Foundation. During the symposium, we also explored a range of topics related to Black LGBT issues among a racially diverse cross-section of academics, activists, and students from the United States and globally.

At the core of Phase I of the Arcus Project was the processing, digital conversion, archival coding, and public unveiling of the Audre Lorde Papers, the most comprehensive documentation of Lorde's life and work as a Black lesbian feminist writer/poet/writer/educator. The papers were willed to Spelman College by Audre Lorde during Johnnetta Betsch Cole's presidency (1987–1997) and are part of the Special Collections of the Spelman Archives, the research component of the Women's Center. Upon the completion of the processing of the papers by project archivist Brenda Banks, the National Archives Publishing Company was hired to undertake the scanning of items from the Audre Lorde Collection. Reproductions were made of 12,000 pages of correspondence, personal letters, journals, notebooks, unpublished poems, essays, speeches, manuscripts, lecture notes, and photographs. The Audre Lorde papers were officially opened in September 2009.

Also during Phase I of the Arcus Project, coeditors Rudolph P. Byrd (African American Studies, Emory University), Johnnetta Betsch Cole (President Emeritus, Spelman and Bennett Colleges) and Project Director, Beverly Guy-Sheftall, completed *I Am Your Sister: The Collected and Unpublished Writings of Audre Lorde* (Oxford University Press, 2009). It would have been difficult to complete this important book project without having access to the Audre Lorde Papers, which the Arcus Foundation grant made possible. In her reflections, Johnnetta Betsch Cole discusses her friendship with Lorde and the circumstances surrounding the papers having been gifted to Spelman College; in her epilogue, Guy-Sheftall chronicles the connection between Audre Lorde and Spelman College and her impact on the mission of the Women's Center; in his introduction, Byrd articulates the significance of Audre Lorde in the development of Black feminist studies.

Phase I of the Audre Lorde Project established the Women's Center at Spelman College as a major site for the exploration of Black LGBTQ issues in the academy. As a result of Arcus funding, the Spelman Archives (attached to the Women's Center), is becoming a major repository for the work of contemporary Black feminist scholar/activists. We remain committed to exploring LGBTQ issues in multiple racial/ethnic communities, especially in the African Diaspora, and in stimulating further exploration of these important issues at historically Black colleges and universities. We are also committed to stimulating additional research about LGBT matters at HBCUs. In this regard, one of the most exciting and important aspects of the Arcus Project was reconnecting with Spelman alumnae who had been involved with advocacy around sexuality issues, which included the founding of our first LGBT organization, Lesbian and Bisexual Alliance (LBA). It is now possible to chronicle that early history, as well as engage in a more comprehensive analysis of LGBT issues at Spelman, which will be similar when it is completed to Howard University's Lavender Report.

According to the testimony of Spelman alumna Wendi O'Neal (Class of '96), Kendra Johnson was the first student to approach then President Johnnetta Cole in 1992 about chartering an LGBT organization in response to an earlier homophobic incident on campus. At that point, there were about eight students who were meeting secretly in the counseling center with a supportive staff member; among them was an out domestic exchange student as well. Wendi (see the new LBA/Afrekete list-serv) attributes events in their own lives, the contentious public debate around gay rights, and the rise of the Christian right's mobilization in Black churches as factors that motivated them to push for a chartered student organization so that they could address the needs of lesbian and bisexual women in the AUC. They called themselves the LBA (Lesbian and Bisexual Alliance), so that students would know they weren't hiding. The following year only two of them returned—Antonia Randolph and Wendi, the first copresidents of LBA. Wendi indicates they were able to keep the small organization going with help from friends and allies, especially Women's Center staff. In the fall of 1993, President Cole wrote an open letter to the College community in which she joined the debate about the recently chartered LBA. Her goal was to affirm her commitment to diversity and to help create a "beloved community" at Spelman, including students who marked sexual difference. Excerpts from the letter are reprinted in *Gender Talk: The Struggle for Women's Equality in African American Communities* (2003), which Cole and Guy-Sheftall coauthored some years later.

Given the fragility and size of LBA and the departure of its founding presidents in 1996, the organization might not have survived were it not for Donna Hope who attended Spelman from 1995–1998 and returned to graduate in 2000. When they left, Donna was asked to carry the torch and articulates the genealogy of the organization, which is still a vibrant organization:

> I admit I was very reluctant! I was in the very intense Dual Degree program with very little free time; LBA had no faculty advisor, no meeting space, and our beloved and progressive Dr. Cole was resigning as President. It wasn't easy, but I was determined to make the LBA thrive. I placed ads in the paper, petitioned several faculty for support, and fliered all around the AUC each week for meetings. I was just making some headway sophomore year when my mother expectedly passed away in January '97. I decided not to take time off, but requested a domestic exchange that spring semester at Barnard College. I returned to Spelman my third and final year in fall '97 with bold ideas. I decided that the LBA needed a new name to reflect the new, fierce, bold, proud and OUT lesbian/bisexual Spelman sister. I had just read Audre Lorde's Zami and Catherine McKinley's Black lesbian anthology, Afrekete, and knew that Afrekete was the perfect name. Voila! This rich legacy of Spelman student activism around LGBT issues has not had a public face until the Arcus Project, and we are determined to write a more complete history of this important phase in the College's evolution.

Our Howard University liaison, Victoria Diane Kirby, graduate assistant in the Office of the President, and author of their *Lavender Report*, shared with us important aspects of their LGBT history as we struggled to make more visible these hidden histories at HBCUs. Howard was the first HBCU to have a recognized LGBT organization on campus as early as 1980 but, like Spelman's, it could be characterized as fragile from the beginning. The first group, Lambda Student Alliance, was recognized by the university as an official student organization and lasted until the mid-1980s. In the 1990s, a new LGBT student group, Oxala, began, but by 1999 it had faded. In September 2000, Sean McMillan and Sterling Washington started a new student group and began the process of having it recognized officially. On October 6, 2000, they met for the first time. Named the Bisexual, Lesbian and Gay Organization of Students at Howard (BLAGOSAH), the new LGBT student group has flourished over the past decade. In 2009, the name BLAGOSAH was officially changed to the Coalition of Activist Students Celebrating the Acceptance of Diversity and Equality (CASCADE).

Kirby also shared with us the variety of ways in which Howard University has been in the forefront of LGBT equality since the early 1900s, beginning with its appointment of Professor Alain Locke to the faculty. Locke was not only the first African American Rhodes scholar but also openly gay. His protégé, Zora Neale Hurston, the cofounder of *The Hilltop*, was openly bisexual and, during the time she was at Howard, along with a group of other students, used The Caverns (now Bohemian Caverns) as an early meeting place for LGBT students. Lucy Diggs Slowe, a Howard alumna and its first

Dean of Women, had a female partner during her tenure at Howard (see Ruby Nell Sales's commissioned paper). Howard is also seen as the birthplace of the Black Pride Movement, an international movement celebrating the unique experiences of Black people who are same-gender loving (SGL); the first Black Pride celebration was held across the street from Howard at Banneker Field.

Howard alumni, such as Darlene Nipper of the National Gay and Lesbian Task Force (NGLTF), and Sterling Washington of the International Federation of Black Prides (IFBP), started the first black LGBT churches in Washington, D.C., and are active in prominent black and mainstream LGBT organizations, according to Howard's "Lavender Report." In terms of university policy, Howard was the first HBCU to have an antidiscrimination policy designating gays and lesbians as a protected class; it was approved twenty years ago by the Board of Trustees when most HBCUs were unwilling to do likewise. Howard is one of three HBCUs that grants employee health benefits to the spouses of LGBT faculty and staff and has partnered with the Metropolitan Police Department's Gay & Lesbian Liaison Unit (GLLU) to provide LGBT sensitivity training to its campus police. Religious life at Howard has also been inclusive. Bernard L. Richardson, Dean of the Chapel, has selected openly gay assistants and brought LGBT preachers to speak at Rankin Chapel. Dean Pollard of the School of Divinity and its alumni were instrumental in organizing a group of over 100 D.C. ministers and other faith leaders to support marriage equality in the nation's capital. University chaplains Rev. Franklin Vaughn (Anglican/Lutheran/ Episcopal) and Reverend Frazier (United Methodist) have made their ministries open and affirming, becoming beacons of light for students struggling to reconcile their same-gender affections with their religion. This academic year (2010–2011), the Office of the Vice President of Student Affairs launched an LGBT learning cohort for the entire campus community that served as an important site for discussion of LGBT issues, art, and literature.

Phase II of the Audre Lorde Project—"Facilitating HBCU Campus Climates of Pluralism, Inclusivity and Progressive Change"—is an expansion of Phase I, which focused on Spelman College and the AUC. It engages in research, outreach and community-led change at ten HBCUs. Our broad goals are to raise awareness, inspire critical dialogue, and explore senior administration-endorsed strategies to facilitate progressive change around inclusivity and difference in a variety of Black colleges and universities. During the first year of the project, we engaged in extensive data gathering and analysis relative to institutional policies and practices at our partnering institutions:

Philander Smith College, Morgan State University, North Carolina Central University, Bennett College for Women, Clark Atlanta University, Southern University, Howard University, Fisk University, Morehouse College, and Spelman College. We commissioned a case study of Dillard University during Michael Lomax's presidency because of its LGBT-friendly campus climate and culture, given a set of criteria that we identified. Because of the uniqueness of Dillard during Lomax's presidency, we engaged a consultant to write a report based on interviews with key administrators; we were interested in an analysis of the specific conditions and circumstances that situated Dillard in this unusual place among HBCUs. The consultant we chose was the former director of International Programs both at Dillard and Morehouse Colleges and a doctoral student at Clark Atlanta University. Our assumption was that this consultant's report would enable us to ascertain what constitutes gay-friendly Black colleges and universities so that we would be able to more effectively advise and make policy recommendations for other HBCUs. We used Campus Pride's "LGBTQ-Friendly Campus Climate Index: National Assessment Tool" as our primary instrument for assessing campus cultures at the Black colleges with whom we collaborated.

During the first year of the project we also wanted to ascertain the nature of already existing projects that might have addressed LBGT issues at HBCUs. In this regard, three important national initiatives were identified: the Human Rights Campaign Foundation's HBCU Program whose Hype '08 involved ten HBCU campuses; SoulforceQ, whose Equality Rides visited fifteen Black colleges, including Spelman and Morehouse in the fall of 2008; and Campus Pride, whose collaborative questionnaire we would be encouraging all of our partner institutions to complete and use in the working groups they would form for their own individual assessments of their campus climates. We also commissioned an additional four papers which constitute the intellectual underpinnings of this historic four-year Audre Lorde project. Collectively, the five papers represent the most comprehensive scholarship to date on a broad range of LGBT issues at Black colleges and universities, some of which challenge conventional notions about the nature of homophobia in African American communities or the experiences of Black gay and lesbian faculty in particular institutional contexts.

Much of the work during Phase II focused upon cementing our partnership with ten carefully selected HBCUs and hiring the appropriate staff to carry out this challenging but important work. We hired a senior professor, M. Jacqui Alexander (Women's and Gender Studies, University of Toronto), who was Cosby Chair at Spelman (2008–2009) and Aaron Wells, a Hampton

University alumnus who served as part-time research coordinator. We also hired Taryn Crenshaw, a Spelman alumna who had assisted with our Zami Salon in Phase I of the Arcus Project; she gathered data about a variety of issues at a range of HBCUs, including curricula matters and institutional practices around gender and sexuality. The primary activities during this year were securing buy-in from our partners, which began by soliciting presidents to partner with Spelman; conducting campus visits; finalizing the four commissioned papers that would provide the intellectual backdrop for the project; and planning for the culminating activity, which would be a historic Summit that focused on HBCUs.

Our campus visits were informed by particular sets of data: 1) pertinent information from the respective college's website (history, mission, diversity programming, curricular, and institutional policies); and 2) the LGBT campus climate index that was developed by Campus Pride. The index scans college campuses to determine their level of LGBT inclusion and engagement or what they call "gay-friendliness." The questionnaire that colleges complete (after registering with Campus Pride) includes a broad range of questions, especially services, that relate to campus climate around issues of inclusion. During campus visits we met with presidents, provosts, student life professionals, faculty, a broad range of staff, and students. We were attentive in our discussions to whether campuses addressed issues of diversity broadly and the extent to which gender/sexuality issues were perceived to be connected to racial/ethnic, class, or religious diversity. We made use of what we had learned from the Dillard case study which explored strategies that shifted the usually chilly climate for LGBT persons on campus. The case study turned out to have been an indispensable orienting document for us as we planned our campus visits. We undertook extensive preparations prior to each campus visit. Initially, we contacted presidents and provosts requesting that they designate a campus liaison who would coordinate our visits; in some cases, project staff identified campus liaisons based on our having already worked with them in Women's Center projects. We stressed the importance of identifying administrators/faculty/staff whose administrative, policy, pedagogical, curricular, or political work bore on dimensions of the Arcus Project. Faculty advisors to LGBT student organizations, as well as members of those organizations, were critical during our campus visits. Fortunately, there was widespread enthusiasm for our visits among most of our collaborators. Despite the logistical challenges associated with scheduling all-day visits with a variety of participants (including presidents and provosts), we managed to complete all of the visits by the third year of the project. There were only two campuses where we were unable to meet with presidents.

And finally, there are recommendations that we believe will be useful as Black colleges and universities expand their efforts to facilitate campus climates of inclusivity and progressive change. A Luta Continua! The struggle continues.

Curricular Issues: Section Two

Despite their history of exclusion and commitment to providing a quality education for students who have been marginalized elsewhere, HBCUs have been conspicuous by their absence, with a few exceptions, in national debates about diversity in the academy. Exploring diversity at HBCUs may seem to be an oxymoron, but only because of the ways in which curriculum transformation projects on college campuses have been conceptualized. Nationally, these projects assume a predominantly white institution whose students and faculty of color constitute a minority. A main premise of these efforts to bring about a more inclusive curriculum has been that white students have not been prepared to deal adequately with an increasingly multicultural, multiracial world.

Spelman College's Women's Center (in an atypical occurrence within the HBCU context) began its curriculum transformation efforts with a Ford Foundation–funded mainstreaming women's studies project in 1983 ("Curriculum Development in Black Women's Studies"); a decade later, in 1994, it embarked upon another Ford-funded project to infuse diversity in the liberal arts curriculum. As in other diversity projects at predominantly white institutions (PWIs), we addressed issues of race/ethnicity, gender, class, religion, disability, and sexuality. In our survey of curricula at other HBCUs during the '80s, we discovered that while race and class may be dealt with routinely, there are silences about other diversity issues, especially gender and sexuality. When Spelman initiated a Women's Studies minor in 1981, it was the first HBCU to do so; in 1996, it expanded the program to include a major in Comparative Women's Studies, the first and only HBCU with a women's studies major. If Women's Studies has been slow to become institutionalized at HBCUs, Gay and Lesbian Studies is virtually absent, though there has been some attention to sexuality, broadly speaking.

At HBCUs, courses on sexuality have been offered in a variety of disciplines, including social work, sociology, psychology, Women's Studies, family and consumer sciences, the natural sciences, schools of medicine, and theology. In the data-gathering phase of Phase II of the Arcus Project, the Women's Center found that from a random sample of 29 HBCUs, 17 had offered courses with the term *sexuality* in the title and/or course description. Located primarily in the social/behavioral sciences, content on sexuality was typically found in courses like "Sex and Gender" or "Race, Class, and Gender," which are commonly housed in sociology departments, and in Women's Studies, such as "Introduction to Women's Studies: Human Sexuality," a course that preceded the development of women's studies as a field of study, appears to have been one of the more common courses taught at HBCUs, since 10 of the 17 institutions surveyed had at least one "Human Sexuality" course, which was offered in various academic departments. Descriptions of the courses varied tremendously. One such course (offered in sociology) described its objectives as follows: "This course surveys the biological and social components of sexuality. Relevant concepts include reproduction, birth control, venereal disease, emotions, etc." Five of the seventeen institutions offered courses in sexuality that were based in women's studies. Only one HBCU (Spelman) offered a dedicated course that narrowed the pervasive analytic distance between Black Studies and LGBT studies by treating explicitly "queer" scholarship.

Faculty at five of our partnering institutions spoke about integrating LGBT content (some more that others) in their courses in Philosophy, Sociology, Political Science, Women's Studies, Religion/Theology, Performance Studies, and in a cluster of courses at one institution called "Platinum by Design." In two other cases, faculty were in the process of developing new LGBT courses, one on queer theory at the graduate level in English. Our assumption that the humanities might have been a vibrant place for LGBT curricular engagement turned out to be misplaced in most cases. In a few instances, we found that it was possible to teach James Baldwin—one of the most iconicized "gay" authors—without interrogating his sexuality. Audre Lorde, a Black lesbian icon and writer, seems not to have been taught routinely in English departments, including African American literature. No HBCU offered LGBT studies as an academic major, minor, concentration, or certificate program, though, as a result of student advocacy, one of our partnering institutions is in the process of working with consortium schools to construct a possible major or minor. This same institution sponsors what is referred to as an "LGBT learning community/ cohort" that is called "To Be Young, Gifted, Black and Gay." It is offered as a seminar course, but without course credit. It appeared that our partnering campuses did not carry a significant number of LGBT-inclusive books and periodicals on sexual orientation in their libraries, though one bookstore seems to have moved in that direction.

In the absence of LGBT Studies, the intellectual and emotional space for students to wrestle with gender and sexuality as social constructs is understandably circumscribed. In contexts where same-sex sexuality remains taboo, presumably supported by religious dictates that mark it as such, pervasive ideas about heterosexual morality or heteronormativity usurp the place of curricular engagement in ways that make it difficult for LGBT students to locate themselves within a robust intellectual legacy. Additionally, the absence of curriculum helps to perpetuate the myth that LGBT orientation is a lifestyle, one of individual choice, therefore personal, therefore private—and therefore unworthy of scholarly pursuit. One chair of a history department noted, "The curriculum is failing us in regard to sexuality and gender . . . it is disappointing."

An unexpected issue turned out to have been the question of Black faculty living closeted lives, at least on campus. While we must be wary of attempts to collapse identity into scholarship, the pervasive pattern of closeted black faculty may account for the dearth of LGBT curricular offerings. In those instances where there was LGBT content in courses, they were taught mostly by white faculty who were "out." In one case, however, an out Black lesbian faculty member shared that she had designed a Black queer course but no students enrolled in the course. In one faculty discussion, one semicloseted junior faculty member disclosed that he was dissuaded from offering courses on sexuality by the chair of his department whom he thought to be gay. Here is an instance where the boundaries of the heteronormative are being actively maintained by heterosexual and homosexual alike. When on other occasions we asked (presumably heterosexual) faculty why they believed their LGBT colleagues might be reluctant to be out or to offer LGBT courses, they cited "fear of institutional backlash," of being seen as "controversial," and—among junior faculty the idea that being out "would result in refusals around tenure and promotion." One faculty focus group summed it up in this way: "'Don't Ask Don't Tell' is the same policy for professors; most faculty are not out; the idea here is that LGBT people must not be too flamboyant; it will be seen as unprofessional, lead to political backlash . . . damage professional development. Faculty feel they shouldn't get into the conversation in the classroom around sexuality . . . because it will be easier for their lives; better for their reputation; and new faculty are advised not to do this. Departmental committees may not give you the green light when a faculty member wants to introduce a course on queer/gender issues and might say, 'this is not the type of course that we want here.'"

No discussion of academic life would be complete without some mention of the type of classroom culture that obtains in the conflictual arrangements of silence, religious taboo, visibility of LGBT students, closeted black faculty, and an overall climate that enforces heterosexuality. Incidents of homophobia in the classroom figure prominently in alumni accounts of their experiences at HBCUs, though less so in our discussions with students about academic life. Students nonetheless did reference incidents of homophobia in the classroom in which their LGBT status was used to mark negative difference, a matter to which we return later. The point here is not really about whether black faculty use the classroom as the site for coming out, but rather whether the scholarly silence around sexuality forestalls a series of critical conversations that mark the territories of blackness, gender, sexuality, class, nationality and pedagogy.[1] In such a situation, it becomes easy to believe that these very topics are "unspeakable" and therefore lie outside the boundaries of theoretical and intellectual inquiry. In the same way in which the absence of Black Studies/Black history rendered "American" history incomplete, so, too, the absence of Black LGBT studies renders Black Studies similarly incomplete. And perhaps ultimately, the absence might well be ostensible, in the sense that that which is queer is always already contained within Black, not as the absent or the exile, but as the unspeakable and the named and, therefore, as that which always gestures rupture and possibility. Related to these varied engagements with LGBT Studies, we found that women's studies courses, including courses on black women, played an important role in the intellectual and political preparation of students at HBCUs. During our campus visits, we observed a notable difference in intellectual/analytic skills between those students who had been exposed to Women's Studies as an academic discipline and those who were not. Students who had enrolled in women's studies courses, even in the absence of LGBT studies, were more likely to be conscious of the politics and history of their campuses in relation to matters of gender and sexuality and as a result were more likely to view these matters not as private, individual concerns but as public, culturally constructed, and ultimately amenable to intervention. The interplay between the local and the global provided them with a vocabulary to understand themselves and the world at the same time that they were engaged in critical scholarship about feminism and sexuality.

LGBT Student Life

Directors and staff at the Offices of Student Life who deal in an immediate way with the day-to-day realities of LGBT students made several important observations about their experiences. One director with close to three decades of experience framed the general problem in these terms: "One of the challenges we have here is that we are taking young people from much larger adaptive environments and putting them into a microcosm (HBCUs) that hasn't caught up with the real world." They noted a marked increase in intimate partner violence for both LGBT and heterosexual students over the number of years they were employed at a given HBCU; they outlined the ways in which gender perceptions shaped the degree to which heterosexual students embraced ally relationships with their LGBT peers. They knew of situations where vocal LGBT students felt that they had been singled out, silenced, or were involved in organizations that had been refused a charter; and that gay male students have been told in the classroom "to put some bass in their voice." They commented as well on the kind of distortions that result from gender imbalances and uninterrogated ideas of masculinity. In one instance where women students outnumbered men, it was men, "gay men [who] tended to assume more leadership positions."

Most often, Offices of Student Life were focal places for LGBT programming, though there were two instances in which proactive Women's Centers also assumed that role. These Offices sponsored diversity workshops and panel presentations and otherwise assisted in organizing training for *Safe Zone* programs. Faculty, students, and staff complete *Train the Trainer* workshops to become Safe Zone facilitators by agreeing to serve as a campus resource. The goal of Safe Zone is to provide a network of persons who would be "understanding, supportive and trustworthy if a sexual minority student or employee need[ed] help, advice or just someone to talk with." Still, in many instances, administrators sounded the urgency of designing structural mechanisms for gathering data about the experiences of LGBT students and developing tailored programs. One director of an Office of Student Life put it flatly, "There is simply no institutional capacity to do the strategic work we know needs to be done."

The dire need for tailored programs is evident in complaints by student life staff that they could not identify proactive and consistent programming that their offices had undertaken to shift the culture of silence at their respective schools or attend effectively to the incidents of violence that had occurred among students. While they knew of some of the more egregious and public incidents of violence at HBCUs, such as suicide, an attack on a gay student by members of a school's marching band, and the beating of a male student with a baseball bat, there seemed to be an implicit sense that they were not those institutions. Somehow, then, egregious violence was something that occurred elsewhere. As is the case at PWIs, LGBT students are severely harmed, attacked and harassed for their sexual orientation on HBCU campuses; they have been the survivors of hate crimes, and some have harmed themselves. On the same day that we visited one campus, LGBT students learned that, only a few months earlier, a lesbian student had withdrawn from the university and taken her own life. Admittedly, this incident occurred after she had withdrawn, but there has been one reported incident of suicide at an HBCU, and students revealed in conversations with us that they, too, had considered suicide. This suggests that HBCUs are indeed microcosms of the national picture with respect to violence. It is important to remember that nationally Black LGBT youth are nearly 35 percent more likely than other youth to be homeless or commit suicide, even though they are a mere 1 percent of the overall youth population.[2] While the term *hate crime* rarely surfaced in our discussions of violence against LGBT people, it would be useful to introduce the concept in future discussions of campus violence on HBCU campuses. Much like violence in the larger society, these incidents of violence might well be flash points that signal certain ruptures in the social systems of gender-sex at schools. It is thus another area that requires deeper investigation.

From students in our focus group discussions, mostly with LGBT organizations, we heard a variety of disturbing occurrences: LGBT students drop out or transfer when campus pressures become psychologically unbearable; they experience peer pressure to acknowledge their racial identity but not their sexual orientation; they have experienced homophobia in the classroom; they have been harassed by faculty with apparently little recourse as policies that prohibit sexual harassment do not routinely include harassment on the basis of gender identity; they live in fear of being ostracized; they have struggled with coming out on campus; they have heard whisperings about the presumed damnation of their souls because of their sexual orientation; "butch" women have been dubbed "the aggressives" by virtue of how they presumably look and what they wear; lesbians have been told they are "too cute to be lesbian;" gay men have been told that "sissies are not real men." There were two instances in which students were required to adhere to a "dress code" and codes of "appropriate attire." Though LGBT students in the case of the latter were divided on the intent of the policy, they were nonetheless the most vocal opponents of the policy on campus. More work will need to be done to determine whether the focus on looks and dress works to displace engagement with other issues that pertain to gender and sexuality.

On campuses where loyalty to race dovetailed closely with heteromasculinity, students believed it was "easier to be out as a lesbian than as a gay man"; while in other coed contexts, they felt that "heterosexual women accepted lesbians far more easily than heterosexual men accepted gay men." Other campuses seemed less polarized and polarizing. In the absence of student organizations, especially on small campuses, one out LGBT student can bear the onus of all that signifies LGBT on that campus, assuming a level of hypervisibility and taking on a level of extra work that borders on danger. Some LGBT students live on campuses where their student handbooks prohibit them from "showing affection"; and others revealed that they feel compelled to hold administrators accountable for "creating a hostile environment." All of these experiences can be understood as violences of different kinds.

But perhaps the most consistent area of collective student discontent about academic matters pertained to epistemic violence, the erasure of LGBT knowledge and ways of knowing, evidenced in the absence of focused LGBT curriculum across different disciplines. It was often difficult for students to identify LGBT courses. They also alluded to closeted faculty and administrators whom they believed perpetuated the culture of silence and therefore made it difficult to be held accountable by virtue of their remaining in the closet. For them, closeted black faculty resulted in most instances in advisors to their organizations being white. A white gay faculty member on one of the campuses captured the dilemma in this way: "Students have said to me that one of the hardest things on this campus is that there are no role models who are out and proud . . . the fact that they have an old white guy as their LGBT advisor speaks volumes. . . . I was hired as an openly gay man in my department and I can say that it is easier being an out white man than it is for my Black colleagues. . . . When I brought up LGBT issues in 1999, there was a multitude of really concerning responses, from total ignorance to really hateful remarks; there is much less of that these days. I've seen students lead the way on this issue."

Indeed, LGBT students and their allies are the catalyst for change at HBCUs. Political organizing on the part of LGBT students at our partner schools is one clear indication that gender-sex systems are being publicly contested and renegotiated despite the cost. But there is also substantial benefit in the sense that political organizing assists in building a collective consciousness among LGBT students that reduces the tendency to individualize social injury. Some organizations are of long standing—two decades and more—while others have been formed recently. Where organizations were small and embattled, they experienced the arm of the administration as long and retaliative, and of "being pushed around a lot." On some campuses, strong cultures of heteromasculinity conspire to keep gay men away from LGBT organizations, in which case such organizations tend to be small and comprised mostly of lesbians. Such cultures can produce a certain amount of homophobic polarization among students as this statement indicates: "As a heterosexual male, I would not join . . . LGBT groups. . . . [They] promote segregation. They are promoting themselves . . . segregation is an inevitable result." This occurred on the very campus where we noted the hypervisibility of the single lesbian student. The comment helped explain the failure of events that she almost singlehandedly organized: "I organized this event *Gay Questions, Straight Answers* . . . [S]ides were set up for the gay side and a straight side . . . nobody from the straight side came out to support us, only some high school students that were brought in by another woman from off campus." Aware of the costs of her own hypervisibility, she yearned for an organization: "If we had a gay/straight alliance on this campus, it would give people a place to go so they could come out; it would help lines of communication."

In all but four of our partner schools, students had important experiences in building vibrant organizations. Thus, the LGBT student organizations with whom we held focus group discussions comprise approximately 23 percent of all LGBT student organizations among HBCUs. While their missions vary, SafeSpace at Morehouse, CASCADE at Howard, B.R.I.D.E. at Bennett, RAINBOW SOUL at Morgan State, COLORS at North Carolina Central, and Afrekete at Spelman all agree on the importance of combating "heterosexism and homophobia," on providing "support and company," on building a "safe, respecting and affirming campus," and on creating relationships with allies. They have lobbied administrators and their peers for LGBT programs and curricular interventions, which they believe will benefit the entire campus. They understand that misogyny and patriarchy undergird and prop up heterosexism, therefore the slogan, "No More No Homo," at one campus, and they have likened sexual injustice to racial injustice: "Is Gay the New Black?" In collaboration with faculty and offices of Student Life, they have organized for "Dinner After Sex," and have sponsored film series. They have created magazines, set up e-portals to facilitate quick and easy communication, and have documented their lives. They have joined fraternities and sororities, sometimes in tense, sometimes in accommodative, relationships to them. They have staged days of silence on their campuses to coincide with April 10, the National Day of Silence.[3] SafeSpace and Afrekete have worked collaboratively in the Atlanta University Center to sponsor their first Pride Week at Spelman College (November 2009). Among other events in November 2010, the second Pride Week, they featured "a drag fashion show . . . to normalize concepts of gender and gender expression that have been deemed 'alternative' by mainstream society." They have also worked collaboratively and in conjunction with Equality Ride, a project of SoulforceQ, "a traveling forum that gives young adults the chance to deconstruct injustice and the rhetoric that sustains it." Our campus visit to Howard coincided with CASCADE's celebration of 30 years of LGBT student organizing on its campus; here, we read its *Lavender Report*, written by Victoria Kirby, a model for other HBCUs interested in chronicling their LGBT history. LGBT students have called for a variety of changes on their campuses: "resource centers with paid dedicated staff" to serve as the springboard for conferences, symposia, and research; the establishment of "safe space"; clearly articulated and consistently visible nondiscriminatory LGBT policies; LGBT training for faculty, staff, health professionals, police officers, and residence hall directors; active LGBT recruitment; substantive LGBT presence at Open Houses and New Student Orientation; signage for gender-neutral/family bathrooms."

Much of LGBT student organizing has come about in the wake of campus violence and in closely aligned partnerships with organizations such as the National Black Justice Coalition (NBJC), Campus Pride, and the Human Rights Campaign (HRC). The HRC began its HBCU initiative in 2001 in response to an incident in which the founder of an LGBT student organization was threatened with a gun as he walked on campus with his boyfriend; he was later attacked on campus. HRC intervened on behalf of the gay student and since that time has worked closely with LGBT student organizations at 22 HBCUs.[4] They also maintain their Equality Forward Research Project/Resource Guide to Coming Out for African Americans. They provide resources; assist students in chartering their organizations; identify advisors; engage in succession planning; and organize student empowerment sessions as well as dialogues on sexuality.[5] In 2009, HRC worked in concert with members of Rainbow Soul to launch a letter writing campaign in support of the Employment NonDiscrimination Act (ENDA) that prohibits workplace discrimination on the basis of sexual orientation and gender identity; and with CASCADE a panel titled, "Legalize Gay: A Dialogue on Race, Faith and Marriage."[6]

Working at the intersection of various identities of "race/ethnicity, gender, religion," Campus Pride offers resources and programs in conjunction with some HBCUs. Its *Voice and Action National Leadership Award* grew out of a scholarship program for HBCU students—Camp Pride Summer Leadership Camp—which is based on a social justice model of leadership development. It is under the auspices of this leadership camp that JeShawna Wholley (2011), past president of Spelman's Afrekete, was recognized in 2011 as the first African American awardee.[7]

In 2010, The National Black Justice Coalition, which works at the confluence of Civil Rights and LGBT rights, placed HBCUs at the heart of its work. Among other projects, they have "provided leadership opportunities to HBCU students from around the country to participate in the 2010 "OUT on the Hill," an NBJC conference that brings together Black LGBT leaders to Washington, D.C., to hold members of the Congressional Black Caucus accountable for taking on these questions. They have also met with twelve senior level administrators at HBCUs on the climate issues that are the subject of our campus visits, and were instrumental in highlighting HBCU visibility (along with HRC) at the National Coming Out Day at the White House.[8]

Generally, all of these organizations have brought legitimacy to the concerns of LGBT students on our campuses. One outstanding question remains about how to make inroads and create a ripple effect with other HBCUs who have not yet begun to consider these questions. Very recently The Human Rights Campaign has created a partnership with the United Negro College Fund to explore ways to reach additional HBCUs. Out of 103 HBCUs, 26 have LGBT student organizations.

LGBT Recruitment and Retention Efforts

To be explicit about LGBT recruitment and retention of students suggests that institutions have been simultaneously explicit about the range of policy and program matters that shape the cultural and academic lives of LGBT communities. We were unable to find such explicit policies. As administrators at HBCUs shy away from being known as a magnet for LGBT students, citing at times pressure from alumni, it is left up to students to use the mechanisms at their disposal to recruit other students in order to build a critical mass. Gay friendliness is often a determination that students make and they tend to make that determination not so much on the basis of the existence of policy, but on numbers, on the presence of a few—yet important—faculty and administrator allies and on the basis of vibrant student organizations.

LGBT Policy Inclusion

In our review of their public documents, we found that nine of our partner schools prohibit discrimination on the basis of sexual orientation and include the words *sexual orientation* as part of a list of other possible categories of discrimination, such as race, color, national or ethnic origin, religion, sex, age, marital status, and disability or physical challenge. Three schools explicitly prohibit discrimination on the basis of gender identity by including the words gender identity in their policy; one school explicitly outlawed discrimination on the basis of HIV status. Perhaps the most inclusive of all these statements of nondiscrimination indicated that the school was "committed to ensuring equal opportunity without regard to race, color, national or ethnic origin, sex, actual or perceived gender, age, religion, creed, disability, sexual orientation, gender identity and expression, genetic information or parental, marital, domestic partner, civil union, military or veteran status."

Three of our participating schools offer health insurance coverage to their employees' same sex partners. As posed on the questionnaire, the query asked: What other benefits does your campus offer equally to both opposite-sex spouses of employees as well same-sex partners of employees? The options listed twelve possible benefits ranging from dental and vision insurance to tuition remission for spouse/partner and employee discounts. From a lengthy discussion on one of our campuses as part of the LGBT working group on LGBT issues convened by the president, we learned that in some instances certain benefits were not included in any employees' compensation packages while others would require negotiations with health insurance companies. A benefit such as tuition remission for spouse/partner/dependents, for instance, bears on larger legal questions about whether LGBT persons are prohibited from adopting dependents, from marriage, and from registering/claiming domestic partnership. This is one major area where clarification and ongoing discussion will be most needed. Access to this information also emerges as an area of concern. In one of our faculty discussions and in conversation with one director of human resources at the same institution, it was revealed that although same-sex partner benefits were provided, the information had not been made public. The director of HR immediately noted that it was an omission and promised a correction. The correction has since been made.

However, in light of the varied accessibility of printed materials that would send a clear signal about LGBT inclusion to all segments of the campus community and the concern voiced by some, mostly senior, administrators about outside perception of their schools as havens for lesbians and gay men, a question emerges about whether the inconsistency of visible materials contributes to the self-presentation of the school as heteronormative. In some instances, we observed a gap between a vision of inclusion at the senior level of the institution and implementation that would have been evidenced, for instance, in proactive strategies to train faculty and administrators about what LGBT policy inclusion would entail for themselves, the students whom they served, and the larger campus climate as a whole.

LGBT Support and Institutional Commitment

Questions about diversity in higher education have gained widespread attention over the last two decades, so much so that there is perhaps no institution in higher education today whose intellectual culture has not been shaped by it. But diversity means different things and while it has been pervasive both as ethos and as practice, these meanings shift within and across campuses and disciplines, depending on the play of social demographics and political will. Notably, HBCUs have been missing from these national debates about diversity.

One of the pivotal questions we posed in focus groups on various campuses had to do with public conversations about diversity, whether they had been undertaken, what had been the impetus for them and whether sexual orientation or sexual diversity figured as important constituents of those conversations. According to one vice president for Academic Affairs: "When I first got here five years ago, we didn't have the infrastructure for diversity programming . . . the majority of diversity work was around food, music, and fashion. Most student activities are centered around Homecoming, since we are a traditional HBCU." That situation has certainly changed, but most of our partnering schools revealed that more deeply contextual conversations about diversity would be of enormous benefit to their institutions.

In many instances where inclusive discussions about diversity had occurred, they came in response to incidents of physical violence against LGBT persons. They have taken the form of mandated workshops and professional training that engaged the multidimensionality of diversity. Such workshops are critical not only for building sensitivity but also for opening up the analytic parameters of a way of thinking, a new consciousness about diversity that is not exclusionary and that can imagine all different kinds of people within its ambit. For campuses that are in the early stages of building awareness and instituting critical dialogue on matters of sexual orientation and campus culture, these workshops are foundational to establishing a learning curve. But the question arises: Where does sensitivity training end and implementation begin? Is there a sustained institutional commitment to move ahead of the moment of acute crisis or preempt it, by adopting practices and programs that anchor the multidimensional experience of diversity?

Support for and commitment to these understandings of sexual orientation as diversity can be demonstrated in the following ways: assigning full-time professional or dedicated staff to address the unique needs of LGBT students and continuing the ongoing work of legitimating sexual diversity on a campuswide basis; creating a student resource office that provides information on gender and sexuality information; creating a safe zone, a web of visible people on campus who identify openly and therefore publicly as allies for LGBT concerns; establishing a standing committee that advises the administration on all dimensions of diversity; facilitating the creation of an LGBT alumni group within the existing alumni organization; providing gender neutral/single-occupancy restroom facilities in various buildings throughout the campus. One could imagine in such a context senior-level administrators utilizing gender and sexuality inclusive language both in spoken and written statements about diversity in ways that legitimate the existence of actual programs and the building of new understandings of identity. These are some of the underlying assumptions that the Council for Advancement of Standards in Higher Education (CAS) adopted in a widely disseminated document that deals with the imperatives of establishing targeted programs and services that can reverse the disproportionate harassment, discrimination, and hostility that LGBT students face on our campuses.[9]

When asked to gauge the climate in one of our joint administrator/faculty focus group discussions, one chaplain responded: "We do not have a climate." He went on to explain that one piece of work that needed to be undertaken on his campus was the deconstruction of religious belief systems and that in those instances where religion was a firm part of the "cultural narrative" of an institution, the task of deconstructing those belief systems was an uphill battle. "How does one establish a climate?" he asked. "How do we get from point A to point B?" These are critical questions in light of the strong links many HBCUs have with the churches out of which they originated. In one instance we found an HBCU president who initiated a blog, "Time for HBCUs and the Black Church to talk about Sex." In 2011, the School hosted its first Sex Week, "its goal [being] to provide a forum for frank and honest dialogue among the students, faculty and staff . . . to promote healthy behaviors and good decision making with regard to sex . . . The topics included STD and HIV education, sexual harassment and Christian relationships."[10] Still, a certain silence persists.

Many faculty and administrators attributed the continued silence and taboo around talking sex, sexuality, and sexual orientation to the pervasiveness of Christianity in campus cultures and the more dominant Biblical interpretations that promote a conservatizing ethos by branding homosexuality as sin and a "lifestyle" to be condemned and converted rather than as a minoritized identity formation that needs to be engaged. But, data from the Centers for Disease Control confirm that both Black heterosexual and LGBT people of color are disproportionately affected by HIV, thus making it an ethical imperative for HBCUs to provide sex-positive and inclusive information that is clearly missing from the larger society.[11] Now, as part of a small but growing movement within Black religious communities to reexamine their beliefs and move toward the affirmation of LGBT people, prominent ministers have also visited campuses and addressed questions of homophobia and heterosexism head on.[12] We found that chaplains have an important role to play in reframing the language of "worship" and "prayer" to be inclusive of multiple belief systems; in advancing plausible Biblical explanations for some of the thorniest theological issues that pertain to sexuality such as the fall of Sodom and Gomorrah (interpretations that do not reside in the "sin" of "homosexuality," but rather in "inhospitality"); and, where possible, in participating in coalitional strategies between the university and wider community. One such strategy was undertaken in Washington D.C., in which the Divinity School of one of our partners worked collaboratively with LGBT groups in the area on the successful passage of same-gender marriage. This is an example of a community/university alliance, one that challenges pervasive beliefs concerning disproportionate homophobia within Black communities versus White communities.[13]

LGBT Housing and Residence Life

Questions about the creation of inclusive housing environments for LGBT students pertain to an area that requires attention at HBCUs. On our partner campuses, there seemed to be no formal mechanisms to match LGBT students with LGBT-friendly roommates in their application for student housing, though in many instances students were free to choose their roommates; or to provide for gender neutral single occupancy rest rooms; or to install individual showers to protect the privacy of transgender students. Housing and residence life staff noted that training on LGBT issues was insufficient for the task that confronted them and that often they worked without formal mechanisms in place. It is in this context that dorms become the flashpoint for the fractures and unevenness in the campus response to the growing and visible presence of LGBT students. Proximity, intimacy, friendship, and the sheer dailyness of living push competing sexual anxieties to the fore in ways that provoke dormitories to become living incubators of things denied and unexplored.

There are several sexual cultures that reside often uncomfortably in the tight space of the dorm and that therefore make interpersonal relationships especially fraught. Students are required to adhere to the etiquette of shared living, but they are also bound, especially in single-sex contexts, by sexual codes for visitation and the like. In those instances in which heterosexual coupling takes place between and among schools that are in close proximity to one another, both administrators and faculty report a marked increase in both intimate partner violence, and physical violence among women in particular, as they compete for the same male partner. At times the details of relationships were posted on Facebook and other social media causing women to experience a double shame—the shame of violence as well as the shame of compromising sexual exposure. But there were also instances reported to us in which off-campus partners were physically abusive to their student partners who lived in the dorms. And there is evidence as well of partner violence among the smaller, yet growing numbers of LGBT students.

Increasingly, LGBT students are refusing to inhabit the closet or to choose silence as a way of living. In a context in which they are made to be hypervisible, they are thus targeted by heterosexual students. Residence life staff sometimes referenced a number of reasons why LGBT students were targeted: perceived loud and aggressive behavior on the part of LGBT students; the fact of an LGBT student being unapologetically out; and presumed favoritism, where requests for friendly rooming choices by LGBT students were perceived by heterosexual students as an unfair bending of rules. Paradoxically, this latter form of reverse heterosexism has reared its head on single-sex campuses where heterosexual students claim disproportionate injury. Some administrators were of the view that if rooming choices were made on the basis of sexual orientation it would open the door for sex in dormitories to become the norm. Central to this claim, however, is the assumption that two LGBT students living together is motivated by sex alone. It is another claim that operates in the wider society as well in ways that circumscribe the possibilities of kinship, support, and chosen family in which LGBT people engage. These arrangements could potentially open the door for deepened conversations about different family configurations, about sex, and about the complicated sexual cultures that these particular generations of youth inhabit. As the packed rooms at fora such as "Dinner After Sex I & II" and "Sex Week" indicate, all students stand to benefit from such conversations.

LGBT Campus Safety

All of our partner campuses, like other campuses in the country, are mandated under the terms of the Clery Act to have clear procedures for reporting and processing complaints, bias incidents, and hate crimes.[14] But as one president put it, "Federal regulations such as the Clery Act require certain things of us, but to move from regulations to intentional programmatic efforts is a whole other thing." During our campus visits, we did not collect information on specifically LGBT-related incidents as hate crimes. Yet in one publicized case on one of our campuses, we learned that one incident that could have been recorded as a hate crime was reported instead as "disorderly conduct."[15] The significance here lies in the naming and the use of specific language that could assist in the development of particular procedures and response structures for "LGBT bias incidents and hate crimes." As one of its HBCU campus initiatives, Campus Pride has developed a Stop the Hate initiative that involves the training of public safety staff in strategies to monitor and prevent incidents of bias and hate crimes against LGBT people.[16]

LGBT Counseling and Health

From a survey of websites, there were no counseling centers on our partner campuses that promoted and advocated for services that address the unique needs of LGBT students. They do not make specific mention of serving the needs of LGBT students as there are no targeted support services for coming out and addressing LGBT concerns in relationship to those multiple dimensions of diversity that institutions vow to protect in their statements of nondiscrimination. In follow-up correspondence with one of our partner institutions, however, we found out that the university had created an Empowerment Committee that was being led by a member of that University's Counseling Center. Located within the department of Student Health and Counseling Services, its purpose "is to provide a venue for faculty, staff, students and community partners to develop and implement support services to the LGBT community on campus." The committee is currently working on the following initiatives: i) assessing the university climate for readiness regarding [specific] services for the LGBTQ community; ii) assessing the current needs of the LGBTQ community; iii) developing "inclusive" outreach materials during health awareness screening activities; iv) developing culturally competent peer educators within the Student Health and Counseling Services; and v) increasing professional cultural competency within the division of Student Affairs by means of in-services regarding LGBTQ support services."[17]

While no formal mechanisms appear to have been established to train staff and increase their sensitivity to meet the particular needs of LGBT students, individual counselors, however, by virtue of their own professional training, counsel LGBT students who seek their services. At one school, the counseling center was at the forefront of a major outreach effort to LGBT students that ultimately served as the catalyst for the formation of their student organization. In one focus group discussion with administrators, we learned that another school had pioneered a sensitive model of HIV testing and services for counseling that in the words of the counselor "created an environment where students knew they could bring their concerns and knew that they would be cared for"; while at another institution, one student noted, "we can't get birth control on campus and health services will only test for STDs if you have symptoms." Given what has been reported about the incidence of violence of different kinds, including violence against LGBT persons, services for survivors and perpetrators of homophobia, bi- and transphobia and those that address domestic and relationship violence are critical in getting to the underside of the causes of such violence and in implementing strategies to reduce it. The large absence of designated counselors was one of the reasons students cited for not using counseling centers as a place to address their problems.

In an overall context where silence prevails and where violence has occurred, students reported a complex of emotional and psychic responses to coming out: confusion, shame, loneliness, anger, and fear of being ostracized by their families and their peers. Some have considered suicide. It is a long and difficult process to come to the point of asking, as one lesbian student did: "Should I stuff who I am in the closet because I'm simply trying to get an education at a university that happens to be in the Bible belt?" This refusal to continue to stuff oneself, to come into oneself, to move in and out and beyond the boundaries of the closet requires scrutiny, intentional support, advocacy, and visible safe space services that send a clear signal to LGBT students that institutions care about what matters to them as LGBT persons.

Conclusion

The major goal of this advocacy project was to raise awareness and engage in critical dialogue with various segments of the campuses of ten HBCUs on climate issues that shape the experiences of LGBT communities. In several cases, we were informed that this was the first time the conversations our Arcus Project had initiated had taken place on their campuses, especially among high-level administrators, faculty, and staff. Underlying both the questions we posed and the discussions that were generated, was a tacit adoption of the essence of the epigraphs with which we began this book. We are referring to Audre Lorde's trenchant insight: "It is not those differences between us that are separating us. It is rather our refusal to recognize those differences, and to examine the distortions which result from our misnaming them and their effects upon human behavior and expectation." And the equally trenchant recognition of Rev. Dr. Martin Luther King Jr.: "(We are) caught in an inescapable network of mutuality, tied in a single garment of destiny. Whatever affects one directly, affects all indirectly. . . ." Thus, this project has placed the valuing and respecting of difference at the center of institutional transformation at HBCUs. What affects LGBT communities affects everyone.

We know from the higher education literature that both campus climate and campus culture play a formidable role in a student's educational success, in the scholarly achievement of faculty, and in the productivity of all employees.[18] We know as well that the cultures of racial justice, which HBCUs have intentionally cultivated are, in large measure, responsible for our success in educating and matriculating high-quality graduates and undergraduates. We are now at a crucial juncture where a new challenge awaits us—that of creating cultures on our campuses in which academic excellence, inclusion, and equity are at the forefront of our institutional imperatives. If the color line was, as W. E. B. Du Bois so wisely predicted, the problem of the 20th century, attending to multiple dimensions of difference and our inescapable mutuality, is the problem or rather the opportunity of the 21st. They are the cognates for structuring some of the most vibrant educational communities imaginable.

Notes

1. Bryant Keith Alexander, "Embracing the Teachable Moment: The Black Gay Body in the Classroom as Embodied Text," in E. Patrick Johnson and Mae G. Henderson, eds. *Black Queer Studies: A Critical Anthology* (Durham: Duke University Press, 2005), 261.

2. Department of Health and Human Services, Task Force of the Secretary on Youth Suicide, 1989, Washington, D.C.

3. The national Day of Silence is now being annually held on the third Friday of April.

4. www.hrc.org/hbcu (accessed August 27, 2018).

5. Email correspondence with Donna Payne, Associate Director of Diversity, HRC, March 2011.

6. http://hrcbackstory.org/2010/04/race-faith-and-marriage-equality-dialogue-at-howard-university (accessed August 27, 2018).

7. www.campuspride.org (accessed August 27, 2018); email correspondence and conversation with Shane L. Windmeyer, Executive Director/Founder Campus Pride, March 2011.

8. Email correspondence and conversations with Tarrance Laney, resource person, National Black Justice Coalition, March 2011.

9. CAS Professional Standards in Higher Education, "The Role of Lesbian, Gay, Bisexual, and Transgender Programs and Services: CAS Contextual Statement," Washington, D.C., 2000 and 2010; www.cas.edu (accessed August 27, 2018).

10. See http://newsone.com/newsone-original/newsonestaff2/time-for-hbcus-and-the-black-church-to-talk-about-sex/ (accessed August 27, 2018). Dr. Walter Kimbrough, President of Philander Smith College, February, 2011.

11. CDC. Subpopulation Estimates from the HIV Incidence Surveillance System—United States, 2006. MMWR 2008; 57:985-9.CD.C. Prevalence and Awareness of HIV Infection among Men Who Have Sex with Men—21 Cities, United States, 2008. MMWR 2010; 59:1201-7. Hall I, Song R, Rhodes P, et al. Estimation of HIV Incidence in the United States. *JAMA* 2008; 300: 520-9; see also, Office of National AIDS Policy, National HIV/AIDS Strategy. Washington, D.C.: Office of National AIDS Policy, 2010. Available at http://www.whitehouse.gov/administration/eop/onap/nhas (accessed November 1, 2010).

12. http://www.theroot.com/views/black-church-and01lgbt-community (accessed August 27, 2018).

13. For this discussion, see Howard University's unpublished Lavender Report. See also E. Patrick Johnson, *Sweet Tea: Black Gay Men of the South* (Chapel Hill: University of North Carolina Press, 2001), for a compelling account of the ways in which Black gay men weave their day-to-day lives into the church. For an expansive and moving treatment of the varied spiritual lives of Black same-gender loving people, see G. Winston James and Lisa C. Moore, *Spirited: Affirming the Soul and Black Gay/Lesbian Identity* (Washington, D.C.: RedBone Press, 2006). Also in that vein, see Randy P. Conner and David Hatfield Sparks, *Queering Creole Spiritual Traditions: Lesbian, Gay, Bisexual and Transgender Participation in African-Inspired Traditions in the Americas* (New York: Harrington Park Press, 2004).

14. The Clery Act requires higher education institutions to collect crime data, report, and disseminate this information to the campus community and to the Department of Education. The Act is intended to provide students and their families around the country with accurate and complete information about the safety of colleges and universities in the United States. To comply with the Clery Act, the Office of Public Safety is responsible for compiling and reporting specified crime statistics and certain referral information for the campus, on a monthly and/or annual basis, to the U.S. Department of Education (USDE), the (relevant state's) Bureau of Investigation, and the Metropolitan Police Department (MNPD). In addition, the Office of Public Safety is responsible for publishing the University's policies pertaining to crime prevention and awareness on the campus. This overview of the terms and regulatory procedures of the Act is reproduced on many campuses. The Act clearly

states that in compiling statistics, colleges and universities "must indicate whether a specified crime is a hate crime." See also Federal Register 22314 et seq, April 29, 1994. Also, Title 34, Code of Federal Regulations.

15. The Matthew Shepherd and James Byrd Jr. Hate Crimes Legislation of 2009 underscores this point as it specifically addresses crimes that are motivated by a victim's "actual or perceived gender, sexual orientation, gender identity or disability."

16. Conversation and email correspondence with Shane L. Windmeyer, Executive Director/Founder Campus Pride, March 2011.

17. Email correspondence with Chimi L. Boyd-Keyes, Director, Women's Center, North Carolina Central University, March 2011, and our Arcus campus liaison.

18. See A. Kezar and P. D. Eckels, "The Effects of Institutional Culture on Change Strategies in Higher Education," *Journal of Higher Education* 73 (222): 435–460; see also Shawn R. Harper and Marybeth Gasman, "Consequences of Conservatism: Black Make Undergraduates and the Politics of Historically Black Colleges Universities," *Journal of Negro Education* (Fall 2008) 77(4): 336–351.

6

From Exile to Healing

I "Too" Am a Womanist

SUSIE L. HOELLER

Given womanism's origins with Black women and other women of color, many people wonder who can be womanist. There is a consensus among most progenitors of womanism, namely [Alice] Walker, [Chikwenye Okonjo] Ogunyemi, and [Clenora] Hudson-Weems, that people other than Black women or women of color can be womanists. Indeed, these authors all suggest that womanism is a perspective open to all humanity. The womanist idea is not owned by Black women and women of color; even if it was developed, launched, articulated, and elaborated primarily by Black women and other women of color . . . White women have questioned whether they, too, might be womanists (Layli Phillips [Maparyan] *The Womanist Reader*, 2006, xxxvi).

I am an American woman seen to be white in the 21st century. Why am I included in a book about womanism? It is not because I have suffered like Black women and women of color have under slavery, Jim Crow, and continuing institutional and personal racism. It is because I wish to share my unusual experience of white privilege shattered by exile and how it leads me to a place not of bitterness but of healing. It is because I have embraced Alice Walker's definition of a womanist, especially related to her "not [being] a separatist . . . [but] [t]raditionally universalist."

What Is Whiteness?

Before I describe my modern-day exile experience, I wanted to note that my paternal grandparents were poor Slavic immigrants from Eastern Europe. At the time they entered the United States through Ellis Island in the early years of the 20th century, Slavs were not considered to be fully "white." Of course, they were not black like the descendants of African slaves. Rather they were ethnic immigrants "in between" and disparaged as "hunkies" by the White Anglo Saxon Protestant (WASP) establishment. They worked in the steel mills and factories of the industrial North. David Roediger, a historian of race and labor describes the hunkies in his book *Working toward Whiteness: How America's Immigrants Became White*. Hunkies were thought to be brawny but stupid and only fit for the dirty jobs in the mills and factories. Many hunkies were even compared to hunks of dirt because of their darker complexions and the jobs they performed. When laborers were injured in industrial accidents, typically caused by the unsafe working conditions, they were said to be "hunked."[1]

At the time of their arrival, immigrants like my paternal grandparents were part of the huddled masses and wretched refuse, celebrated in Emma Lazarus's famous poem inscribed on the base of the Statue of Liberty; but in reality, they were welcomed for only a short time as a source of exploitable cheap labor. In 1920, Congress reacting to white nativist outrage closed the door to further immigration from Eastern Europe. My grandfather died from lung cancer after a life working in the steel mills of Youngstown, Ohio. My aunt also died of lung cancer since she grew up across the street from the belching mills. My father was also a millworker as a young man. He and his sisters learned English only after they went to school.

My father was able to move up the economic ladder thanks to his naval service in World War II and the GI Bill. He met my Anglo-Saxon mother at college in Ohio. When they were married, they moved to Chicago, her hometown, where I was born. Since my mom is of Anglo-Saxon stock, she was always considered white and so were my brothers and I. By this time, my father, despite his slightly anglicized, Slavic name, was college-educated, and he would be accepted as white except by people like the prejudiced steel mill manager who would not hire a "hunkie" for a management training position even one with a college degree. But my dad never forgot his Slavic immigrant roots. He always championed the underdog.

I Was a Minority Growing Up in Quebec, Canada

In 1960, when I was six years old, my father went to work for a Canadian company. Our family moved to a small town on the west island of Montreal in Quebec. I grew up as a minority—not only as an American immigrant in Canada but more significantly as an English speaker in Quebec, the largest province in Canada, where French speakers have always been the majority population.[2] Most residents were descendants of the original colonists who sailed from France and founded Quebec in the early 1600s. The French Crown lost this colony after its army was defeated by the British in 1759. The British took control over Quebec (and all the other territory north of the U.S. border which later became known as Canada).

In the 1960s and 1970s, in the Montreal metro area, most people were French Canadians (aka Francophones) but there was a substantial English-speaking minority.[3] Francophones dominated the other cities and most rural areas of Quebec province, too. At the time, Montreal was correctly described by Jean Drapeau, its visionary mayor, as the "undisputed metropolis" of Canada. It was comparable to New York City in the United States. It was the center of everything financial, industrial, social, cultural, culinary, fashionable and sporting. It attracted people from all over the world as the place to see and be seen.[4]

As I was growing up, there were two separate school systems that taught in either French or English. I went to English schools but we studied French every year. It was textbook French and most of my classmates and I never became fluently bilingual. But language was not an absolute barrier. We did business with French-Canadian merchants and my parents had some French-Canadian friends and business associates. We had experienced no problems on a personal level. Our life in Montreal seemed so peaceful and idyllic, especially when at the same period of time, the Unites States was rocked with the murder of civil rights activists in the South, riots in Detroit and Watts, the assassinations of JFK, MLK, and RFK, and the violent anti–Vietnam War protests.

The Quiet Revolution Begins

In the 1960s, what became known as the "Quiet Revolution" started, something we were not aware of it at first. French-Canadian intellectuals began challenging the social control of the Quebec hierarchy of the Roman Catholic Church, which was closely allied with an autocratic provincial government dominated by French-Canadian politicians. Quebec was a near theocracy. For decades, the wealthy French-Canadian elite sent their sons into careers in the law, politics, the priesthood, academia, or journalism. Careers in big business and high finance were frowned upon by the Catholic Church hierarchy in Quebec. The hierarchy viewed Anglo-American corporations and American-style consumerism and media as dangerous competitors for the hearts and souls of the Church's parishioners. Even so, there were many wealthy French-Canadian industrialists, bankers, and a *petite bourgeoisie* merchant class.

Most French Canadians in Montreal were working class. The French Canadians did not have a free public school system for decades. Many children dropped out of school early because their parents could not afford the fees. Furthermore, children needed to work because the French-Canadian families were so large, often with 19 to 20 children. Large families were encouraged by the Catholic Church and French-Canadian politicians to increase the demographic power of their bloodline, which they called the "pure laine."[5] This was especially true because for decades thousands of French Canadians had migrated to New England in search of better economic conditions. Once settled there, they became assimilated Franco-Americans. To counter this loss of numbers, the Quebec provincial government paid monthly baby bonuses to women in Quebec. The more babies, the larger the bonus check would be.[6]

The Separatist Movement

In the 1960s, French-Canadian workers became fed up with the low wages paid by the giant industrial corporations. Some French-Canadian politicians preached socialism or communism, but most of the solution became directed toward separation. If we could only separate ourselves from the rest of Canada, they exclaimed, we would become "maitres chez nous"—"masters of our own house." They conceived of separatism as the ultimate solution. A new economic system could follow after a separate Quebec was established.

Pierre Vallieres was the leading intellectual father of the separatist movement in its violent incarnation, the Front de la Liberation du Quebec (FLQ). In 1968, the year of worldwide revolutions, Vallieres wrote his seminal work *Negres blancs d'Amerique* (*White Niggers of America*). He compared the maltreatment of French Canadians to what American blacks had endured under slavery and Jim Crow. In my opinion, his comparison was greatly exaggerated. The French Canadians were always the majority population in Quebec. After the British Crown took over in 1763, they were allowed to keep their language, their Roman Catholic Church, and their own schools. They were always the elected political leaders of Quebec. They were never slaves. There was no legally imposed segregation. There were no antimiscegenation laws. There was no organized violence like lynching and murder as a means of social control.

There was a higher rate of poverty due to the huge size of the French-Canadian families and the lack of universal public education. But there were many poor working-class English Canadians as well. However, many English Canadians looked down on French Canadians. For generations, Anglo-Saxons have been taught that they are a superior race and, of course, English was the dominant language in the other nine provinces of Canada and the United States.[7] Some English Canadians told mean, hurtful jokes about French Canadians. I see this as a form of "classism" like the way American white elites disparage "rednecks." It was nothing like the terrible way African-Americans were treated in the States. But regardless, large numbers of French-Canadian intellectuals and workers were aggrieved. They never focused on how their real oppressors were the politically engaged Quebec "branch" of the Roman Catholic Church and their own often corrupt politicians. It was easier to blame everything on the English Canadians who controlled most, but not all, of the corporate and banking institutions.

Soldiers in Our Streets

The first major separatist violence in Montreal occurred in 1970 during what was later called the "October Crisis." Our newspaper headlines were filled with reports of bombings and kidnappings conducted by the FLQ. On Thanksgiving weekend of 1970, there was something other than a celebration of family or a bountiful harvest. There were tanks and soldiers in the streets of Montreal. Canadian Prime Minister Pierre Elliott Trudeau[8] had to invoke the National Defence Act and he had deployed the Canadian Army in Montreal. The FLQ had committed atrocities that heavily damaged its reputation but not the cause of separation itself. Kidnapping and murdering a political opponent, the Quebec Labour Minister Pierre Laporte, and stuffing his dead body into the trunk of a car was horrendous. Kidnapping and holding the British trade commissioner James Cross for months was another vile terrorist act. Placing pipe bombs that killed an innocent night watchman and bystanders at commercial businesses and in English neighborhoods did not succeed. The Canadian Army deployment quashed the FLQ. Several FLQ murderers and terrorists were tried and jailed. Some fled to Cuba.[9]

The Reincarnation of Quebec through Anglo-Cleansing

Even though Prime Minister Trudeau stomped out the political terrorism in 1970, the separatist movement survived and grew larger under a different name, the Parti Quebecois. Its cagey, chain-smoking leader, Rene Levesque adopted a nonviolent strategy. This would become a legally sanctioned form of "Anglo cleansing"[10] after he was elected to head the Quebec Parliament in 1976. Unlike the FLQ, the Parti Quebecois would not use terrorist tactics. Levesque knew that another violent uprising would be stopped by the

Canadian Army. Levesque had a legitimate political goal, which was to protect French as a viable language and the "Quebecois" culture. He did not want the French language and culture in Quebec to wither away like it has in Louisiana. But however legitimate his goal, he used illegitimate means. For the Parti Quebecois and its supporters, the only way to create this new Quebecois Utopia was to eliminate the Anglophones because their presence and economic strength was seen to threaten the survival of the Quebecois Collective.

How did Rene Levesque engineer a mass exodus of over 600,000 Anglophones from Quebec, which included our family?[11] The exodus was started by the 1977 passage of "The Charter of the French Language," aka Bill 101, a law specifically designed to reincarnate Quebec from a bilingual province to a unilingual French province. Unilingualism would drive out Anglophones by taking away their language rights. Bill 101 severely limited the use of the English language in the workplace and on commercial signage, commercial invoices, product labels, and other material. It established "La Regie de la langue francaise" to enforce the new law. The immediate results were very effective, even if ludicrous in many respects. In 1977, Regie inspectors seized doughnut bags from "Dunkin' Donuts" franchises in Montreal because "Dunkin' Donuts" was an English name, even if grammatically incorrect. This made the U.S. national news and Americans laughed about the Quebec doughnut bag raids. All the previously bilingual red "Arret/Stop" signs in the province were torn down and replaced with unilingual red "Arret" signs.

In 1978, the Regie inspectors arrived at my father's place of business and ordered him to change the name of his company into French. They instructed him to send out his commercial invoices in French even if they were being sent to customers in the States.[12] At the beginning, many businesses, like my father's, ordered by the Regie to take down their English language signs and replace them with French signs just took down the signs altogether. To anyone unfamiliar with the Quebec of the 1970s, this sounds comical and even ridiculous. But it was very serious business. In addition to Bill 101's pressure on public signage and commercial business to convert to unilingual French, Levesque needed to stop the tide of newly arriving English-speaking immigrants to Montreal. A very effective way to do this was to restrict English schooling. After all, at the time, the headquarters of public companies were located in Montreal, not in Toronto as they are today. It would not be possible for companies to entice their employees to move to Montreal if their children could not receive their education in English.[13]

"The Last One Out, Please Turn Off the Lights"

The first major corporation to move out of Quebec after the passage of Bill 101 was the Sun Life and Trust Company of Canada. Think about what would happen if JP Morgan or Citibank suddenly abandoned New York City. This venerable Canadian financial institution left its "wedding cake" landmark office building on what was then known as Dorchester Street. The street has since been renamed as Boulevard Rene Levesque. Once Sun Life pulled out of Quebec, the dam broke and almost all corporate headquarters followed, devastating Montreal's economy over the short and long term. The real estate market immediately crashed. My mom lost her home construction business. She could not sell or build new homes because the Anglophones were moving out quickly, not hanging around, and waiting for Quebec to separate from Canada. The tradesmen and construction workers, mostly French Canadians, lost their immediate livelihoods when building and construction came to a halt.

The Parti Quebecois victory, their platform to break away from Canada, and the passage of Bill 101 caused the banks financing my father's inventory and accounts receivable to call their loans because of political instability. Without cash flow financing, his international valve business ended up failing. My father and his 40 employees lost their livelihoods overnight. In my father's case, the bank foreclosed on our family's personal assets—there were no protective bankruptcy laws like those in the United States. My parents lost their home and most of their possessions. They had to start all over and move back to the States, which was ironic considering the fact that my dad had become a naturalized Canadian citizen in 1975.

Our neighbors who worked for large corporations and whose families had lived for generations in Montreal, were transferred to the new corporate offices in Toronto. They were forced to sell their homes at a steep loss and pay much more for housing in Toronto. Housing prices there spiked higher with all the ex-Montrealers moving in. The small merchants we traded with lost most of their valued customers. Almost every family we knew moved out—to Toronto, Ottawa, the rest of Canada, and some to the States. There were handmade signs posted next to the westbound lanes on the Trans-Canada Highway just before the Ontario border that read: "The last one out, please turn off the lights." Montreal lost its stature as Canada's largest city to Toronto. Before this happened, my dad used to say that Toronto was so dead at night, one could fire artillery cannon on Bloor Street, its main street, and no one would get hit.

The Aftermath

In 1976, when the Parti Quebecois came to power, Montreal was the greatest city in Canada. Toronto was a relative backwater. Today, the roles of the two cities are reversed. A new word entered my vocabulary: *diaspora.* Diaspora is from the Greek and it means "a scattering" or "dispersion" and over time it has come to mean the scattering of an entire population, such as the Jewish people from biblical Israel. Ours was not the grim, violent dispersion occurring in so many global hotspots throughout time. Ours was relatively silent and subtle. It existed, though, an unwanted scattering of a community, tossed like seeds to the breeze.

Prior to the rise of Quebecois separatism, our family had planned on staying in Montreal forever. But we reluctantly and sadly joined the Anglophone Exodus. We were driven away because the Parti Quebecois and their followers believed that they could not save their language and culture unless they built walls around Quebec and forced us out—not at the point of a gun but by using unjust laws. Even today, almost 40 years later, the few Anglos still remaining face constant criticism of their presence and keep their heads down. Most recently, the Quebec government's language police even tried to force global retailers like Walmart, Costco, and Best Buy to change the names of their stores in Quebec. These well-financed retailers won in court because their corporate brands are internationally trademarked.[14] However, the language police continue to bully small merchants into removing English signs and product labels, even targeting an Italian restaurant in Montreal to prevent the use of the word "pasta" on the menu.[15]

I believe Quebec could have preserved its unique French character without separatist and nationalist politicians running it into the province's present economic coma. Montreal today has bridges and highways that are in serious disrepair. The province of Quebec has currently amassed public debt that is the highest in Canada, and corruption scandals in public works projects never end. Quebec is much more French speaking than it was in 1976, but it has suffered economically, and I would argue culturally, as a result of its xenophobic language policies and separatist politics. Critics of my conclusions will counter that Quebec is still part of Canada,[16] some Anglophones still live in Quebec and that the Quebec government has admitted immigrants in the past three decades from other parts of the world.[17]

No matter what has happened since the Parti Quebecois turned Quebec upside down in the late 1970s, I was blessed and privileged to have grown up in what was once the most dynamic city in Canada during the best years of its history. I love the Montreal I was raised in. I think it was morally wrong for the Parti Quebecois to pass laws that arbitrarily denied Anglophone Quebecers free exercise of their language and educational rights. We loved Quebec as much as the French Canadians and Quebec's long history was not exclusively French. Many other nationalities and the indigenous peoples helped build the colony and the province over the centuries.

I would suggest that the experience of Miami, Florida, is instructive. In today's Miami, there is a vibrant Hispanic culture, and many people are speaking Spanish in their workplaces, the marketplace, schools, and homes. The English language is not dominating or erasing Spanish like it did the French language in Louisiana in the distant past. Miami actually has become more Hispanic and more prosperous in the past 30 years by transforming into an immigrant and trade gateway for Latin America. The state of Florida did not pass Bill 101-type laws restricting the use of Spanish in the state. Instead of driving intelligent and entrepreneurial Anglophones away, Quebec separatists and nationalists could have taken another road. They could have worked harder to make their culture even more attractive than it already was. They could have encouraged more English speakers to learn French, not with punitive laws and coercive language inspectors but with kindness.

Going to the extreme of legally banning most commercial uses of English and restricting English schooling has isolated Quebec from the rest of North America and the world, instead of making it the place it used to be—where everyone would want to live and work. Today, in the United States, salsa has replaced ketchup as the number-one selling condiment. Just as one hears Spanish spoken everywhere in the United States, I believe Quebec could have preserved its authentic French culture and language without driving the Anglophones out.

Reflections

Do I hate or resent French Canadians? No. I have only fond memories of growing up among them. But I do not respect Quebecois nationalistic collectivism because it is exclusionary and at its core racist. French-Canadian nationalists wanted to become masters in their own house. They have essentially achieved that dream. The Quebecois philosophers always put the ethnic-based collective above individual rights and diversity. History shows that cultures which do this become stagnant and depressed. Quebec is much more French than it was in 1976—but to what end? Celine Dion, the province's greatest singer, lives in Florida, earns her living in Las Vegas and mostly records in English. The Montreal Canadians have not won the Stanley Cup since 1993. The Blue Jays play baseball in Toronto and the wonderful Montreal Expos baseball team was moved out to become the Washington Nationals.

If only Rene Levesque and his followers, including the current generation of separatist politicians and intellectuals, could understand the future. The future is not Montreal, a unilingual city turned insular. It is found in cities like London, Toronto, Miami, New York City, and other places where people can learn about the past but not wallow in historical grievances. The Quebecois nationalists are like the white Southerners who still fly the Confederate flag—always dreaming of their lost cause. When the Parti Quebecois took over, they changed the automobile license plate slogan from the "La Belle Province" to "Je me souviens." The former means "The Beautiful Province" and the latter means "I Remember." What the Quebecois are remembering is the defeat of the French army in 1759.

What does Quebecois nationalism and separatism have to do with womanism? The connection is not immediately obvious. My response is that all womanists should teach young people about the past and the ways in which incredibly strong and resilient black women and women of color, helping each other, survived inhumane conditions. Yet, a community of people working together to overcome oppression should never become a "collective" that seeks to separate or isolate itself from others. As Alice Walker conceptualized the womanist in *In Search of Our Mothers' Gardens*, she (*or* he) must be "committed to survival and wholeness of entire people, male *and* female (xi). Moreover, in Walker's vision the womanist is "[t]raditionally universalist, as in: 'Mama, why are we brown, pink, and yellow, and our cousins are white, beige, and black?'" The mother's response is compelling. She says, "Well, you know the colored race is just like a flower garden, with every color flower represented" (ibid.). From this standpoint, *we* as human beings are all related—across *all* our differences. Therefore, those committed to womanist thinking embrace all people who stand against systemic and institutionalized oppression. As white womanist thinkers, we must cultivate a vision in which all white women and white men stand as allies to all black people and people of color instead of their oppressors or remaining indifferent to the continuation of racism in our society.

Tragically, we still have white racists and political leaders living among us causing continuing mayhem. It remains much easier for whites to navigate their lives in a society where they are the majority (soon to change due to immigration). Many whites bristle when they hear the term "white privilege," especially because in recent years, the economic status of the white working class has been battered by the forces of globalization and outsourcing. The bristling occurs because the term "white privilege" is misunderstood. It does not mean that white people in the United States do not struggle and have pain in their lives. Rather, it means that merely by being "white," they receive many socially structured benefits especially as compared to blacks and other people of color.

Ironically, I am a white woman whose family lost our beloved home because of a hegemonic linguistic/ethnic group's collective fear of our presence in a place they falsely claim only belongs to them. We should celebrate our unique heritages and experiences, but as former President Bill Clinton told a crowd at the Human Rights Campaign's annual black tie dinner last year:

> I believe that in ways large and small, peaceful and sometimes violent, that the biggest threat to the future of our children and grandchildren is the poison of identity politics that preaches that our differences are far more important than our common humanity.[18]

Why is my personal experience in Quebec relevant to African-American womanists? Am I foolishly declaring that I suffered like a slave or as black Americans did under Jim Crow or as blacks who are forced to cry out even today that "Black Lives Matter." No, I have not experienced cruel savagery against my physical body or racial slurs. I have never gone hungry. I have never been afraid of the police. But I have suffered emotionally like a refugee because our family was forced from our home. Not like the Syrians and other refugees we see on our TV screens today. But all suffering is not physical hunger or bodily abuse. Everyone who is stripped of their home and their rights by an intolerant collective suffers. My identity was shaped by my life lived in Montreal from childhood through early adulthood. But for the Quebecois separatists, our family would have remained in Montreal. We loved living there. Those happy days are lost forever but our memories live on.

The Anglophones forced out of Montreal are dispersed all over North America and around the world. If you run into them, all of them will share their special memories of a place that was once what we all hoped the future would be—a city where people of *all* identities and backgrounds could live together in peace and harmony, not a place where only the members of the "pure laine" collective are embraced. I can honestly say that my early life was spent in a kind of earthly utopia and, of course, that was lost. But not to despair because the lessons I learned from it were many. It led me to work for three decades to provide pro bono legal assistance to refugees and immigrants coming to the United States from war-torn and/or poverty-stricken places—little hells on earth, really. It led me to develop empathy for others because overnight our family's wealth and position disappeared. It led me to understand why the Jews, persecuted for centuries, developed such an intense attachment to education—something that cannot be stolen from you by political and social upheavals.

I had a unique experience for a white American girl/woman. I grew up as a minority. Not a financially impoverished minority but still a minority. As a result, I believe that I have a unique insight into problems minorities experience that many whites do not have. This is what attracted me to the universalist values taught by Alice Walker and the womanist movement. In addition, losing a material foundation to our lives when we were forced out of Quebec led me to seek a spiritual foundation. What does this mean? It means that I am called away from self-love to love God and my neighbor as myself. It means that I must put doing what is right over what is profitable or expedient. It means not only taking up my cross daily but helping others to carry their crosses.

As a Christian, I have nothing to fear in this world—

> So do not fear, for I am with you;
> do not be dismayed, for I am your God.
> I will strengthen you and help you;
> I will uphold you with my righteous right hand. (Isaiah 41:10 NIV)

Notes

1. David R. Roediger, *Working toward Whiteness: How America's Immigrants Became White* (New York: Perseus Book Group/Basic Books, 2005), 43–45.

2. I am using the English Canadian spelling of place names, individuals' names, law, and other references rather than placing accents over various letters as the French spelling does.

3. In Canada, English speakers are referred to as "Anglophones."

4. Just a few: Richard Burton and Liz Taylor for their wedding; the Beatles on their first North American tour; Barbara Streisand to date Canadian Prime Minister Pierre Elliott Trudeau; The Supremes, Ed Sullivan, Lyndon Johnson, Charles de Gaulle, and many others at the most successful World's Fair in history, Expo 67; John and Yoko Ono for their famous "Bed-in for Peace"; the Soviet Red Army hockey team to play against the Montreal Canadiens; Bruce Jenner, Nadia Comaneci, and Sugar Ray Leonard to dazzle at the 1976 Summer Olympics.

5. Large families were needed to maintain the French-Canadian presence in Quebec because the province was surrounded by the ocean of English speakers in the United States and most of Canada. There are small numbers of French Canadians in other provinces like New Brunswick, Ontario, and Manitoba.

6. The irony was that my mom and other English-speaking Quebec women also received baby bonuses. My mom loved receiving her monthly check but it did not motivate her to have more than three children.

7. The notion of white supremacy is a myth but too many white people still believe in it.

8. His son Justin Trudeau was elected Prime Minister of Canada on October 19, 2015.

9. The FLQ still exists and its supporters commit occasional acts of intimidation and violence but it is not a political force today.

10. It was later called "genteel ethnic cleansing" by Morley Safer on February 8, 1998, during the CBS News program *60 Minutes* when he was reporting on the continuing saga of the Quebec language laws and their enforcement.

11. The 600,000 Anglophones did not leave Quebec in one year—this number is an estimate of the multiyear exodus available from studies conducted by Statistics Canada.

12. When Canadians refer to the United States, they typically say "the States." I speak this way as well.

13. Levesque's plan did not take the immediate step of simply closing all the English elementary and high schools like the ones I attended. That may have provoked too harsh a backlash, even among mild-mannered English Canadians. Levesque, being clever, devised a slower strangulation of the English school system. Anglophones already living in the province could attend English schools, but brand-new immigrants, with no previous Quebec ties, would be forced to attend French schools.

14. The Canadian Press, "Wal-Mart, Best Buy win court battle against Quebec government: Superior Court rules major retailers with non-French trademarks won't have to translate signs," *CBC News*, April 10, 2014, http://www.cbc.ca/news/canada/montreal/wal-mart-best-buy-win-court-battle-against-quebec-government-1.2605615 (accessed December 19, 2015).

15. Lorraine Mallinder, "Rebelling against Quebec's 'language police,'" *BBC News Magazine*, May 7, 2013, http://www.bbc.com/news/magazine-22408248 (accessed December 19, 2015).

16. Two separation referenda were held in 1980 and 1995 and both failed by small margins. The people who voted against separation were the remaining Anglophones, new immigrants, and French Canadians who wanted to stay in Canada as patriots and/or worried that a separate Quebec would not be economically viable.

17. Most of the welcomed immigrants have arrived from former French colonies and/or unstable countries. Many of them have moved on to Toronto because they realize that their children's future is limited in Quebec.

18. Matthew Larotonda, "Bill Clinton: Gender and Racial Politics 'Greatest Threat' to Country's Future," *ABC News*, October 26, 2014, http://abcnews.go.com/blogs/politics/2014/10/bill-clinton-gender-and-racial-politics-greatest-threat-to-countrys-future (accessed December 19, 2015).

7

Nepantlera as Midwife of Empathy

PAUL T. CORRIGAN

Alice Walker's definition of womanist speaks of *love* repeatedly. A womanist "Loves music. Loves dance. Loves the moon. *Loves* the Spirit. Loves love and food and roundness. Loves struggle. *Loves* the Folk. Loves herself. *Regardless*."[1] For Walker, womanist love is a love that spans the divide between one place and another, "as in: 'Mama, I'm walking to Canada and I'm taking you and a bunch of other slaves with me.'" This love bridges the distance between "male *and* female." It bridges the distance between "brown, pink, and yellow, . . . white, beige, and black."[2] This love connects, sustains, heals.

We live justly and peaceably with one another only when we recognize others as not wholly other, only when we see—and *love*—others *as ourselves*. We develop "a healthy moral relationship to others" only, as Martha Nussbaum writes, through "[t]he imaginative activity of exploring another inner life."[3] We step closer toward the flourishing of all only, as Gloria E. Anzaldúa teaches, by building bridges—by "living on the slash between 'us' and 'others.'"[4] Importantly, this is not an idea but a practice. It's not enough to consider our neighbor as ourselves. We have to *love* them that way. It's not enough to acknowledge our neighbor's shoes. We have to *walk* in them. It's not enough to know bridges exist. We need to actually, actively build them. How? Literature contributes much to this work. As Nussbaum insists, through reading literature, we can "see the world through another person's eyes."[5] Artists help us develop empathy for people who are different from ourselves. While artists of all backgrounds may practice empathy, the writers in womanist anthologies—such as *This Bridge Called My Back*, edited by Cherríe Moraga and Gloria E. Anzaldúa and *this bridge we call home*, edited by Anzaldúa and AnaLouise Keating—undertake this work in particularly vital, purposeful ways.[6] In this essay, I will follow the thread of empathy through several texts from *this bridge we call home*.

In reading theory, a painting, a work of fiction, and a memoir from this anthology to see how they may help readers build bridges between themselves and others, I situate the practice of empathy at the heart of Anzaldúa's theory of *nepantlera*. Specifically, I propose understanding nepantleras as *midwives of empathy*. In the Preface to *this bridge we call home* Anzaldúa describes "nepantleras" as "those who facilitate passage between worlds."[7] Poets, storytellers, and other artists who undertake this task perform work akin to that of midwives who facilitate passage from womb to world. Nepantleras facilitate passage from self to other. Nepantleras help us give birth to empathy. While each text I look at offers an insight about, or representation of, this practice, the deeper point isn't to abstract ideas from the texts. What these texts offer cannot simply be lifted out of these specific artifacts and turned into general propositions. These texts do thematize nepantlera. More importantly, they *enact* it. Nepantlera is not just what they are *about*. It's what they *practice*, what they *are*. Helped by these texts, the same may also become so for those who read these and other works in the same spirit.

1

In *Light in the Dark/Luz en lo Oscuro: Rewriting Identity, Spirituality, Reality*, her final book, published after her death, Gloria E. Anzaldúa roots her concept of nepantlera—a term she derives from *napantla*, "the Nahuatl word for an in-between space"[8]—in practices of art and empathy. Anzaldúa writes:

> La napantlera, artista-activista, with consencia de mestiza offers an alternative self. As intermediaries between various mundos, las nepantleras "speak in tongues"—grasp the thoughts, emotions, languages, and perspectives associated with varying individual and cultural positions. By living on the slash between "us" and "others," las nepantleras cut through isolated selfhood's barbed-wire fence. They trouble the nos/otras division.[9]

Anzaldúa further urges:

> In seeking the truths of our lives, let's not draw back from what frightens us. Let's look toward our nepantleras (poetas, artistas, queer, youth, and differently abled) who have a tolerance for ambiguity and difference, la facultad to maintain numerous conflicting positions and affinity with those unlike themselves.[10]

Nepantleras are in-betweeners. Nepantleras are people whose liminal experiences—often stemming from the way their marginalized identities situate them in the world—allow them to develop liminal perspectives and who then, from that place, create art or activism that helps separated people move toward one another. In other words, nepantleras build bridges; nepantleras *are* bridges.

In the Preface to *this bridge we call home*, Anzaldúa declares, "To bridge is to attempt community."[11] As an example, she narrates a conflict that broke out in a email discussion among contributors to the anthology: "The contentious debates among Palestinian women and Jews of Latina, Native, and European ancestry churned a liquid fire in our guts."[12] As these conflicts irrupted from places of real and painful differences, they could easily have caused irreparable ruptures. But some of those participating in the discussion, rather than choosing sides, sought to work healing instead: "Where others saw borders, these nepantleras saw links; where others saw abysses, they saw bridges spanning those abysses. For nepantleras, to bridge is an act of will, an act of love, an attempt toward compassion and reconciliation, and a promise to be present to the pain of others without losing themselves to it."[13] What Anzaldúa describes is the practice of empathy—or, more precisely, the practice of some people helping other people develop the practice of empathy.

We often think of empathy as a feeling, whether the feeling of love or the feeling of pity. But even as empathy involves feelings, empathy itself is not a feeling but a practice, specifically a practice of imagination. While imagination is often considered individualistically—creative individuals, working imaginatively inside their own individual heads, thinking up new or unusual things—the most vital uses of imagination are not individual but empathetic. Empathy means imagining what is already: what others feel, what their motivations are, what their lives are like, what histories brought them to that place. Empathy also includes imagining what is not but could be, imagining better possible futures.

Empathy often begins with pain. As Anzaldúa writes, "Like love, pain might trigger compassion—if you're tender with yourself, you can be tender with others." We can use our "wounds as openings to become vulnerable and available (present) to others."[14] Our experience of our own pain allows us to imagine how others experience pain. Even if our pain is different from others,' even if it is significantly less acute, it serves as a starting point, a place to build, through imagination, a bridge of empathy between ourselves and others. Of course, even with pain as a beginning, practicing empathy also includes imagining others' joy—imagining the whole of others' lives, including the wide range of mundane or mixed or ambiguous experiences that fill most days for most people.

I once heard a white male graduate student insist he could not fully empathize with the women of color whose work he had read—and then directly proceed to truly empathize with them, connecting his suffering with the suffering expressed in their texts. Of course, he was correct. One cannot *fully* empathize, whatever that means. At the same time, he demonstrated that one can *truly* empathize. We build bridges we can only partially cross. But that partial crossing remains essential. Neither "you are just like me so I know exactly how you feel" nor "you are nothing like me so I cannot know how you feel" will do. We are neither exactly nor nothing like each other. We are adequately alike. As people, we share enough with all other people to do the work.

The work takes place in many forms and forums, including conversation, food, touch, work, play, and all other aspects of daily life. But aesthetic texts have an irreplaceable role. At least once, Anzaldúa even uses *artista-activista* as a synonym for napantlera.[15] Aesthetic texts allow for interactions among people who—because of the segregation that continues in the United States—might never otherwise interact. Because texts are mediate—that is, not *im*mediate but mediated and mediating—they provide safe space for risky encounters with others. Literature allows for much deeper engagement than the typical business-only or shooting-the-breeze many people resort to when talking with people different from themselves. Texts also provide nonliteral elements that allow readers to explore what might otherwise not be able to be put into words. Where silence or repetition might become prohibitively awkward when speaking with a stranger, texts invite us to pause, to linger, and to return to certain points over and over again as long as we need—the sort of slow, recursive engagement transformation usually requires. While reading does not replace lived, embodied experiences and relationships with others, reading does help us develop the practice of empathy, which we may then bring with us out into the world.

2

The body of *this bridge we call home* opens with "Open the Door," a painting by Nova Gutierrez. The image's broad brush strokes, printed in shades of gray, give the impression of smudges or shadows.[16] The painting includes both representational and abstract, even surreal, elements. It will certainly yield to more than one interpretation. I will consider several now, landing on the interpretation that the painting puts flesh on Anzaldúa's idea of nepantlera. To get here, I lean on the context of this piece; as the doorway to the rest of the anthology, I assume this painting leads us to whatever work the anthology undertakes, which is, of course, the work of womanist writers, the work of nepantleras.

"Open the Door" presents a woman kneeling on a surface. A dark area of paint encircles and encloses her body, which appears naked, with smudges of paint indicating fleshy curves of calf, thigh, stomach, breast, shoulder, back. Her arm reaches forward and downward. Her hand takes hold of something round. At this point, at least two possible readings diverge. The round something she holds could be a doorknob. A light, vertical panel behind and above the possible doorknob could be a door. If so, then the shadow surrounding the woman could be either the dark cloud of oppression or depression or isolation that she may escape by going through the door or else the dark aura of midnight's wisdom that she will bring with her through the door. The title of the painting points toward this door reading.

At the same time, certain elements of the painting itself point in another direction: the woman's body, without clothes, fills the frame, belly and breast visible; the shadow around her resembles a womb. Most strikingly, the round object, too close to the ground to be a doorknob, strongly resembles a vulva. In this reading, the painting speaks to the door through which humans, and all other mammals, enter this world—the vulva, vagina, and uterus. In this reading, the painting may speak to the sexual wounding so many women experience, whether from rape or assault specifically or from male control of female bodies in general. To the degree that the painting has a particular message, that message may be that in order to heal from the sexual trauma of patriarchy, women have to embrace their own bodies, to take hold of their own vaginas, to take back control of reproductive and other rights, yes, but even larger than that to develop a sense of ownership of and belonging in their own flesh. In this, perhaps the religious and spiritual metaphors of rebirth become relevant. Women may be reborn through reclaiming their bodies.

Yet, if we may read the painting as representing a woman taking hold of her own vagina, then we may just as well read it as representing a woman taking hold of another woman's vagina. In this case, the painting speaks to the need for women to love other women. In the broadest sense of the term *womanist*, as Alice Walker defines it, this may mean as lovers or friends.[17] In either case, women must hold one another, must affirm one another's bodies. In this same direction, still one more possibility emerges. A woman kneeling and taking hold of another woman does not have to be about either lovemaking or close friendship. It can be about healing or about birth. The kneeling woman could be doctor, nurse, doula, or midwife. With gratitude, I remember the nurse massaging and rubbing oil inside of my wife's vagina as she was about to give birth to our daughter. Acting as a midwife, this woman facilitated a birth. She stayed with us, with my wife, through the pains of contractions, transition, pushing, and birthing. In addition to working with her hands and simply being present, she also spoke calm, sometimes firm, knowledgeable words that guided my wife through the loud, wet, beautiful process of birthing something new into the world. We might read this painting in the same way. And I do, finally, take the woman kneeling as a midwife.

Read as midwife, this painting sheds light on nepantleras. If nepantleras "facilitate passage between worlds,"[18] then nepantleras may be understood as midwives—for that is precisely the task of midwives, to facilitate passage between worlds, the passage of the birthed from womb to world and from fetus to infant, the passage of the birther from pregnant to motherhood, the passage of the wider family from one state to another, even the passage of the world itself from one condition to a slightly new condition. In this reading, Gutierrez's painting represents a nepantlera who stands in, most immediately, for the writers in *this bridge we call home* and, more broadly, all womanist artists and all others who facilitate the passage between worlds, most especially the passage from the world of the self to the world of another. That passage is itself a birth and those who help it happen are midwives. In that passage, we are reborn, transformed by the birthing of empathy within us, for empathy is precisely the practice, the ability, the habit, the ongoing process and state of moving from the self to the other. Womanist nepantleras help the labor along through stories, poems, paintings, theories. As we read and listen, our imaginations massaged by stories, by pictures, by images, by voices, we give birth to empathy.

3

In her short story "Chameleon," Iobel Andemicael narrates nepantleras of several sorts: a troubled nepantlera, a failed nepantlera, and two nepantleras who succeed in helping people make their way between worlds. The story revolves around An, the troubled protagonist, a college student who bridges races with her body and cultures with her life—whether or not she understands that, whether or not she wants it. The story begins and ends with An in front of a mirror. In the beginning, she stands looking at herself, troubled about her body, troubled, in particular, about how others perceive her body: "Was she so pale and soft-featured as to be mistaken for white? Was she dark enough to be *Latina*? Discernibly Colombian? Or did she simply look mixed—too indefinable to be seen as anything authentic at all?"[19] In fact, she is mixed, her mother Colombian and her father Anglo. Although considered "white" in Colombia, she knows she and her family are considered "all black here" in the United States.[20] In the course of the story, An feels torn between identifying with her family, with her roommates, and with her friends in the Black Student Center, an extension of feeling torn between identifying with one or another of the different parts of herself. In this state, An is the troubled nepantlera. She *could* be one who helps people build connections with others. But first she needs to build these connections for, and within, herself.

For help, she turns to her poetry professor, a white woman who has traveled extensively in Latin America. Along with the reading, writing, and teaching poetry she has done, this travel should allow the professor to serve as a nepantlera for An. But she fails at precisely this. Telling An about her travels and about the cultural artifacts displayed in her office, the professor patronizes and exoticizes Latin America: "Very compelling, colorful, historical. . . . Loved the food. Adored the people. . . . Such a sad and beautiful place. Passionate. Caught my imagination."[21] To make matters worse, the professor then steps into an adjacent room to take a phone call from her son who, on his own travels, appears to have begun a relationship with a Latina. In response to this news, his mother tells him, with "clenched jaws," loud enough for An to overhear, "I don't care what you do with her. Just take precautions. I don't want or need any third world babies."[22] In this, we see that this white woman's supposed love for Latin America pointedly excludes its *people*. Given this attitude, it is little surprise that, when she returns to the room with An, the professor refuses to even try to genuinely understand or help her. An's identity crisis has left her unable to write poetry. But the professor rudely dismisses her crisis as "Bo-ring," tells her to pick one "side" or the other as her identity, either black or white, and then to get on with it.[23] What makes this scene so painful is that this professor *ought* to be one who helps An, not just with poetry but with empathy. She ought to show An compassion. She ought to teach An how to make the passage between worlds. But as a failed nepantlera, she does not help An at all, not with writing and definitely not with living—except, perhaps, indirectly by shoving An further into her crisis, which leads, eventually, to labor, to the birthing of empathy.

Where An's professor fails, her grandfather comes through. In the story, her Abuelito encourages her in overtly nepantlera terms: "Instead of thinking of yourself as not fitting in, can't you think of yourself as a bridge between groups?"[24] Distraught by the idea of being caught in-between, An responds, "Bridges may join two places but they themselves are nowhere. . . . A bridge is what people trample to get where they are going."[25] But, as a true midwife of empathy, her grandfather touches "his forehead to hers" and tells her: "Take strength from who you are, corazón, not weakness from who you're not. . . . [I]f it's in the space between things [that you fit], then that's your place. Who are you to question it?"[26] With these words, he encourages her journey from confusion and pain toward acceptance and healing. And he is not the only one—or thing—in the story to do so. After speaking with her grandfather and professor, An finds and reads a book that helps her take the next step: itself the labor of many nepantleras, the anthology *This Bridge Called My Back* now serves as a nepantlera for An. Upon reading the book, she locks herself in the library bathroom after hours. Shoved by her teacher, encouraged by her grandfather, and empowered by *This Bridge Called My Back*, she now faces herself alone. She strips naked in front of the bathroom mirror. She looks closely at her entire body, inch by inch. In this process, she begins to understand and accept herself in all her complexity. As the story ends, she begins writing the poetry that had given her so much trouble.[27] With compassion for herself, she can now help others as well.

4

In his memoir, "Bridges/Backs/Books: A Love Letter to the Editors," Jesse Swan pays homage to nepantleras in his life, particularly his mother and the anthology, *This Bridge Called My Back*. While *This Bridge Called My Back* includes only women contributors—reserving space for traditionally excluded voices—Swan appears in *this bridge we call home* as one of several men included. Nepantleras are all who build bridges. And womanists are all, regardless of gender, who love, and support the work of, women of all colors. Men are vital, and equal, participants in this work—as Swan demonstrates. In the course of his essay, he shows himself to be a nepantlera, building bridges between himself and his mother, on one hand, and readers, on the other, bridges that potentially span great distances. In particular, toward the end of his essay, Swan writes two long sentences that each become a bridge, one from the reader to the author's mother and one from the reader to the author himself.

The first of the two sentences presents a portrait of Swan's mother, with her voice (or his memories of things she has said to him) represented in italics:

> There's injustice—*My counselor* [at "Fox Tech" high school] *told me, "Little Mexican girls can't be doctors. Some can be nurses, but you look better as a secretary"*—there's anger—*I know you think you're white and so better than me, but you're mine, too, and so remember you're just a Mexican, too*—there's passing—*"This is Mrs. Stanley Swan. We need to negotiate some acceptable alternative to Pee, Eee for my Jesse: I cannot have him in such programs, as you, no doubt, can understand"*—there's betrayal—*I'm your mother, mi hijito,* [sob] *please stop calling me "Mrs. Swan"*—there's some attempt for rational justice—*Yes, okay, I do love your brother more, but only because he needs it more*—there's genuine respect for humanity—*Mi hijito, you know, not all boys like girls . . . like Ricardo, you know, my hairdresser, he doesn't like girls. You don't have to. I mean, you know, like that*—there's abiding love—*mi hijito.*[28]

This tour de force is followed quickly by another. The very next sentence presents a portrait of Swan himself, written as an apostrophe, a direct address to the absent editors of *This Bridge Called My Back*:

> If I had not come across your book—quite nervously in that huge used bookstore on Broadway in San Antonio—and only consulted furtively because I was too afraid to buy it from the tall, cute white guy smoking and affecting a loitering demeanor at the cash register (I was afraid that he'd recognize the book and all that it meant to me and realize that I was a fag and a Mexican, a realization I was afraid would ruin all my chances of getting him to fall in love with me, since, in my bizarre, childish, self-hating yet desiring dream-mind, he'd only fall in love with me if he thought I was another straight, white guy like he appeared to be), I may never have been able to know or understand my mother's back, my mother's bridge, my mother's greatness, my mother's open, redemptive love for everyone, including for herself, including for those who hate, including for me.[29]

Each sentence deals with suffering caused both by oppression and by the ordinary circumstances of life; communicating suffering is central to helping people develop empathy. At the same time, neither empathy nor these sentences are about suffering alone. While empathy may begin with suffering, it does not end there. Empathy encompasses, must encompass, whatever others go through. Accordingly, while these sentences are rooted in pain, they travel varied terrains, containing complexities, nuances, ambiguities, and pain, yes, but also infatuation, anxiety, bravery, love, and other messy aspects of life. In this way, as the second sentence notes directly how Swan's mother and *This Bridge Called My Back* were nepantleras for Swan—how they both were bridges for him, how they both taught him to love others and to love the other in himself—so both sentences undertake the work of nepantleras, the work of allowing people to reach out of themselves toward others.

Almost poems in themselves, these two sentences do a lot of work. The articulation of the characters' plights works to pull readers in. The minimal, though carefully chosen, details of dialogue and setting evoke vivid scenes for readers to visualize. The excessively long, winding structures reflect how long and winding the bridges may sometimes have to be to reach between people—between this Latina woman and queer Latino man from the Southwest and, for instance, a white straight male reader from the East. Of course, the sentences do not allow us to "fully" understand Swan and his mother since, when it comes to understanding, there is no "fully." But there are degrees of relation. Readers traveling these sentences may become several degrees more deeply related.

5

Summarizing what it means to build or be a bridge, Chela Sandoval cites the "Mayan code of honor": "In Lake'ch: I am another yourself."[30] Love gestates within us already. But we cannot easily give birth without help. We require someone to address us with these words or to speak to or act toward us in a way that carries the same meaning—"I am another yourself"—so that we may respond in kind, so that we may respond in kindness. The womanist texts discussed above undertake this very work: Anzaldúa articulates the theory of nepantlera, Gutierrez offers an image of nepantleras as midwives of empathy, Andemicael illustrates nepantleras in action, and Swan helps readers bridge the distance between themselves and him and his mother. These writers, like all nepantleras, may help us to understand and undertake the act of empathy, the act of building and crossing bridges between ourselves and others—perhaps beginning, like Swan, like the Gutierrez's character An, and like many others, with the fragmented parts of ourselves.

We need nepantleras now as much as ever. Sociologist Eduardo Bonilla-Silva documents that most people in the United States, particularly whites, live with, work with, learn with and from, befriend, and marry only people of the same race: "Despite the civil rights revolution, whites, young and old, live a fundamentally segregated life."[31] That common refrain by white people—"some of my best friends are black"—turns out to be, empirically, inaccurate for most whites. Interracial interactions, when they do occur, usually remain superficial. Bonilla-Silva writes, the "lack of empathy" whites have on certain racial matters "should not be a shock or mystery to readers. People cannot like or love people they don't see or interact with. . . . [F]riendship and love emerge when people share activities, proximity, familiarity, and status."[32] In this state of segregation, Samantha Blackmon observes, people rely by default on popular media to learn about each other—and this has devastating, sometimes deadly, consequences for those, particularly people of color, most absent or most misrepresented in movies, video games, and television. In this situation, Blackmon writes, "the ability to empathize" becomes "almost non-existent." This is the context that makes the work of nepantleras of such vital spiritual and political urgency.[33]

We need texts by women of color (and other "others") as counternarratives. Nepantleras are midwives to the birthing of empathy and compassion. The towels and hot water they use take many forms, not least the story but also the poem, the song, the picture, the phone call, the visit, the meal, the protest sign, and so forth. May we surround ourselves with nepantleras, with artists like Anzaldúa, Gutierrez, Andemicael, and Swan. May we read deeply the work of Alice Walker, Naomi Shihab Nye, Lucille Clifton, Joy Harjo, bell hooks, Rita Dove, Nikki Giovanni, Gwendolyn Brooks, Zora Neale Hurston, Louise Erdrich, Toni Morrison, Marylin Chin, Cathy Song, Octavia Butler, Sandra Cisneros, Julia Alvarez, Maxine Hong Kingston, Claribel Alegría, Isabel Allende, Ntozake Shange, Helena Maria Viramontes, and so many others to whom I and so many others owe so much. May we join them in this work, all of us, readers, writers, teachers, parents, lovers, spouses, friends, sojourners, embracing the maternal within, giving birth to empathy and helping others do the same.

Postscript

I wrote the first draft of this essay as a doctoral student in 2012 in Gary Lemons's course titled: "Literature by Radical Women of Color." That course blessed me deeply, not least for introducing me to the anthologies of Anzaldúa and other nepantleras. Though I've now revised this essay, some four or five years later, it retains more than a trace of its initial existence as a pedagogical artifact. I find this fitting because the site of teaching is the site for so much of this work. In the time since that class, I've come to learn in my own teaching that what calls out to me so deeply—to truly hear and care about the lives and works of others who are different from me, particularly those whose voices have so often been marginalized—does not always resonate in the same way with students. So it seems the first part of the work will always be to help students become open to the work. While this process can be slow and difficult, and doesn't always succeed, I am comforted by the words of Ann Jurecic in her essay on empathy and literature. "Literature matters," she writes, "not because it changes our brains, hearts, souls, or political convictions, but because the practice of reading literature slows thought down. . . . [A] book provides a rare opportunity for sustained focus, contemplation, and introspection."[34] Literature does not change us; it invites us to be changed. How we respond is up to us; how our students respond is up to them. Midwives don't give birth to other people's babies. Nepantleras don't bring forth other people's empathy. We can only help. But help we must, by inviting engagement; by providing space, time, and aesthetic texts; by living transformed, empathetic lives ourselves. I am grateful for those—including Gary, the writers in these anthologies, and many others—who have helped me in this journey. I hope to pay it forward.

Notes

1. Alice Walker, *In Search of Our Mothers' Gardens: Womanist Prose* (New York: Harcourt, 1983), xii.
2. Ibid., xi.
3. Martha Nussbaum, *Not for Profit: Why Democracy Needs the Humanities.* (Princeton: Princeton University Press, 2010), 109.
4. Gloria Anzaldúa, *Light in the Dark/Luz en lo Oscuro: Rewriting Identity, Spirituality, Reality* (Durham: Duke University Press, 2015), 82.
5. Nussbaum, *Not for Profit*, 96.
6. Cherríe Moraga and Gloria E. Anzaldúa, eds., *This Bridge Called My Back: Writings by Radical Women of Color*, 2nd ed. (New York: Kitchen Table, Women of Color Press, 1983), and Gloria Anzaldúa and AnaLouise Keating, eds., *this bridge we call home: radical visions for transformation* (New York: Routledge, 2002).
7. Anzaldúa, "(Un)natural Bridges, (Un)safe Spaces," in *this bridge we call home*, 1.
8. Anzaldúa, *Light In the Dark*, 28.
9. Ibid., 82.
10. Ibid., 94.
11. Anzaldúa, "(Un)natural Bridges," 3.
12. Ibid., 4.
13. Ibid.
14. Anzaldúa, *Light in the Dark*, 153.
15. Ibid., 82.
16. Nova Gutierrez, "Open the Door," in *this bridge we call home*, 27.
17. Walker, *In Search*, xi.
18. Anzaldúa, "(Un)natural Bridges," 1.

19. Iobel Andemicael, "Chameleon," in *this bridge we call home*, 28.
20. Ibid., 34.
21. Ibid., 37–38.
22. Ibid., 37.
23. Ibid., 39.
24. Ibid., 34.
25. Ibid.
26. Ibid., 35.
27. Ibid., 42.
28. Jesse Swann, "Bridges/Backs/Books: A Love Letter to the Editors," in *this bridge we call home*, 61.
29. Ibid.
30. Chela Sandoval, "AfterBridge: Technologies of Crossing," in *this bridge we call home*, 23.
31. Eduardo Bonilla-Silva, *Racism without Racists: Color-Blind Racism and the Persistence of Racial Inequality in America* (Lanham, Md.: Rowman and Littlefield, 2014), 172.
32. Ibid.
33. Samantha Blackmon, "Beware the Magical Negro: On Tropes, Race, and Black Lives Matter," *Not Your Mama's Gamer*, August 4, 2016. http://www.nymgamer.com/?p=14468 (accessed August 4, 2016).
34. Ann Jurecic, "Empathy and the Critic," *College English* 74.1 (2011): 24.

8

A Deeper Shade of Consciousness

My Voice Is My Resistance

ATIKA CHAUDHARY

I have always known I wasn't white, even when I was the lightest shade in a slew of browns. I knew I wasn't black. I spent decades being pushed out of and pulled into categories of brown, yellow, and even off-white. Mostly passing but always close enough. It was not until recently that I realized I didn't have to pick a color and started identifying as a woman of color and a feminist/womanist. I had been practicing limited feminism since I was a young girl but I'd had no contact with formal feminist/womanist theory or the multitiered challenges of race, class, gender, and sexuality until I encountered writings by women of color in my undergraduate and graduate studies.

Writings by womanist female authors and Alice Walker prompted me to call on and explore the significance of an all-inclusive love. Walker's definition of a womanist is rooted in a universalist love, a womanist is, "A woman who loves other women . . . women's culture, women's emotional flexibility . . . and women's strength . . . loves individual men . . . Loves music. Loves dance. Loves the moon. *Loves* the Spirit. Loves love and food . . . Loves struggle. *Loves* the Folk. Loves herself. *Regardless.*"[1] Being a womanist means to "outrageous[ly], audacious[ly], courageous[ly] or *willful*[ly]"[2] practice an exemplary acceptance, of self and of all people, rooted in love. A womanist is, "Committed to survival and wholeness of entire people, male and female" regardless of ethnicity or color, regardless of being "brown, pink, and yellow . . . white, beige, and black."[3] By practicing this all-inclusive love, I learned how to navigate my life, my identity, my ethics, and my learning through the bridge between womanist and feminist thought. This bridge of radical love and acceptance provided me with a blueprint for self-reflexive discovery and healing.

Reading *This Bridge Called My Back: Writings by Radical Women of Color* (eds. Gloria Anzaldúa and Cherríe Moraga), *This Bridge We Call Home: Radical Visions for Transformation* (by Gloria E. Anzaldúa and AnaLouise Keating) and *Colonize This! Young Women of Color on Today's Feminism* (eds. Daisy Hernandez and Bushra Rehman) introduced me to my identity as a woman of color. These invaluable texts opened my eyes to the types of oppression faced by women of color and my personal responsibility of coming to consciousness, coming to voice and the urgent need to establish coalition, not only among women of color but with women and men of all classes, genders, sexualities, and ethnicities.

Human beings are innately innovative. We create, recreate, and fix what does not align with our version of the world. We create what we find missing. We recreate what we have already created in order for it to better serve our ever-expanding ideal vision. We fix what we create to overcome the shortcomings of our creations and recreations. Each of the above mentioned processes require a distinct set of tools. We all come equipped with basic tools of intellect, vision, voice and ambition. We can only make a difference, create and recreate change or fix its shortcomings by first recognizing the possession of our basic tools and then developing our basic set of tools into (em)power(ment) tools. The project of feminism/womanism undertaken by women of color cannot be accomplished using a box of primary tools. In order to dismantle systems of oppression women of color feminists/womanists need a box of power tools. Power tools of directed vision and articulated voice to achieve the complex ambition of an all-inclusive feminism/womanism. Through my voice in this essay, I aim to share my struggle in recognizing the tools of voice, written word and personal experience to build a bridge to my identity as a woman of color feminist/womanist and to construct a bridge to reach out to women of color who are yet to uncover their tools of empowerment and inclusion.

Transnationality: The Dilemma of Two, Too Many

> Who am I? When am I? The questions that are asked in the street, of my identity, mold me. Appearing in the flesh, I am cast afresh, a female of color—skin color, hair texture, clothing, speech, all marking me in ways that I could scarcely have conceived of.
>
> —Meena Alexander, *This Bridge Called My Back*

> They would chop me up into little fragments and tag each piece with a label Who, me confused? . . . Not so. Only your labels split me.
>
> —Gloria Anzaldúa, *This Bridge Called My Back*

I am talking, thought after thought rolling off of my tongue. My sentence is halfway out of my mouth when I'm interrupted: "Wait a minute, wait a minute." My listener looks at me confused. He goes on: "So, I've been trying to listen to you and pick up some type of an accent but I can't, and then I'm looking at you, trying to place you, but." his voice trails off. He looks more confused than before, "So what are you?" I fight the urge to roll my eyes and say, I wish you would try harder to listen to what I'm saying instead of figuring out how to categorize me.

I have been repeating, "Don't put me in a box!" for years now, but my voice goes unheard when I fill out a simple form that asks me to check a box for race/ethnicity. Placing that tiny checkmark of "I submit" within a neatly printed box is suffocating on so many levels. I've always despised the "Other" box, and generally, yet begrudgingly, check the "Asian or Pacific Islander" box. People have had the audacity to tell me I should check the "Other" box. As I hear them out, I feel my humanness slipping right out of my hands. I frantically try to hold on as I hear, "In America we have Whites, Blacks, Hispanics/Latinos, Asians, and Others. You should check the 'Other' box." One too many alarms are going off in my head. I have been disqualified. I'm not even a race/ethnicity that is recognized on most paperwork in America. If I don't belong to a recognizable race/ethnicity and I'm categorized as "Other," does that even leave room for identifying as a real human being? The word "Other" has a harshness of alienation attached to it that cannot be removed. Why must I identify as Alien or Outsider? I refuse to be slapped with the label of "Other," an assault on my humanness. Being introduced to multiplicity by *This Bridge Called My Back* and *This Bridge We Call Home*, made me realize that a transnational woman of color does not neatly fit into a box or easily fall under a preconstructed generalization. Transnationality is an inescapable everyday dilemma of identity, entitlement, and authenticity.

My ethnic roots lie in the Punjab region of the Indian Sub-Continent (now India, Pakistan, and Bangladesh). Partition of the Sub-Continent and a divided Punjab (half remains part of India and the other half part of Pakistan), after British occupation, forced my grandparents to migrate across the newly formed border from the Indian Punjab to the Pakistani Punjab that would house most of the Punjabi Muslims. The history of the Sub-Continent is a diverse collection of cultures formed and influenced by the people who came to the region to settle, invade, conquer, and rule. The region has been home, or a conquered and colonized territory to peoples of varying ethnicities. Most people from the Indian Sub-Continent are very comfortable in their belief that they are a particular race and shun the idea of being mixed race. I, on the other hand, am continuously curious of my potentially mixed racial background. Ambiguous racial identity combined with my transnationality as a South Asian American makes checking boxes and picking sides undesirable.

When I was younger, I used to find it amusing, at times funny, when I could pass for something I was not. As I got older, I got darker. My hair developed a big personality, full of waves. I could still pass, usually for Latina, white mixed with "something," Caribbean Islander, and occasionally Middle Eastern. I was yet to be recognized, or mistaken, ironically, for South Asian (Indian/Pakistani). Even in a slew of browns in Queens, New York, weaving in and out of *Desi* (from the Indian Sub-Continent) people, I shocked people when I greeted them in Urdu, Hindi, or Punjabi. People would ask me where did I learn my greetings so well? Offended, I would inform them of my ethnic background. "Really? I didn't think you were *Desi*? Are both your parents from Pakistan?" I was continuously criticized for not acting, speaking, dressing, and behaving *Desi*-enough and was readily labeled too Americanized by my family and my relatives. At the same time I was criticized and praised by Americans for both assimilating and retaining part of my so-called exoticness.

As I grew older, passing no longer amused me. It became a painful series of being continuously disowned. I passed as off-white until I got older and darker. I passed for Latina until my limited Spanish speaking skills would fail me and I would switch from Spanish to English after very basic conversation in Spanish. Muslim women in hijab would take one look at my clothing choices and discount me as a Muslim woman. I can count the number of times a *Desi* person in the United States recognized me as one of their own. Passing is painful. Passing from one world to another, and another, I became a gypsy ghost of myself. Always passing. Always close enough but never truly belonging. In order to belong, I had to abide by the societal requirement of picking a box—only one—and making sure I fit neatly and precisely into that box.

Multiple identities make people uncomfortable. Checking more than one box is believed to not be an option because the multiple boxes cannot fit into each other or are viewed as contradictions. I despise checking boxes, checking into boxes and checking out of boxes. The speculating eyes that rove my face, body, hair, and wardrobe choice as I go about my everyday activities of grocery shopping, attending school, and going to work become overbearing. Passing is a well known, much-lived phenomenon in my life. Being stigmatized by South Asians for being too Americanized is just as hurtful as being called an "Other" in my home country of America. My transnationality should not be a struggle between my South Asian and American identities. It is simply the establishment of my own individual identity, which is a complex selection of Pakistani and American traits that best define me as a person and a woman of color. Reading Milczarek-Desai's piece from *This Bridge We Call Home*, in which she quotes Bharati Mukharjee, truly justified my American identity: "each time one of us becomes American we change the very definition of that word and change everyone else who refers to themselves as American as well."[4]

I am often urged and pushed to choose sides, for multiplicity seems to be an incomprehensible predicament in a country as diverse as the United States. On one hand, I am labeled an outsider. On the other hand, people who share my background regard me as not ethnic enough, too Americanized, too independent, too outspoken. If I had not gotten up on my feet and yelled "Stop!" my life would have become a series of being put into boxes and being kicked out of boxes. I am who I am, in all my complexity and diversity. In the words of Rebecca Hurdis, "To live a life of multiplicity is difficult . . . we are asked to find one identity that will encapsulate our entirety. . . . Yet where is the space for multiplicity?"[5] When I identify as Pakistani and American simultaneously, why do I become a contradiction? There are days I am deeply troubled by ignorant questions asked by people too comfortable with boxes. My many identities are authentic and coexistent for me but are hostile contradictions to most people around me. I refuse to apologize for any of my multiple selves, no matter how uncomfortable they may prove to be for people who like the idea of diversity but choose to not invest in understanding it. Transnationality comes with its challenges, but my identity as a woman of color feminist/womanist has taught me to embrace the challenge of multiplicity. I am able to recognize multiplicity as a tool of empowerment to carve out a more refined identity for myself.

"Gallina Ciega"—Reaching Out with Hand and Heart

> The threat of difference has been no less blinding to people of Color.
> —Audre Lorde, *This Bridge Called My Back*

I was sitting in my backyard reading *This Bridge We Call Home*, half distracted by my housemates' three cats that hissed and clawed at each other occasionally. I wondered why they couldn't get along. What separated them and made them hostile to each other? I tried to focus on reading "Gallina Ciega: Turning the Game on Itself" by Leticia Hernandez-Lineres. My thoughts kept straying to a conversation I had the night before. I was speaking to an older male relative. He politely asked when I was planning to get married. I told him that, unlike the traditional South Asian women, it is not my goal to be married in my twenties.

He continued as if he did not hear my response and advised that I must seek a partner who belongs to the same ethnic and religious community as myself. I was appalled. I replied that I would not be inclined to limit myself to a certain race, ethnic background, or religion, if and when I decided to pick a partner. He considered my perspective and informed me that if I were to choose someone outside of my race or ethnicity, my first choice should be a white man, then a brown man, and definitely not a black man.

Here I was, the next morning, reading in my backyard, still upset about my conversation the night before. No, not merely upset, I was angry! So angry that I couldn't focus. I forced my attention to reading "Gallina Ciega" again. Hernandez-Linares recalls playing a game called Gallina Ciega or Blind Hen with the neighborhood children when she was young: "I remember, girls, boys, running around me, light, dark, black hair, red hair, migrants, speakers of more than one language. We saw our differences, but more important to us as children were the things that brought us together."[6] The game required the children to close their eyes and learn to see through their other senses, as one child is blindfolded and trying to catch the other children singing Gallina Ciega. Hernández-Linares's words were reaching out of the pages to hold and comfort me, to give me hope, to share my pain.

As I read about the blindfolded children, I wondered how my life would be different if I could not visually perceive diversity. What if I were blind and had never seen varying skin tones? What if I had no concept of race and color? What if I could not comprehend those ideas because I had never seen race or color? Would I, then, not be judged for choosing someone who is not the same color as I am? If I could not witness whiteness or blackness, would I have been exempt from the conversation I had? Would my blindness have protected me from the pain and sorrow I felt after? Would I have been a person free from and unrestricted by societal notions of right and wrong in accordance with a color chart that always puts white or light on top? Would I be free or would I be more limited than I already am? Would my life choices and decisions then be made for me because I cannot see what society deems right or acceptable? Would my blindness set me up to be oppressed by the people who could see color and difference but are unable to appreciate it or cannot help but categorize and stereotype it? Would my choices be made for me because I would be deemed unfit to choose correctly for I cannot see that light is right?

Hernández-Linares plays the game Gallina Ciega as an adult while she is working with children of migrant and working-class families in Santa Barbara. She finds herself relearning the Gallina Ciega game and applying it to her adult life, emphasizing: "the game doesn't ask us to be color blind, it just demands that we learn to expand our ways of seeing."[7] What if we all were to play Gallina

Ciega in our everyday lives? If only we could reach out, out of our boxes, out of our skins, to touch each other, to feel, know, and see in ways other than race, class, sexual preference, and gender. We must unlearn our fear of difference and relearn the Gallina Ciega game as adults, to "look for each other's voices, to seek others in their words and not simply their color, culture, gender assignment," and religious values.[8] Unlearning and relearning is not enough. We must reach out with hand, heart, and voice to break the cycle of pain and oppression. We must look for each other, for a bridge, for common ground by "learning how to see in alternative ways—instead through preconceived static notions of how people should act, look, be."[9] We must not be silent, we must sing "Gallina Ciega" so that the ones among us wearing blindfolds of racism, sexism, classism, and heteronormativity, may be urged to take reluctant, clumsy steps out of their comfort zone and stumble upon difference.

Bridging the Gap: The Indelible Bridge of Articulation

> I had to write so that somebody would realize what my life is like.
> —Ntozake Shange, *This Bridge Called My Back*

When I was younger, I considered silence my most reliable tool. I could avoid conflict, verbal and physical, and carry on with my life. I wrongfully believed silence won me peace because it deterred altercations. It was not until I realized that outward silence led to intrapersonal arguments and painful imploding that I started speaking up. I look back at my life and find myself sometimes astonished, other times ashamed, that my silence pushed me to the brink of self-destructive depression before I decided to put into words the pain in my heart. During my years of silence "I hadn't yet figured this out: I don't have to die, leave, silence myself to show the world how bad I feel from oppression. But maybe I do have to scream a little."[10] Reading Nadine Naber's "Resisting the Shore" brought back memories of yelling and screaming bouts between my mother and me when I was growing up. I was trying to figure out what part of me was Pakistani/American, Muslim/secular and traditionalist/nonconformist, with the color of my skin always serving as the base, means, and problematic end of our screaming matches littered with physical altercations. I remember choosing silence and I remember admitting to myself years later that I had made and lived the wrong choice for far too long.

As I read the section "'a place at the table' . . . surviving the battles, shaping our worlds" in *This Bridge We Call Home*, I couldn't help but wonder why coming to voice for women of color is such a battle? How much will we endure? With how much patience? For how long? Why live in silence, with broken hearts, bleeding egos, and fractured identities? What will it take to come to voice? Rape for Chandra Ford, hunger and poor health for Judith Witherow, the killing of an Arab for Nadine Naber, and attempted suicide of her sister by the anonymous author of "For My Sister." None of the situations mentioned above are by any means mild, which again, begs the question: What will it take to come to voice? How much patience? How much suffering? How many broken hearts?

Coming to voice is only the first step to conquering the distances between women of color and building bridges to connect our worlds. Speaking up is the initial step we are still struggling with. To voice and share our stories as a point of connection is an act of bridging. It elevates the personal to political. The time has come to "smash the walls of pretense, shame, and silence to really show ourselves—and not just as victims of oppression, but with the motivation of communicating . . . for others and hopefulness about organizing for change."[11] Reading "For My Sister" opened my eyes to the oppression I had blocked out and had chosen not to address as a South Asian American woman of color. It was the very same oppression that led me down the dark path of silence and life-threatening depression. There is a price one pays for silence, a price that easily exceeds the price for coming to voice. Silence eventually, inevitably breaks the heart it guards and resides in. Breaking down walls of silence is a labor-intensive endeavor; it requires commitment and courage. Above all, it requires love. Love for oneself, for another, for listeners and readers, for community, and for healing.

I have learned to incorporate my newfound passion for voice into my everyday life instead of keeping it in the confines of neatly typed papers for school. I recently discussed details of my personal struggle with depression with another "Other." For the first time in my life, I willingly laid bare painful truths and undesirable experiences that comprise my account of hitting rock bottom and not wanting to get up again. I willingly opened up and spoke about one of my most difficult experiences in dealing with depression. Like Chandra Ford, I shared my story "to complete my own healing process, and hope that in my so doing, other[s] are reminded of their own healing process [and] their own unique capacities for tremendous growth in the face of adversity."[12] I came to voice to bring another to voice; exposing myself, putting myself out there, discarding my masks and cloaks to share the personal pain of another by offering my own experience as a point of connection. I did so with the knowledge that I may be left exposed, cold, unreceived and judged, and all the above may hurt. Following my cue, I heard a story surprisingly similar to my own.

From El Mundo Zurdo to El Mundo Unido (From a Left-Handed World to a United World)

> For separatism by race, nation, [ideology] or gender will not do the trick of revolution. . . . Ultimately, we must struggle together. Together we form a vision [to keep] the embers of revolution burning.
>
> —Gloria Anzaldúa, *This Bridge Called My Back*

Week after week, our classroom for "Literature by Radical Women of Color" buzzed with talk, debate, and agreement of coalition. But I still saw fingers pointing. I still heard, "You don't know me!" "Do you see me?" "If this isn't white privilege then what is?" "Do you hate all white people?" Eyes roll, tongues click, heads shake in disagreement as often as they do in agreement. I sit there and I take it all in. Absorbing it in the place where I held on to the love of El Mundo Zurdo. Over a period of four months this bustle in the classroom slowly eroded the bridge in my mind to El Mundo Zurdo. Will we cross over? No. We need more than El Mundo Zurdo. We don't need to migrate, cross a bridge and build another world. We need to stay where we are. We need to own the mess we have made—all of us—and we need to unite our worlds. My vision of El Mundo Zurdo has been displaced by an all-inclusive vision of El Mundo Unido (A United World). Together, by reaching out, communicating with written and spoken words, affirming by actions and touch, by learning and practicing spiritual activism, we can achieve the vision of El Mundo Unido. Together we can! Gloria Anzaldúa, Chrystos, and Cherríe Moraga's pieces from "Speaking in Tongues" and "El Mundo Zurdo" in *This Bridge Called My Back* led me to the vision of El Mundo Unido.

I am not a delusional woman of color. I know we have been programmed, generation upon generation to shy away from difference, to fear it, to blame it, to run away from it, to approach it only to perform an exorcism. As Anzaldúa states: "It is easier to repeat the racial patterns and attitudes, especially those of fear and prejudice, that we have inherited than to resist them."[13] We hold on to our destructive old ways. We hold on because we are afraid of change. We fear what is new and different. It is unbearably painful to acknowledge that we view togetherness as a concept chaste and unpracticed, a radical goal yet to be achieved. What a shameful slap in the face of our collective humanness! As women of color feminists/womanists, we need to extend the invitation to practice the erotic, spiritual activism to people of all races, classes, genders and sexualities as a path to freedom and to El Mundo Unido. We, as women of color, must raise our voices and put our pens to work in order to reach out to all people of difference, the people who practice indifference, the consciously and unconsciously ignorant and fearful alike. Women of color may ask, why us? Why must we be the bridge? I say why not us? Who can do it better than women of color feminists/womanists who live to free ourselves and others from oppression, who live to build bridges and to establish coalitions?

Anzaldúa believes we are all to blame for our state of oppression. People of color cannot play victim and point the finger of blame at light or white skin. According to Anzaldúa, we all are "accomplices to oppression by our unwittingly passing on to our children and our friends the oppressor's ideologies" consciously and unconsciously.[14] We all *seem* to agree, but we all *do* agree only as a safe collective. We are shy to take the blame as an individual and work on ourselves to open our hearts and minds to other people's difference. We are quick to shun, expertly casting responsibility on collective humanity or preconstructed societal notions, but unwilling to be vulnerable to accepting blame, to live with the shame of aiding and abetting oppression. Anzaldúa leads by example and takes an individual stand: "I cannot discount the role I play as accomplice, that we all play as accomplice, for we are not screaming loud enough in protest."[15] There is an urgent need for all of us to commence a personal revolution by tapping into the spiritual and the erotic. We must start with ourselves, within ourselves, tackling the demons within. Driving them out, out of ourselves, out of our skins, out of our communities and out of our world/s. In Anzaldúa's words: "I believe that by changing ourselves we change the world, that traveling El Mundo . . . [Unido] path is the path of a two-way movement—a going deep into the self and an expanding out into the world, a simultaneous recreation of the self and a reconstruction of society."[16]

We choose to fragment and distance ourselves from "Others" due to difference instead of realizing that our commonality is the fact that we all are different. We all must take on the challenge to pursue "the blend of common elements to make a common thing," the common thing being a point of connection.[17] In "La Prieta," Anzaldúa mentions that our oppressions, ideologies, and affinities may not be the same, but we can "empathize and identify with each other's oppression."[18] We must actively look beyond the fear and oppression society has instilled in us to realize our differences can be a point of intersection. Cherríe Moraga emphasizes and repeats "we all come from the same rock," but we forget or we ignore the fact "that we bend at different temperatures / that each of us is malleable."[19] We must not forget that we are soft enough to bend and change, and empowered enough to make change. Change will occur only if we turn on the heat of passion and urgency. Moraga confirms, "Yes, fusion is possible / but only if things get hot enough / all else is temporary adhesion, patching up."[20] We must start with our individual selves and come together to build an unshakable frame of connectedness and a collective consciousness. We have the power within ourselves. Our empowerment is buried under fear, resentment, and distrust of difference. We must uncover, rediscover, and use this power. We all must make a commitment to be "The Welder" and pledge "I am taking the power / into my own hands" to make change.[21]

The most influential discourse for transformation is breaking silence and reaching out to each other with the aim to transcend all systems of oppression. Gloria Anzaldúa's piece "Speaking in Tongues: A Letter to 3rd World Women Writers" emphasizes the urgent need for women of color to come to voice, to risk disclosure and to facilitate change through our writing. As stated by Anzaldúa: "The meaning and worth of my writing is measured by how much I put myself on the line and how much nakedness I achieve"[22] and "I write because I'm scared of writing but I'm more scared of not writing."[23] We must probe and prod the darkest corners of our mind. We must write, digging deeply, diligently, fearlessly to drive out the demons of internalized oppression. Writing is essential for women of color to generate a spiritual activism from within ourselves to create a new order in the outside world.

When engaging in internal revolution fueled by spiritual activism to free ourselves from our intrapersonal oppression, we must remind ourselves that it is too easy to blame an outside source (white society and men or white feminists). Anzaldúa reminds us: "What we say and what we do ultimately comes back to us, so let us own our responsibility, place it in our own hands and carry it with dignity and strength."[24] Our responsibility is to write for change, to facilitate the voices of others and the commitment of coalition. We, third world women of color, do have privileges. Our challenges are our empowerment; our oppression is our privilege: "Even though we go hungry we are not impoverished of experiences."[25] We have had the privilege to experience what people who have class and race privilege will most likely never experience. We, marginalized women of color, are eager to point out that those at the center don't want to give up their privilege. However, we are guilty of the same offense. We, as women of color must be willing to share the privilege of experience—of hurt, solitude, struggle, seized empowerment, and wrested self-love—that allows us an in-depth understanding of the need and urgency for El Mundo Unido. We must share our privilege of knowledge and experience with the oppressors to free them of their ignorance, hate, and guilt. Anzaldúa puts it best: "To touch more people, the personal realities and the social must be evoked—not through rhetoric but through blood, pus and sweat."[26]

It may seem as if women of color are responsible for the majority of reaching out, giving, teaching, and bridging. My third world sisters of color may retort that the oppressors don't deserve all this love and understanding. If we put out love and understanding, it will come back to us. We fear getting hurt if we extend our hand and our affections, but love requires faith. One must believe in love and cast away fear. There will be no bridges to El Mundo Unido if there is no naked trust, stripped of fear, to hold up those bridges. Giving, loving, and bridging are acts of fearlessness.

Chrystos highlights the importance and necessity of giving fearlessly in her poem, "Ceremony for Completing a Poetry Reading," which opens with the words: "This is a give-away poem."[27] As the poem progresses she coaxes her readers to "Come closer" to receive the gifts out of her "basket" of "kind words," which "is only the beginning."[28] She gives and gives, verse after verse, but without the expectation of receiving in return. To me, "Ceremony for Completing a Poetry Reading" is a love poem, a celebration of unconditional giving and loving. Chrystos is sharing not only the words of her poem but everything she can possibly offer from within herself and of herself:

> Come take it
> Take as much as you want
> I give you seeds of a new way[29]

She imparts gifts of simplicity, beauty, thoughts, words, and peace. From beginning to end, Chrystos is inviting, giving, and loving. She does not get tired of it; she ends by saying: "I will be full."[30] The last few lines of the poem depict a dire, almost desperate need to give. Her unmatched feeling of liberation and empowerment can be achieved only by unconditional giving and loving.

Love is what we must cultivate our minds and spirits with in order to achieve the vision of El Mundo Unido. We must cultivate our colored skins with fearless love. For people who will hesitate, I will extend an invitation, like Chrystos did, to "Come closer" to the bridge to El Mundo Unido.[31] For the people who will say it doesn't work that easy and you can't do it, I will say, "I am a change in the making." I am called to create El Mundo Unido. I will not wait and linger for change to come about; I will make it. I will be the revolution. As a woman of color feminist/womanist, I am a firm believer of the ideology that the personal is political. Hence, a personal revolution will inevitably be a political revolution.

The people "who have made a circle with me" with whom I partake in the acts of giving, receiving, and loving in my personal life, are men and women of nearly every race, class, sexual orientation, and religion.[32] In my personal life, I live in a small version of El Mundo Unido. I practice reaching out and saying: "Come closer."[33] I write about love because I have no fear of being judged for writing about something that is deemed unacademic. My written words about political change are backed by actions of personal magnitude. The vision of El Mundo Unido is attainable, but we must start with the personal to achieve the political.

Are We There Yet? How Far Is This Bridge?

> In loving ourselves for who we are—American women of color—we can make a vision for the future where we are free to fulfill our human potential. This new framework will not support repression, hatred, exploitation, and isolation, but it will be a human and beautiful framework, created in a community, bonded not by color, sex, or class, but by love and the common goal for the liberation of mind, heart, and spirit.
>
> —Merle Woo, *This Bridge Called My Back*

I am a listener and thinker in the classroom. In the world outside the classroom, I am a speaker and doer. I have written vigorously about coming to voice, practicing voice and resistance in the world outside the academe to build bridges and foster connections through differences. Yet, I found myself striving to create a space for my voice and body in the "Literature by Radical Women of Color" classroom, which seemed to be only Black and White. I was the only undergraduate in a class of graduate students. I was also the only nonwhite, not-black individual in a class where I continuously heard white academics questioning their robust black colleagues on how they really feel about white people. And I heard responses from certain black women in class along the lines of "S/he did not just say that" or a booming, "But do you see me?"

There were times when I wondered whether everyone in class saw any other color but Black and White? If anyone did see other colors why didn't she or he care to include them in conversation on a regular basis, especially in a course on "Literature by Radical Women of Color"? Did anyone else in class notice how most (not all, but most) class discussions revolved around or boiled down to strictly Black and White dynamics. I wondered if I were invisible. In these moments, I would start raising my hand and speaking up. My voice lent me existence. Reflecting on the racial dynamics of the class, I believe my biggest challenge throughout the course had to do with the prickly question of belonging. Did I belong in this class? Did I have a voice in it? Ultimately, did I claim a space for myself in this course of study?

During one of our class meetings, the topic and possibility of re-segregation was discussed. I was apprehensive about considering re-segregation as a viable solution to issues of difference. The discussion made me uneasy and damaged my hope for coalition politics in and outside the classroom. After I had started reading *This Bridge Called My Back*, I realized with horror and urgency, we're not there yet! Thirty years after *This Bridge Called My Back*, we are still trying to talk about how to build bridges. I had been a fool in love with the vision of El Mundo Zurdo and then with the dream of El Mundo Unido. Is this really how far we have managed to come? We're building walls and mapping boundaries and we wonder why we feel fractured. Why we feel alone. Why we still talk about building bridges. When will we—a truly all inclusive "We," anyone and everyone human—get there? How far is this bridge? I am sick of it like Donna Kate Rushin declares in "The Bridge Poem."[34]

If we, humans of all colors, races, classes, genders, and sexualities are holding our breath for change, we are suffocating ourselves. Rushin's poem is about being sick of being the bridge for everyone around her. She is tired of bridging the gaps for her friends and family. She is sick of being the "sole Black friend to 34 individual white people."[35] However, Rushin doesn't propose distancing herself and shutting out her 34 white friends and reinstituting segregation. Instead, she cautions against Othering people by shutting them out or shutting oneself in: "I'm sick of reminding you not to close off too tight for too long."[36] Here I was, with twelve other people, meeting week after week for four months, to build bridges, to open up to each other, to take in each other's differences, to stretch and reach out to one another. Our class discussion around the possibility of re-segregation left me shocked and hurt.

Rushin stressed that we must recognize the power we each possess to make change. Change starts with the self—"I must be the bridge to nowhere / But my true self / And then / I will be useful."[37] If we are holding our breath in denial of difference and similarity or resisting change, we are indulging in conscious suffocation. Our evolution as a race—the human race—starts with feeling each other's pain, "The pain of racism. The pain of it all . . . people of color are [not] the only ones hurt by racism."[38] Racism hinders everyone. Racism sets us up to live our lives with a disabled humanness. The oppressor and the oppressed are both disabled, they both hurt. They are both blinded by ignorance and by pain, simultaneously. Anyone who partakes in racism, classism, sexism, homophobia, and so forth, and anyone who accepts it, doesn't speak up against it, ignores it, or makes excuses for it contributes to the ignorance and oppression. Cherríe Moraga says it best: "Coming to terms with the suffering of others has never meant looking away from our own. And, we must look deeply. We must acknowledge that to change the world, we have to change ourselves—even sometimes our most cherished block-hard convictions."[39] In order to form coalitions, one must let go of "block-hard convictions such as separatism of any kind, for separatism will only lead to reinforced fragmenting and splintering."[40]

To make a movement, we must seek coalition, we must "Stretch" as Rushin states, and be the bridge. If we "turned our backs on each other—the bridge collaps[es]—whether it be for public power, personal gain, private validation, or more closely, to save face, to save our children, to save our skins," what will we be left with?[41] Will we even be left with our skins? Would an All-White, All-Black, Chinatown, Chicana/o town, *Desi*-town, Arab-town, Latin-land, and so forth, help us save our skins? What would be the next degree of separation? For example, would *Desi*-town have a separate section for Muslim, Hindu, Sikh, Christian, Jain, Bahai, Buddhist, Parsi? Would the Muslim section then have Sunni, Shia, Wahhabi, Ahmadi streets? What next? Class separation? How many more degrees of separation?

Even if we do form individual communities based on skin color, race, ethnicity, or religion, color politics would still exist. There are color politics in our extended families and even in our very homes, as Moraga states in the introduction to "Children Passing in the Street": "We grew up with the inherent contradictions in the color spectrum right inside [our] homes: the lighter sister, the mixed-blood cousin, being the darkest one in the family. It doesn't take [much] to realize the privileges or lack thereof, attached to a particular shade of skin or texture of hair."[42] An All-Black, All-*Desi*, All-anything town will not end color games nor will it disable color charts. It will only serve to separate and fragment us more than we already are. Do we, women of color, not have color charts and color politics in our own black, brown, or mixed homes? Would those color charts magically cease to exist in segregated towns? There will be varying skin tones in an All-Black, All-Brown town, and so forth. What would happen to our darker sisters in our own towns? Would they be invisible even then? Would they suffer the same way they would in an unsegregated town? I think not; they would suffer more. I ask the question Barbara Cameron asks: "What's worse than being invisible among your own kind?"[43] And then I ask, is it really worth the pain?

I refuse to settle for the mentality that if the current situation or established social/cultural set up is not working, let's get up and leave. I accept that racism in America is real. However, picking up and moving to a racially segregated town will not grant anyone justice. It will not protect anyone. In fact, the distance, alienation, and mistrust between groups would skyrocket. Segregation would lead to mistreatment, assaults, and violence every time a person would cross the boundary of one's segregated town into a place where one does not belong. As Dykewomon states: "What we wear on our skins—race, ethnicity, money, country of origin, physical ability, appearance, religion, age—creates troubling barriers [but it is] absolutely necessary . . . to find ways to bridge the divisions that institutions use to keep us powerless."[44]

Powerlessness and shame is what was on Ednie Garrison's mind as she wrote her essay, "Sitting in the Waiting Room of Adult and Family Services at SE 122nd in Portland, Oregon, with My Sister and My Mother Two Hours before I Return to School (April 1995)." Garrison states: "The only privilege I can count on is whiteness."[45] Garrison picks up her pen to write about her experience of shame; she is not oblivious of her white privilege and has an understanding that "even that [privilege] is no guarantee. The poverty of [Garrison's] youth, and the continued poverty of [her] family reminds [her] that whiteness doesn't have to signify security. So [she] rel[ies] on knowledge."[46] In my opinion, knowledge of privilege or lack of privilege does not increase security either. It only heightens awareness, which in turn increases responsibility. Garrison takes on that responsibility and comes to voice to share the experience of her shame and her privilege to extend herself in coalition in *This Bridge We Call Home*, to find intersection through her difference and her similarities. The same responsibility falls on the shoulders of the underprivileged, i.e., my colleagues and me for starters. To borrow Anzaldúa's words: "Our goal . . . [should] not [be] to use differences to separate [ourselves] from others" but to extend ourselves in coalition.[47]

As a woman of color feminist/womanist, I believe radicalism is about doing something that has never been done before. Building coalitions is radical. Finding connection and similarities through difference is radical. Thinking and stepping out of our respective race/color boxes is radical. We cannot alter the past, but we can teach about it and learn from it. We can come together and challenge the present inequalities to truly change the future of race relations in America. If Black and White are polar opposites, then there is a world of color in between those polarities, and America is home to every color and shade imaginable. America is colorful[l] and not just black and white. Coalition will seem an impossible goal, if one is unable to comprehend that to build coalitions one must first recognize that diversity exists.

I had to speak up in class and mention how I had been taught all along that light is right. I had stereotypes drilled into my head about other races, classes, religions, cultures, genders, and sexualities. My parents did not want me to mingle with any outsiders—anyone who wasn't part of my immediate family. If behaviors of acceptance and rejection of difference are learned by how one is raised, then what happened to me? If I was raised to mistrust difference, to keep myself separated from the "Others," then why is my life so rich with people of difference? Why am I not quick to hate, to label, to stereotype, to separate, to turn away? How did I, a Pakistani American Muslim woman, find it bearable to share a house that is inhabited by a white Midwestern Scientologist, his part-Venezuelan son who is openly gay and agnostic, and an Israeli man and his girlfriend of similar origin? What happened to my sorry excuse of undiversified upbringing? What happened to the Pakistani-Muslim-box I was raised to be confined in? Why didn't I stay in that so-called comfort zone where I didn't have to think about difference or suffer the criticism of family and relatives for going against what is traditionally and culturally expected of me. I am outside the box because I chose to be. I built a bridge to the unfamiliar world/s outside my box, and I have strived every day to consciously live outside my box.

There is an inexplicable, incompatible joy in bridging, in reaching out with my humanness to seek another's, to witness their dreams, to feel their pain, to touch their skin, to understand their difference, and to cherish their humanness. Bridging is described by Anzaldúa as: loosening our borders, not closing off to others. Bridging is the work of opening the gate to the stranger within—and without. To step across the threshold is to be stripped of the illusion of safety because it moves us into unfamiliar territory and does not grant safe passage. To bridge is to attempt community, and for that we must risk being open to personal, political, and spiritual intimacy.[48]

I have tried to imagine how my life would change if I were to perpetuate boundaries of difference I had been indoctrinated to believe would be enforced as a "normal" standard of practice. In this vision, I see myself and loved ones, friends, and friends I call and know as family having to pick sides. My life would be a ruin. I would lose my best friends, the people I love, the families with whom I celebrate Christmas, Thanksgiving, and Fourth of July. Maybe the right to be upset over that would be lost, too, since there are plenty of people who think these holidays are not mine to celebrate since I'm not Christian by religion or not American in their eyes or by their standards. What would my white friend, who is a mother to four biracial children do? What side would she pick? What about my African American male friend who is married to a Pakistani woman? Where would they live? Would their young daughter have to pick sides? Would my LGBTQ+ friends be safe in communities based on skin color but intolerant of their gender and sexual identities and preferences? How would I cope without the people I love? Would I survive? My heart would surely break, since it can't segregate.

Our goal should not be to wipe the slate clean and start from scratch to build strong segregated communities and then to try and build bridges between them. I want to start from where we are right now. I don't want to go back several hundred years to come to consciousness. I don't want to build metaphorical walls. I want to build real bridges. If everyone takes personal responsibility to be a bridge, no matter how insignificant a personal bridge may appear, it makes a difference, because the personal *is* political. All it takes is one voice, one step, one outstretched hand, one open mind, one accepting heart to initiate a revolution. If each of us makes a commitment to a personal revolution against racism, sexism, classism, homophobia, and heteronormativity, it would make building bridges a habit, a way of life. "The work: To make revolution irresistible" would come naturally and would spread like wild fire.[49]

Notes

1. Walker, Alice. *In Search of Our Mothers' Gardens: Womanist Prose.* (New York: Harcourt Brace Jovanovich Publishers, 1983), ix–iix.

2. Ibid., ix.

3. Ibid.

4. Milczarek-Desai, Shefali, "Living Fearlessly with and within Differences: My Search for Identity beyond Categories and Contradictions," in *This Bridge We Call Home: Radical Visions for Transformation*, eds. Gloria E. Anzaldúa and AnaLouise Keating (New York: Routledge, 2002), 134.

5. Hurdis, Rebecca, "Heartbroken. Women of Color Feminism and the Third Wave," in *Colonize This! Young Women of Color on Today's Feminism*, eds. Daisy Hernandez and Bushra Rehman (Seal Press: Emeryville California, 2002), 287.

6. Hernández-Linares, Leticia. "Gallina Ciega: Turning the Game on Itself," in *This Bridge We Call Home*, 111.

7. Ibid.," 115.

8. Ibid., 111.

9. Ibid., 115.

10. Anon., "For My Sister: Smashing the Walls of Pretense and Shame," in *This Bridge We Call Home*, 295.

11. Ibid.

12. Ford, Chandra, "Standing on this Bridge," in *This Bridge We Call Home*, 304.

13. Anzaldúa. "La Prieta," in *This Bridge Called My Back, Writings by Radical Women of Color*, 2nd Edition (New York: Kitchen Table: Women of Color Press, 1983), vi.

14. Ibid.

15. Ibid.

16. Ibid., 208.

17. Moraga. "The Welder," in *This Bridge Called My Back*, 219.

18. Anzaldúa, "La Prieta," 209.

19. Moraga, "The Welder," 219.

20. Ibid., 220.

21. Ibid.

22. Anzaldúa. "Speaking In Tongues: A Letter To 3rd World Women Writers," in *This Bridge Called My Back*, 165–173.

23. Ibid., 169.

24. Ibid., 171.

25. Ibid., 172.

26. Ibid., 173.

27. Chrystos. "Ceremony for Completing a Poetry Reading," in *This Bridge Called My Back*, 191.

28. Ibid.

29. Ibid.

30. Ibid., 191–192.

31. Ibid., 191.

32. Ibid.

33. Ibid.

34. Rushin, Donna Kate. "The Bridge Poem," in *This Bridge Called My Back*, xxii.

35. Ibid.

36. Ibid.

37. Ibid.

38. Moraga. Preface, in *This Bridge Called My Back*, xv.

39. Moraga, Foreword, in *This Bridge We Call Home*.

40. Ibid.

41. Moraga, Preface, in *This Bridge Called My Back*, xvii.

42. Moraga, Introduction: "Children Passing in the Street," in *This Bridge Called My Back* 5.

43. Cameron, Barbara. "Gee, You Don't Seem Like an Indian from the Reservation," in *This Bridge Called My Back*, 50.

44. Dykewomon, Elana. "Body Politic—Mediations on Identity," in *This Bridge We Call Home*, 450.

45. Garrison, Ednie Kaeh. "Sitting in the Waiting Room of Adult and Family Services at SE 122nd in Portland, Oregon, with My Sister and My Mother Two Hours before I Return to School (April 1995)," in *This Bridge We Call Home*, 472.

46. Ibid.

47. Anzaldúa. Preface, in *This Bridge We Call Home*, 3.

48. Ibid.

49. Bambara, Toni Cade. Foreword, in *This Bridge Called My Back* viii.

PART III

Speaking and Acting Out in Womanist Solidarity

9

Transgenero Performance

Gender and Transformation in Mujeres en Ritual

DORA ARREOLA

Founding Mujeres en Ritual

In 1991, I founded a theatre group in the Universidad Autónoma de Baja California (UABC), in order to conduct my own theatre research and connect with indigenous cultures from the North of Mexico. As a mestiza from the North of Mexico, I was looking for my own roots, rituals, myths, and legends. Before that, I had directed several theatre productions by famous male playwrights, such as *Tartuffe* by Moliere and *An Open Couple* by Dario Fo. As I began to create original work, I noticed a tendency to put male characters who create the world and dominate it in the center of the spectacle, which also meant that the male actors always had the lead roles and more voice. The women in my productions, during this time, served as extras or in support roles, always in the background, during the artistic process as well as in the show. I realized that I was not conscious about the sexism inherent in the material, that I was projecting my own internalized sexism, the normalcy of a patriarchal and misogynist society, and my fears of not pleasing society with my artistic work. With time, I realized that this tendency made no sense for me as a lesbian artist.

In the mid-nineties, I was invited to direct a production of *Giving Up the Ghost*[1] by Cherríe Moraga, in San Diego, California. It was my first experience directing a play by a feminist, queer woman of color. At that time, I also was inspired by Alice Walker's definition of a *womanist* from *In Search of Our Mothers' Gardens: Womanist Prose* (1983), especially part 2: "A woman who loves other women, sexually and/or nonsexually. Appreciates and prefers women's culture, women's emotional flexibility (values tears as natural counterbalance of laughter), and women's strength. Sometimes loves individual men, sexually and/or nonsexually. Committed to survival and wholeness of entire people, male *and* female."[2] With Moraga's and Walker's concepts, I began to channel my own voice into my work. I became more interested in exploring women's relationships and empowerment through theatre. For this reason, in November 1999, I founded a company in Tijuana called Mujeres en Ritual Danza-Teatro, with the intention of creating a safe space to produce performances from the experiences of women, with women's issues and women performing at the center.

The idea of creating the company Mujeres en Ritual was to confront my own internalized sexism, classism, and racism, and to represent the power of women when we work together in solidarity against the systems that perpetuate hatred and separation among us. The particular geographic and historical context of Tijuana, and the experiences of women in the U.S.-Mexico border region, became the principal themes of the company. We explored these themes from a feminist and queer perspective to expose the domestic dynamics of power in the city and the power dynamics between the two countries. Mujeres en Ritual became a safe space to share and publicly expose stories of oppression and abuse. The idea of bringing together ten women (the original company) represented an act of solidarity and mutual support. The company also became a space for empowerment and public voice.

With Mujeres en Ritual, I developed a unique physical training process. In addition to grounding in traditional dances and rituals of Mexico, I draw from three techniques that complement each other and sustain the concept of precise movement: Suzuki Technique (stillness), Butoh (high levels of concentration and body poetics), and the theatre tradition of Jerzy Grotowski and Rena Mirecka, specifically Objective Drama, Art as a Vehicle and Paratheatrical phases (body and voice transformation through organic movement). I explore the sources of creativity, and the connection between ancient practices and contemporary performance, through ritual structures.

As a company created in the lineage of Jerzy Grotowski, who very deeply explored the "internal pulse" (as described by Thomas Richard in *At the Work with Grotowski on Physical Actions*[3]), we work from the *impulse* of the performer that comes *before* the manifestation of an expression or movement. With such impulses, the performer can create structures of movement, also called "actions" (which are not confined by realism). To achieve this, the performer should first prepare technically to create the actions and perform them with mastery and precision. This work not only develops the performer's craft, but also emphasizes a perpetual practice, a journey of the performer in working on herself.

The process that Mujeres en Ritual uses to create original performances can be described as Devised Theatre, in which the text is created or adapted in collaboration with the performers, usually through an improvisation process. Our work is animated by the expansion of internal images, the company members' own personal associations, which are derived from the images and metaphors contained in a text, the physical environment of Tijuana, or the themes we choose to investigate. As artistic director, I create structures to explore movement, the reconstruction or invention of rituals, and traditional or contemporary dances. The actions created by the company members are then developed into scenes and choreographies—all of which lead to compositions that sustain the metaphors of transformation and journey.

In the aesthetics of Mujeres en Ritual, text and movement—or voice and body—have their own place and value, without the hierarchy that mainstream culture usually assumes. We employ multiple layers and interpretations through visual, theatrical, and political spectacle. The use of abstraction and symbolism, popular culture and farce create a political theatre that is not narrative or didactic. The audience is called to make sense out of juxtaposed realities in which power is constructed, gained, and deconstructed in vastly different ways.

With Mujeres en Ritual, I have created and directed more than twelve full-length works including: *Mujeres en Ritual*, a game of contrasts that explores the body, motherhood, aging, domestic violence and innocence; *El Sueño de Sor Juana*, based on the epic poem *Primero Sueño* by the first feminist in the Americas, Sor Juana Inés de la Cruz; *Perfecto Luna*, based on a short story by Elena Garro that explores the realities of Latin América through the eyes of an orphan; devised dance-theatre works *Rios de Ofelia*, *De Granadas Mi Vida*, and *Leonidas*; *Fronteras Desviadas / Deviant Borders*, written through a community-based process by Andrea Assaf (which I will discuss further); and *Aqui deberia estar tu nombre / Here Should Be Your Name*, based on the writings of Noé Carrillo, a Tijuana-based poet who disappeared in 2003. Carrillo wrote subliminally and explicitly about homoeroticism in an ultra-oppressive and homophobic context through themes of silence, invisibility, and absence. Additional themes of our work have included political corruption and feminicide in *Antigona en la frontera/Antigone at the Border*, migration and colonization in Telares (o el olvido) by Fabiola Ruiz, and more.. Recurrent images include journeys, rites of passage, bridges, doors or thresholds, borders, vehicles (elements, not necessarily physical, that carry you from one place to another), and death.

Over time, Mujeres en Ritual developed as a binational ensemble of women artists, all women of color, from Mexico and the United States, rooted in the exploration of techniques of the body. Our artistic practice is in constant transformation and is framed by crossing boundaries and breaking paradigms to expose and stretch perspectives, and build strong group dynamics. We are always searching for acts of liberatory transgression and the experience of transformation.

Women's Bodies and the Border

There are many ways to perceive Tijuana: as the first corner of Mexico, or the last, or as the doorway to Latinoamerica. I grew up in the hills above the city, overlooking the Pacific Ocean and the San Diego skyline, watching the border patrol cars and helicopters chasing migrants who were trying to cross to the United States, every day. The border was literally in my back yard, in my face—a horrible stretch of rusting metal, left over from the first U.S. Gulf War, recycled in Mexico as a fence to stop the perceived infiltration of Latinos into the United States. As a child, this nonmetaphorical, very concrete border fence reminded me every day that I was considered inferior, poor, dirty, and criminal; that I was not wanted; that I could not cross. As an artist, as I grew, that fence invited me to transgress . . .

The border between Tijuana, B.C. (Mexico) and San Diego, California (U.S.) is the most frequently crossed border in the world. The United States is Mexico's #1 trading partner, while Mexico is the #2 trade partner of the United States. Several hundred million people cross legally every year, across a border that stretches 2,000 miles across four U.S. states and six Mexican states, with a 60-mile border zone on each side of the line. As described by folklife scholar Maribel Alvarez, "The border includes millions of workers essential to the economic machines of North American agriculture, tourism, and industry: farm workers, low-tech labor, dishwashers, gardeners, maids . . . but also a military machine of low-intensity conflict: Homeland Security helicopters, Border Patrol agents, infrared cameras, detention centers, books of regulations. . . . Violence and death are dimensions of everyday life in the border."[4] These deaths include feminicide—the genocide of women in Juarez, numerous unprosecuted cases of female homicide, and the murder and trafficking of sex workers—as well as desert crossers, deaths related to narco-traffic, and toxic illnesses caused by pollution from maquiladoras (unregulated factories owned by multinational corporations in so-called "free trade" zones created by NAFTA, the North American Free Trade Agreement, in 1994). In 2011, there were over 800 maquiladoras in the Tijuana border region alone. Tijuana's maquiladora industries and sexual tourism industries are among the largest in the world—both predominantly controlled by men, but fueled by the exploitation of (predominantly) women workers.

In the U.S. imagination, Tijuana is often associated with sex, drugs, decadence, and illegality. This "*Leyenda Negra*," as it's called in Mexico, is described by Mexican author Humberto Felix Berumen in *Tijuana la horrible: Entre la historia y el mito*: "People have a stigmatized image of Tijuana, as it can be perceived through radio, literature, film, written press, television, songs, and many other discourses (oral, visual, and written). That image is a social creation and a collective image formed by the syncretic amalgamation of platitudes, legends, stereotypes, prejudices, sociograms and clichés. . . . Tijuana is a city-symbol, the emblem, by definition, of perversion and vice. A myth that has been revealed with a great capacity to renew itself continually."[5] But rarely is there an acknowledgment of U.S. responsibility in creating the political and economic conditions that make this image and these markets flourish, or any accountability for the exploitation and violence that accompanies them. Felix Berumen exposes the founding of Tijuana by Americans in 1916, as an adult entertainment center for U.S. tourists: "Tijuana vice was created by Californians evading the moralizing forces of Prohibition. Americans, in time, acquired more influence in Tijuana than most Mexicans." The Americans were the creators and promoters of the Tijuana image, to attract their own people as consumers in the bars and casinos that they owned.

Today, the bars and prostíbulos of the Zona Norte, the "red zone" of Tijuana, are owned by Mexican, American, and multinational owners, as are the maquiladoras. Poverty, lack of opportunity, and trafficking force thousands of women, children, and transgender people into sex work; in 2004, there were an estimated 8,000 sex workers in the Zona Norte alone, the vast majority women.

All of this systematically diminishes the image of Mexican women in the global imagination, and thereby normalizes and renders violence against women permissible in a region where every woman is potentially seen as a "puta."

Breaking Silence, Breaking Stereotypes: Voice and Embodiment through Performance

Mujeres en Ritual was formed as a response and resistance to the systematic oppression of women at the Mexico-U.S. border, a way of transforming the perception of women, as well as women's perception of ourselves, from object to subject.

I founded the company with a group of nonprofessional women artists, the majority of whom were from the community, or had been my students. To be in the company meant that members first had to train, to practice strenuous physical theatre exercises that gave them the ability to respond with their whole bodies and voices to demanding situations. Physical training helped us deconstruct conventional stereotypes of femininity, such as fragility, high and soft voices, weakness, and invisibility. For performers, training develops presence, or *visibility*, and an open vocal range, and enhances balance, energy, and strength, both internal and external. This process includes liberating blocks in the body and voice to allow greater levels of expressivity—which often means breaking silences, and confronting or expressing our traumas. The intention of embodied practice is to eradicate the vestiges of oppression in the bodies of women, to liberate our voices, and to deconstruct preconceptions of femininity or womanhood. Our training process sustains the aesthetics of the company and is also the starting point for creating theatre from our own experiences, pain, dreams, and hopes.

The work of Mujeres en Ritual de-objectifies women of the border region by demystifying our desires and by breaking myths that, as women of color, we "choose" oppressive systems, or "like it like that," or want to be in positions in which we are dominated. We disrupt stereotypes and false perceptions to expose the systematic exploitation of women, the cruelty and abuse. We also perform agency and strength and intentionally break traditional gender roles that theatre conventionally leaves women performers. As a result of our emphasis on embodiment and voice, Mujeres en Ritual has received recognition for a powerful presence, strong images, and unique scenic sensibility.

There are many plays about the border experience, but the question is how to create new work about women at the border that is not condescending, illustrative, simplistic, stereotypical, or didactic—work that deconstructs the images of women and the *Leyenda Negra* of Tijuana. How do we uncover these voices and forms, as if they were there sleeping, or waiting for a bridge, or a new means of expression to emerge?

Interdisciplinarity is profoundly important in the work of Mujeres en Ritual Danza-Teatro. Divisions or categories of form, discipline, and genre create artificial "borders" between human modes of expression. To break the paradigms of Western theatre is to break the social constructions of gender and representation, and to begin a process of decolonizing our creativity. The European concept of "realism," which has dominated theatre since the mid-1800s, expresses a "reality" created and controlled by men. We create our aesthetic through a seamless exploration of theatre, dance, ritual, feminism, queer theory and border studies; we mix multiple aesthetics and sources of movement; we create our own texts, reinterpret plays, or use no text at all; we employ parody, farce, realism, dreamscapes, poetry and prose, narrative and abstraction, dance and physical theatre, all rooted in ritual structures. Ritual is a source of performance that is precolonial, circular, and highly symbolic. Ritual creates an open, holistic, participatory space. The name "Women in Ritual" implies a belief in the power of women in collective work, structures, and systems.

Mujeres en Ritual pushes the boundaries of sexuality and gender representation by performing a whole spectrum of identities, including male, female, and transgender characters, and brings a feminist as well as queer analysis to all our work. Through the training, members of Mujeres en Ritual develop strong, dynamic, versatile bodies and voices that can perform a range of gender expressions. When women perform men, several things happen: catharsis, parody, political commentary, and discovering the freedom of transgressing assigned gender roles or taboo gender expressions.

In a review of *Fronteras Desviadas/Deviant Borders*, theatre critic Sergio Rommel describes how the work of Mujeres en Ritual "fits in the frame of hybrid and trans-genre traditions; in fact, the transgression of borders in multiple ways (*transgeneridad*) is not only the central theme of the play, but at the same time the most effective vehicle for reassigning meaning to all the elements and signs of the performance . . . the same phrases contain an additional charge [double meaning] that in some way alludes to the theatre of protest . . . theatre-dance, anglo-latina . . . Spanish-English . . . sexual diversity (heterosexuality-homosexuality-bisexuality) . . . geographic borders. Like this, successively, other frontiers are deviated or transgressed throughout the performance."[6] Rommel's analysis led us to understand and articulate the work of Mujeres en Ritual in a new way. On all levels, we have experimented with transgression and transformation to arrive at a *transgenero* performance—meaning both transgender and trans-genre.

Cross-border and Community Collaborations

In Mexico, it is still taboo to speak openly about the prevalence of sex work, and the violence of that underworld. While in the United States, it is still taboo to speak out publicly about U.S. economic exploitation of other countries, such as Mexico, and of women of color globally. As Rosa Linda Fregoso suggests in "Gender, Multiculturalism and the Missionary Position in the Borderlands,"[7] the political position of Mexico in relation to the United States is one of submission to a "masculinist colonial fantasy that authorizes and privileges the white man's access to brown female bodies." Mexico itself is feminized as the "bottom" that must submit to the U.S. position of domination.

Then how is it possible for artists from the United States and Mexico to collaborate equitably? How can a play stage the history and dynamics between the United States and Mexico? What aesthetic could support the coexistence of two cultures, two political realities, simultaneously? In 2004, through a collaboration between theatre artists from both countries, Mujeres en Ritual sought to explore these issues from multiple points of view, to arrive at a more complex perception of the relations between women, in the context of the border. Through a six-month artistic exchange with Andrea Assaf, a U.S.-based Arab American writer and performer, we created *Fronteras Desviadas/Deviant Borders*—a collaboration between women of color from two different socioeconomic and cultural backgrounds, both queer-identified, developing ways to work and create together in mutual support.[8] But this meant we had to confront the complex power dynamics in our own relationship—our own internalized racism, Euro/U.S.-centrism, classism, and fears about sexual violence. This process defined one of the most radical acts of the collaboration.

Fronteras Desviadas/Deviant Borders is a bilingual, interdisciplinary work that explores gender, taboo, and rites of passage at the U.S.-Mexico border. The performance presents a juxtaposition of two parallel realities: A tour guide known as "El Chamuco" (Mexican slang for "devil") leads the audience on a journey from night to day through the red zone of Tijuana, as two actress-dancers embody and give voice to the experiences of women in communities near the border. Through the collision of diverse cultural elements and political realities, *Fronteras Desviadas/Deviant Borders* offers a journey to "the other side" of sexuality, deviance, and culture.

We began the artistic process through an investigation of existing research and visiting key sites, including: Zona Norte, the commercial sex zone, to observe the dynamics of gender exploitation and the U.S. tourists filling the bars of Tijuana; and an Environmental Justice Tour[9] of communities affected by the pollution from the Ciudad Industrial, Tijuana's largest maquiladora complex, and the inhumane conditions for women workers there. At the same time, we began the studio process, exploring movement and popular rituals that women are expected to pass through, from birth to death—such as quinceañeras, weddings and funerals—which gave us a structure for the journey of the play.

An important element of the process was community-based workshops with women on both sides of the border, a process which ultimately generated text for the performance. Andrea Assaf brought a writing process to the workshops rooted in methodologies from the U.S. community-based arts movement; I brought verbal and physical improvisations, movement composition, and techniques that Mujeres en Ritual had developed through the years. This interweaving of approaches led us to create a means of shared facilitation and methodology for community collaboration.

As professional artists conducting workshops in marginalized communities—such as Maclovio Rojas, a defiant community halfway between Tijuana and Tecate, sandwiched between maquiladoras, which the Mexican government wants to evict; and a "Parenting Class" for convicted mothers in San Ysidro, California (all of them Mexicanas) whose children had been taken away by the state. I felt it was important for us not to engage in "missionary art" or anthropological study but to create a means of genuine collaboration with other women of color. Again, we had to confront inherent power dynamics and clarify our practice and intentions. "Missionary art" enters with the idea of wanting to "save" communities, a fundamentally paternalistic approach; while "anthropological art" positions the artist as a falsely objective observer or "expert," and usually creates a situation of appropriation.

As facilitators, we were full participants in the creative process, opening spaces by sharing our own experiences and stories of violence. We were collaborating with other women in order to understand ourselves better, to journey back into our own histories and reveal the complexity of multiple oppressions together. I was born in a marginalized community and grew up in poverty. My family migrated to the border region when I was very young, and I lived for many years in a precarious position, struggling every day just to eat. When I was only thirteen years old, I worked in a restaurant in the Zona Norte, as a waitress and dishwasher. We were not there to speak for others, but to work together to tell a collective story.

In the workshops, we offered writing prompts about gender and identity at the border: *When do I experience myself as "woman"? What is deviance? What is on the other side?* We shared our writings and stories in the workshops (using an oral or written process, depending on the literacy level of the group), as well as created movement and improvisations together. We then invited participants to contribute their writing, stories or movement phrases, if they wished, to the creative process of developing a script and movement score for the performance. All participants chose to donate their work to the collective process. The results were texts charged with meaning, strong content and emotionality, as well as profound movements with intensity and complexity that reflected the life experiences and visions of the women of these communities.

These texts became collective poems, rich with abstraction, metaphors and symbolism, cruelty, and the women's surprising encounters with atrocity. The poems were then layered into the movement composition. In *Fronteras Desviadas/Deviant Borders*, dialogue does not exist in the conventional sense; there is no singular defined relationship among the women characters, but there are many that are constantly changing. In the beginning of the play, their encounters are not by choice; only coincidences propel them forward. One initiates, or prepares the way for the other to advance, or they pass each other. It is not until the final scene of the play that they have a moment of intimacy for the first time, when they take hands and look profoundly in each other's eyes, to discover the same pain, the same suffering, and the same hope.

The environment, or set, is unchanging and the same objects are used in multiple ways to create different contexts—a kind of overuse or recycling that suggests a maximum economy, in sharp contrast to the excess of production in maquiladora zones that renders human bodies disposable, just as the sex industry renders women's bodies, and body parts, disposable.

The character of "El Chamuco," written by Assaf, was created from found text on the internet, as an examination of the male gaze, or popular U.S. perceptions of Tijuana women. The objective of juxtaposing El Chamuco with the women's voices was to establish a discourse of the double realities of the border and to implicate American responsibility in the conditions of the Zona Norte. While the bilingual script interchanged lines of Spanish and English in the women's text, the Chamuco was predominantly in one language, depending on which country we were performing in. Presenting the show to audiences in diverse places—some geographically far from the political, socioeconomic and cultural situations in which the work was created—required a process of cultural as well as linguistic translation. In Mexico, the actress interpreted El Chamuco as a Mexican American from California, thereby implicating men of color in their participation in the exploitation of Mexican women. In the United States however, as performed by a Latina actress, the character became a Texan, with the particular inflections, tones, and expressions of men from that state—which had a different political resonance, given that the performance was touring during the presidency of George W. Bush.

In *Borderlands/La Frontera: The New Mestiza*, Gloria Anzaldúa describes the difference between the literal, physical border, and the notion of Borderlands: "The actual physical borderland that I am dealing with . . . is the US Southwest-Mexican border . . . The psychological borderlands, the sexual borderlands and the spiritual borderlands are not particular to the Southwest . . . the Borderlands are physically present wherever two or more cultures edge each other, where people of different races occupy the same territory, where under, lower, middle, and upper classes touch, where the space between two individuals shrinks with intimacy."[10] With *Fronteras Desviadas/ Deviant Borders*, we explored borderlands and border crossings in many ways. Anthropologist Alejandro Lugo thinks the phrase "border crossing" as a metaphor for identity has become overused and "overly optimistic." Border inspections, are actually more pervasive than "border crossings."[11] The experience of inspection is not only about the counting of bodies in the process of crossing, but more deeply about the denigration, the systematic dehumanization of Mexican people based on facial features, skin color, class markers, and sexuality or gender presentation. No matter how successful a cross-border collaboration is, as artists we must continually ask ourselves, is it "too much metaphor"? I am not against using the metaphors of borderlands and crossings, but I want to always acknowledge the reality of the border, and the consequences of those realities for the women who live there.

Pedagogy: Transposing Process across Contexts

Throughout my career, it has been important for me to teach and work in communities, academic settings, and in collaboration with other professional artists. I create performance through a collaborative process, from the expressive needs, levels of experience or ability, cultural/historical and personal experiences of the participants, and whether they are professionals, college students or community members. My creative work focuses on exploring and staging the physical, inner lives of the performers from a postcolonial and feminist perspective, exploring issues of gender and power, and the intersectionality of identities and oppressions. I am most interested in the transformative possibilities of embodiment, what Anzuldúa and Moraga call the "theory in the flesh," in which the physical realities of our lives—our skin color, the land or concrete we grew up on, our sexual longings—all fuse to create a politic born out of necessity."[12]

Over time, many of the original members of Mujeres en Ritual have become professional artists and theatre teachers; some continue to create new work with the company, and some have started their own companies. Now, I am training a new generation of artists, in Tijuana and as a professor in the Department of Theatre and Dance at the University of South Florida in Tampa.

I consider teaching theatre to be a living phenomenon, which starts with fundamental principles and techniques to provide students with a solid and grounded process. The process of exploring and discovering their own experiences develops a state of being that is self-confident and energetic. It also develops in the performers' physical and vocal freedom, intuition, a strong ability to focus, and a powerful presence, both individually and collectively.

In teaching creative process, the need for clear communication is very high. I aim to give my students and performers multiple tools for communication, inclusiveness, respect, and practices of equality—including awareness of racism, sexism, and homophobia. It is important to open conversations around nationality, sexuality, race, and class. I am open about my identity as a lesbian and endeavor to create a safe space for the conversation about all facets of identity in the classroom. I include plays by Cherríe Moraga and other feminist, queer, and women of color writers as part of the curriculum. As a result, there are more students of color enrolling in my classes, and more freedom to express a range of sexual/gender identities in their work. I challenge my students to articulate their observations of aesthetics *and* political content, and to explore new ideas. I endeavor to increase the support that young women of color experience in the academy.

Theatre is a medium that has the potential to sensitize participants, students and audiences, and through aesthetics and creativity, to make the invisible *visible*. My life and artistic work have placed me in a position of challenging oppression in all ways. My company, Mujeres en Ritual, empowers women to perform our stories and visions with our own voices and bodies, and to have voice in the public sphere through performance. The creative process is one of liberation, a healing process that develops our capacity for connection and creates strong bonds among women, building solidarity and relationships of mutual support across class, race, sexual identity, and borders. In this way, the work of Mujeres en Ritual *embodies* women of color feminism. My pedagogy is rooted in this work. It is a queer, feminist, syncretic, creative, and critical process of building womanist coalitions.

Notes

Portions of this chapter have previously been published in "Transgenero Performance: Gender & Transformation in Mujeres en Ritual Danza-Teatro," published in the *Journal of American Drama and Theatre* (JADT) Special Issue: Border Crossings (Vol. 26, No 2.), Spring 2014; and in the book *Mujeres en Ritual: Género y transformación/ Gender and Transformation* (ed. Sergio Rommel Alfonso Guzmán and Dora Arreola), published by Centro Cultural Tijuana and the Secretary of Culture Mexico 2014.

Special thanks to Andrea Assaf for assistance with translation and editing the English version of this essay.

1. Produced by the Diversionary Theater and Centro Cultural de la Raza, San Diego Calif., March 1998.

2. Walker, Alice. *In Search of Our Mothers' Gardens: Womanist Prose.* Orlando, Florida: Harcourt Brace Jovanovich, Publishers, 1983. xi.

3. Richard, Thomas. *At the Work with Grotowski on Physical Actions.* New York: Routledge, 1995.

4. Alvarex, Maribel. "The Boder is . . ." (Guest lecture presented in New WORLD Theater's "Knowledge for Power" series, Amherst College, Amherst, Massachusetts, July 2006).

5. Félix Berumen, Humberto. *Tijuana la horrible: Entre la historia y el mito* (Tijuana: El Colegio de la Frontera Norte, 2003). Quote translated by Dora Arreola and Andrea Assaf.

6. Rommel Alfonso Guzmán, Sergio. *Texto maroma y representación: escritos sobre teatro.* Mexicali, Baja California, Mexico: Universidad Autónoma de Baja California, 2008.

7. Fregoso, Rosa Linda. *meXicana encounters: The Making of Social Identities on the Borderlands.* Berkeley: University of California Press, 2003.

8. The creation of *Fronteras Desviadas/Deviant Borders* was supported in part by a grant from Contacto Cultural (the U.S.-Mexico Foundation for Culture), awarded to Andrea Assaf for the purpose of being an artist-in-residence with Mujeres en Ritual Danza Teatro in Tijuana, Mexico, in 2004.

9. In June 2004, Andrea Assaf and I participated in an Environmental Justice Tour of the communities of Colonia Chilpancingo, Colonia Murua, and Nueva Esperanza, adjacent to Tijuana's largest Maquiladora industrial complex, organized by the Environmental Health Coalition, a leader in the environmental justice movement based in National City, Calif. www.environmentalhealth.org (accessed August 28, 2018).

10. Anzaldúa, Gloria. *Borderlands/La Frontera: The New Mestiza.* San Francisco, CA: Aunt Lute Books, 1987.

11. Lugo, Alejandro. "*Theorizing Border Inspections*," *Journal Cultural Dynamics* 12 (3) (2000): 353–373.

12. Anzaldúa, Gloria, and Cherríe Moraga. *This Bridge Called My Back: Writings by Radical Women of Color* (2nd Edition), "Entering the Lives of Others: Theory in the Flesh." New York: Kitchen Table: Women of Color Press, 1983.

10

Soy Mujer Cuando . . .

A Collective Poem

ANDREA ASSAF

This poem is an excerpt from *Fronteras Desviadas/Deviant Borders*, an interdisciplinary, cross-border collaboration with Mujeres en Ritual Danza-Teatro. The text that follows was created through a community-based process with women on both sides of the U.S-Mexico border. It is written in two voices, for two or more women to perform together.

1

I am a woman when I dive like a hummingbird, *and realize how short the distance to death.*	Soy mujer cuando me lanzo como colibrí, y entiendo cuan corta la distancia a la muerte.
I am a woman when I spin infinity *and deviate . . .*	Soy mujer cuando giro al infinito y me desvío . . .
I am a woman when I cross my legs. *I am a woman when I confront desire.*	Soy mujer cuando cruzo las piernas. Soy mujer cuando atravieso el miedo
I am a woman when I cannot speak, *and my reflection brings me to myself* *once and once again.*	
Soy mujer cuando siento mis sueños	Soy mujer cuando siento mis sueños

Soy mujer cuando siento mis sueños

I am a woman when I am hit.

I am a woman when I attend a man.

I am a woman of breasts and vagina
fucking and washing, cooking and
cleaning
fucking and washing, cooking and
cleaning

cogiendo y lavando, cocinando y
limpiando
cogiendo y lavando, cocinando y
limpiando

Soy mujer . . . *when I pass through fear,*
Soy mujer . . . *when I feel my dreams,*

Soy mujer *when I vibrate with joy*
for nothing more than being alive

2

I am a woman—guilty!
crying alone
in the stench of memory.

I am a woman when I bathe
repeatedly,
when I wash my cunt
when I can't remember . . .

I'm a woman when I take it—
take it hard, bitch, take it!

Soy una mujer con un cuchillo en la
garganta
en un callejón, prometiendo
al hombre con
mi pezón atado a una cadena,
que jamás hablaré . . .
que por mis hijos no me mate

I'm a woman with a knife at my
throat
in a back alley, promising
the man with
my nipple on a chain
that I will never tell . . .
please, for my children—don't kill me

I am a woman when I keep that promise.

I'm woman furious at a society
that has put me in this position!

And I am a woman when I assume the
position.

Soy mujer cuando me niego,
cuando revuelco en las dunas de
arena
y mi cabello da vida a leones y puerco
espines.

I am a woman when I refuse,
when I roll down sand dunes,

and my hair gives life to lions, and
porcupines.

I am a woman when I deviate.
. . . when I make love.
. . . when I love other women.

Soy mujer cuando me desvío . . .

I am a woman . . . *always.*

3

I am a woman when my eyes brighten
before the sunset of a pineapple,
the taste of papaya,
and the song of a fly.

mis ojos brillan
el ocaso de una piña
la canción de una mosca.

I am a woman when I awake
in the dust of my grandmothers,
the nails of my mother, and the
scorpions lost
in a bottle of alcohol.

en el polvo de mis abuelas
las uñas de mi madre,

y los escorpiones perdidos

I am a woman when I deviate.

when I leave my mark in the desert
at night
in the earth of a sprouting garden—
drawing the future and carrying hope
in the totality of our arms.

en el desierto de noche
en la tierra de un jardín retoñante
en la totalidad de nuestros brazos

Note

1. Assaf, Andrea. *Fronteras Desviadas/Deviant Borders* unpublished script, developed in collaboration with Mujeres en Ritual Danza-Teatro, 2005. Text compiled/created by Andrea Assaf, directed by Dora Arreola. (For an in-depth discussion of the collaborative creation process, please see the previous article, "Transgenero Performance" by Dora Arreola, pages 177-181.) The creation of *Fronteras Desviadas/Deviant Borders* was supported in part by a grant from Contacto Cultural (the U.S.-Mexico Foundation for Culture), awarded to Andrea Assaf for the purpose of being an artist-in-residence with Mujeres en Ritual Danza Teatro in Tijuana, Mexico, in 2004. The performance premiered at the Universidad Autónoma de Baja California (UABC) in 2005, and toured to four campus theatres in Tijuana, Tecate, Ensenada, and Mexicali; followed by U.S. performances at New WORLD Theater at the University of Massachusetts, and Alternate ROOTS in North Carolina. The production also toured internationally, to a symposium on Interdisciplinarity at Concordia University in Montreal, Canada, and an international theatre festival presented by Teatro Rufino Justo Garay in Managua, Nicaragua, in 2006.

11

Now Is Not the Time for Silence

Writing and Directing What the Heart Remembers

FANNI V. GREEN

I title this essay "Now Is Not the Time for Silence."[1] Rightly so; coming to voice as an adult who now teaches *voice* as a black woman who must speak, whether or not what I have to say is valued; as a black woman who will speak, whether or not what I have to say desires to be heard by anyone; as a creative artist whose charge is to speak *out*. In this essay, I say to you as its reader, "Now is not the time for silence." What truths are there that you must tell? What words of yours reconstruct worlds of liberatory possibility and create ones to behold a vision of alliance and solidarity across borders of difference? I write this essay to hold up to myself as a mirror of my journey toward writing and directing the production of *What the Heart Remembers: The Women and Children of Darfur*. Simply put, I write to own my voice in solidarity with the oppressed in and beyond the borders of this land we call the United States. I am a black woman committed to ending the silence of systemic and institutionalized oppression on a global scale. I am a womanist writing, directing, and speaking for the liberation of *all* people. I begin this essay with a poem that introduces my own voice, as it calls out the devastating, internalized trauma that comes with the voice that aims to silence:

"Musings on My Mouth"

"Close your mouth," is what was said to me.
"Don't let me catch you running your mouth"
"Children should be seen and not heard"
"Who told you you could talk?"

"Shut your mouth. Be quiet and listen. Did you hear what I said?"
Obedience became belief.

MOVEMENT I: VOICE-A-RECTOMY

SHHHH. NO talking.
NO yelling.
NO outside voices.
BE QUIET.

Girls should be quiet and demure
Ladies should be soft-spoken, in—deliberate.

SIT DOWN SHUT-UP
and LISTEN
Keep your mouth closed so you don't tell lies.
Keep your mouth closed and no one will find out what you don't know.
Keep your mouth closed and you'll learn something. Keep your mouth closed.

MOVEMENT II: THE BAPTISM OF THE TONGUE

Locked behind tears I blink back into my eyes
It wanders off my voice leaves me
It crawls to the place just below my belly
Sometimes is my voice.
What, my voice asks, is a tongue for?
The mouth is only a conduit

And there below my sex my voice dances
The need is there
It waits to come forth
Then flees
my voice.

Sometimes when it returns its raspy longing
tells me to open my mouth
Sometimes when it returns the heart speaks its notes in palpitations
The jaw bites lips tremor
The body fills with the need
AND TH EN
My voice

Wonder if I Loved My Voice the First Time I Heard It?

In writing this essay, I reconstruct my journey of coming to voice through the collaborative cocreation and conceptualization of the choreo-poem that became the production, *What the Heart Remembers.* The process of this work allowed me to explore private, public, and global acts of atrocity that emerged from the experiences of women, men, and children who survived the war in Darfur,[2] born from the human heart of hatred and greed. In writing *What the Heart Remembers*, I answered the heartfelt call of the women, men, and children. I heard them say to me: "Now is not the time for silence." These words provided me the healing solace I needed to write out my interpretive representation of the atrocities of war they experienced. The production speaks out against human domination, degradation, and the ultimate silencing of death. In coming to know the traumatic, wartime experiences of the women, men, and children of Darfur, I could not be silent. I would speak in solidarity with them against the ravages of war on their bodies, minds, and spirit. I would write and direct *What the Heart Remembers* as an artistic-activist response to the 20-plus years of war over land and resources in the former Darfur (now the Republic of South Sudan [RSS]).

A Choreo-poem for Voice and Dance: The Heart of the Matter

What the Heart Remembers premiered as a student theatre production in fall 2010 at the University of South Florida (Tampa), College of the Arts, School of Theatre and Dance. The production of the choreo-poem would stand as a call to the university and the Tampa Bay area communities to add their voices to the chorus of voices globally declaring the events of war in Darfur as crimes against humanity. Conceptually, the work was staged as a collaborative effort on two levels. In transforming the choreo-poem into a script for actors, I would partner with my colleague Jeanne Travers, a professor in the USF dance department to choreograph the work. Together, she and I would cast student actors and dancers to perform it. *What the Heart Remembers* incorporates choreographed poems interwoven with live-video transitions and connected photographed reproductions of drawings by refugee Sudanese children. Collectively, the production represents a protest of voices declaring, "We too dare to call out these atrocities of war—the burnings of villages and people, the killings, rapes of women, the dismemberment and displacement of men, and children—genocide."[3]

Developed in a university context, *What the Heart Remembers* enabled me as its writer and director to join with Travers as a dance professor and choreographer to model for our students the power of artistic collaboration anchored in political commitment to human rights. Staging the choreo-poem represented not only our dedication to struggle against systemic oppression and domination, it also epitomized our allegiance to teaching our students artistic freedom for the good of all people—across differences of gender, race, class, sexuality, and nation-state affiliation. As a black female actor, writer, director, and professor, I self-identify as a "womanist"; Travers identifies herself as a "feminist." According to Alice Walker, "womanist is to feminist as purple is to lavender."[4] Across our differences, Travers and I joined forces in solidarity to stage this choreo-poem, bridging our collective passion for human rights. We would bring together our expertise in the arts of theatre and dance even in the light of our own initial, personal trepidation regarding our social, political, and artistic privileges as women from the United States. Each of us would bring her own artistic expertise and disciplinary training to create this work.

In the evolution of staging *What the Heart Remembers*, we would bring to the process our individual body of creative research exploring representations of social injustice, cultural history, and popular culture—in and outside the United States In the preliminary stage of our work together, we found each other to be unflinchingly tenacious and dedicated to the vision of a work that would ultimately invoke receptive responses to the finished product we never imagined. In the process of our work together, Travers and I initialized a partnership that parallels the components of a sustained marriage of political commitment, friendship, respect, love, anticipation, and trust, as well as friction (sometimes). In the moments of frustration or disagreement or derailment that arose along the way, we discovered our differences: simple, small things like how we handled student chatter in rehearsal differently, how we each addressed what I called the judgmental "prima donna" attitudes of the dancers and actors who live lives of privilege in the States. How to not sacrifice the beauty of dance in light of our aim to stage the traumatic depth related to the atrocity related to our subject matter. How to challenge the dancers to speak with volume and command, while challenging the actors to move with grace and precision. Or why the costumes could not be "pretty." Or facing the challenge of students struggling to manage a head-covering while dancing. Or teaching an accent and cultural mannerisms—while insisting that the actors and the dancers learn and embrace and slip into the skin and experience of "another" with respect and humbleness.

A Journey of Labor and Insistence

As the writer and director of *What the Heart Remembers*, it was a labor of discovery, doubt, and hope for me —a journey of coming to voice. The process felt much like being pregnant with desire and trepidation. In my work with Travers, I learned about the bridgework necessary to establish a foundation of collaboration between theatre and dance. As the writer, I believe my mission in writing this choreo-poem is bound to my belief in speaking "truth to power"—unflinchingly. Cocreating the work when it first was staged, we viewed our task as providing and facilitating an understanding of the political scope and shape of its liberatory vision. Dare I say reflecting on my role as the writer and director, I believe it was my responsibility to give human experience its *voice*? Dare I say my labor as the work's director was to be driven by an insatiable zeal to *re*-create human experience for an audience to take a stand for the oppressed? Dare I admit that for me, the journey of being both writer and director made me have to wrestle internally with a childhood cultural mandate that said, "Children should be seen and not heard."

To write and direct *What the Heart Remembers* invoked in me a life-transforming process that demanded I give birth to my own voice of experience. More so, in my process of coming to voice in the collaborative production of the acting and dancing that the choreo-poem embodied, I was called to own myself and my voice. The expectancy of co-staging the production with Travers as choreographer and labor with the design team, technical crew, and the cast of dancers, actors, children, and musicians demanded engagement with my voice. Admittedly, it was an engagement in a process insisting on a confidence that I often did not possess during the rehearsal phase. However, it made me examine and focus on the eyes of the women, men, and children in ways that I had not originally discovered in my preliminary research of photographs I had collected. Their eyes spoke words of healing into my spirit. They challenged me to give voice to what I saw in the many eyes that looked deep into my soul, enabling me to see with heartfelt depth the pain of their loss, their memory of it, and their resilient survival related to it. Their eyes empowered me to find the words I needed to write to imagine the words the women, men, and children needed to speak through me about the trauma of their experience of war.

In truth, it would be my looking at a selection of profoundly deep, visionary drawings by children from Darfur that inspired the conceptual foundation for *What the Heart Remembers*. The drawings came from Sudanese children whose mothers were being interviewed in refugee camps by Rebecca Tinsley (a founding partner of the international organization, Waging Peace[5]) and fellow journalists in the effort to bring forth the stories of survival these women had to tell. While the mothers were being interviewed, the children were given pencils, crayons, and paper to occupy and quiet them. The children drew fire-lit villages, bombs, and hooded men on horseback with torches and some with guns. The surprisingly well-drawn depictions showed crayon-colored blood, trees, amber-hued earth, and smoky skies. Some of the children drew people fleeing or with arms outstretched in frozen poses of assault or surrender. Travers and I were taken by the drawings. We felt they spoke into us a charge to create an experiential work on the children's behalf. What would that work be? A single choreographed dance with text projected on a screen? A single choreographed dance of one of the drawings with spoken word? A compilation of choreographed dances with a chorus of actors speaking poetry, in one single work? What did we want that work to say? The children's drawings became our reason to collaborate—to transform the children's drawings into a piece of artistic representation of the horrific effects of war on human beings. For me, the drawings were and remain the place from which the voice for the production came.

Personally, the drawings made me remember being a child with something to say but being sent to another room, just within view and earshot of the adults, while they spoke. As a child, I was not to listen to their conversation nor look into their mouths. I was sent outside to read, color, and be quiet; to be invisible. As the drawings by the children from Darfur became their voice, for me these drawings would become the catalyst for me to regain my voice—to become visible as a black woman, writer, director, actor, and teacher committed to a politics of liberation for all people in and beyond the territorial boundaries of the United States. Who would imagine that these children could create anything or say anything worthy of *drawing* world attention?

Voice: The Acoustic Correlate to Speech

As I stated in the opening, *What the Heart Remembers* is about coming to voice for the oppressed. Remembering the deeply moving impression the collection of Sudanese children's drawings had on me and Travers when we first viewed them would ultimately be about creating words and movement to articulate their life-transforming visual power. The politics of radical resistance embodied in these children's works of art would give voice to the power of the collaborative work Travers and I sought to illustrate artistically on stage. When I composed the poems that would compose *What the Heart Remembers*, I could see the piercing eyes of the children as they drew out their experiences of inner pain and outer material suffering. They provoked me to speak, to give voice to the drawings they had created. As I have shared, the power of their bold visual articulation would lay the groundwork for my journey toward voice reclamation. Through the children's drawings, I heard them telling me to speak in a voice that liberates—that frees the mind, body, and souls of those Travers and I would seek to reach through my words and her choreography.[6] Through the children's works, I had to thereby acknowledge the soul-searching impact they had on my creative voice. They called me to honor the fragility of young lives under the ravages of war, and at the same time to capture the self-empowering legacy of strength and survival their drawings depicted.

As I have stated, I am a black committed to womanist liberation. I teach acting; my secondary area of specialty is voice and speech for the actor. I tell my students that if one is physically and emotionally abled, then giving articulate shape to sound must be fueled by one's primal need to communicate. It is more than desire. The children's drawings and the resilient, querulous eyes I saw in the many photographs of women and men were compelling. Added to these were the documentaries I watched about the children of Darfur, which fueled my need to communicate what I saw *and* what I heard them speak through their artistic works. *What the Heart Remembers* became my poetic attempt to dissect and redirect my childhood training that taught me to "be seen and NOT heard."

In the next section, I use selected texts from the original production to demonstrate my attempt to write out what I was called to speak on behalf of the women and children of Darfur. Through their struggle to be heard, through the poems in *What the Heart Remembers*, I would cast them as *living testaments* to the power of struggle against systemic and institutionalized domination to silence the voices of the oppressed.

Text for the Voices, Action for the Dancers

The following poems are written as they were scripted (*Text* for the Voices, *Action* for the Dancers, and for overall direction of the staged performance)—"My Darfur" (sets the imagined landscape of Sudan), "Walking, Walking, Walking" (depicts the life of displacement in the refugee camps), "Road to Water" (juxtaposes the employment of rape as a tool of war alongside the need for water in the refugee camps), "Teresa" (imagines a fictionalized interview with a female refugee), and "Now Is Not the Time for Silence" (is an ode to resistance and hope).

"MY DARFUR"

FEMALE VOICE: Shall I tell you of my Darfur?
Gold diamonds uranium copper
Water underground

Let me tell you
I remember

The voice of my mother before me:
If you are facing a mountain
KNOW
you can move the mountain
The stories of my fathers before me:
The mountain is the pain of hunger
It is the grass that covers you
The longing that looks from your eyes
It is the fear they will plant in your heart

Let me tell you of my Darfur
Once the home I ran from
Where my black skin split and burnt
Shall I tell you?

I remember
My heart remembers

"WALKING, WALKING, WALKING"

ALL FEMALES: Last night I dreamed of feet
Many feet walking
Walking Walking Walking

ACTION: *a woman stands in the middle of the refugee camp crying softly.*
FEMALE CHORUS is divided in clumps around the camp doing daily chores; Children voices are heard wimpering.

FEMALE CHORUS A: Last night I dreamed
Of my village
Last night I dreamed
I saw the Janjaweed
Last night I dreamed
I saw the Janjaweed come riding to my village

FEMALE CHORUS B: The huts blazed blue
Yellow white and orange
The black smoke choked The
gray white smoke floated up to
I dreamed the children cried
We ran

TWO FEMALE VOICES: We ran
Fire chased our feet
I dreamed we ran
Men cried, I cried

ALL FEMALES: Fire chased our feet

TWO FEMALE VOICES: We fell We ran We fell We ran We fell We ran
Under the trees to the mountains we ran to

ALL FEMALES: Last night I dreamed of feet
Many feet walking
Walking Walking Walking

ACTION: Dancers enter down stage left, walking on second freeze.
Dance of the Women and Children making life in the village
The dance ends; the women and the children settle into poses that reflect this displaced life
Singer moves downstage, collapses; whimpers softly.

FEMALE CHORUS: Sometimes
The children play in the clearing
Sometimes
The children go under the tree to cry
There is no food no water
I am thirsty, I am hungry, frightened
Sometimes
I stand and cry
I am crying for everything
Nothing is left
But the empty

ACTION: *The children are heard crying softly.*

"ROAD TO WATER"

FEMALE CHORUS A: It is my turn to get the water
I will take the road to water
(giggles with girlish expectation as they speak)

FEMALE CHORUS B: It is my turn to get the water
I will take the road to water
Though I know when I return I will not be me
I will be used ruined gutted

ACTION: *VILLAGE WOMAN #1 steps out and travels a path that is the road, carrying a jug on her; The FEMALE DANCE CHORUS as the road, dance memories, warnings, protection, ghosts,—FEMALE VILLAGE WOMAN #1 does not see the FEMALE DANCE CHORUS; she is only aware of a haunting breath, a presence on the road. The MALE DANCE CHORUS, as the Janjaweed, dance taunts, threats, and danger as VILLAGE WOMAN #1 travels the road.*

VILLAGE WOMAN #1: It is my turn to get the water
I will take the road to water
It is my turn to get the water
I will take the road to water

FEMALE DANCE

CHORUS: Though I know when I return, I will not be me
VILLAGE WOMAN #1: It is my turn to get the water
I will take the road to water
I will take the road to water

ACTION: *VILLAGE WOMAN #1 kneels to dip water from an imaginary well.*

FEMALE CHORUS
A & B: Because I am female I must go
Because I am a girl I must go

Because I am a woman I must go
Because I am a mother I must go
Janjaweed will not kill me because
I am so lucky

ACTION: The MALE DANCE CHORUS as the Janjaweed attack and rape VILLAGE WOMAN #1.

FEMALE DANCER: I am not my father I am not my brother
I am not my husband I am not my son

ACTION: As VILLAGE WOMAN #1 heads back to camp with water bucket, VILLAGE WOMAN #2 steps onto the road.

FEMALE WALKER #2: But I must go I choose to go
We need the water

ACTION: The MALE DANCE CHORUS, as the Janjaweed, dance taunts, and danger as VILLAGE OWMAN #2 travels the road.

VILLAGE WOMAN #1: Because I am-was a wife
VILLAGE WOMAN #2: But I must go I choose to go

VILLAGE WOMAN #1: Because I am-was a daughter
VILLAGE WOMAN #2: Because I am-was a sister

VILLAGE WOMAN #1: I must go I choose to go
VILLAGE WOMAN #2 I will take the road

VILLAGE WOMEN: We need the water

ACTION: The FEMALE DANCE CHORUS as the road, the air and the dead bones of former female walkers, dance protection, anger, the heart beats, fear and shame.

ACTION: The MALE CHORUS as the Janjaweed attack and rape VILLAGE WOMAN #2.

FEMALE DANCER: When I return
My happy arms will carry the water

But
My hands will be limp
Crazy
From s-c-r-e-a-m-I n g

ACTION: A FEMALE DANCER and a MALE DANCER dance the struggle and violence of the encounter.

VILLAGE WOMAN #2: PLEASE PLEASE NO PLEASE

ACTION: The rape is done; the MALE DANCE CHORUS as the Janjaweed, discard the VILLAGE WOMAN the FEMALE DANCE caresses then aids her return to the village.

The FEMALE CHORUS A & B echo the individual voices of the FEMALE DANCE CHORUS.

FEMALE DANCER: When I return, my cracked feet will run no more
FEMALE CHORUS A: Run no more

FEMALE DANCER: Swollen blows will throb no more
FEMALE CHORUS B: Throb no more

FEMALE DANCER: The blood . . .
FEMALE CHORUS A: The blood

FEMALE DANCER: on my legs from my private place
FEMALE CHORUS B: The blood

FEMALE DANCER: That runs then drips upon the sand
Will be my tears
FEMALE CHORUS A: Will be tears
FEMALE DANCER: I will be no more

ACTION: VILLAGE WOMAN #2 collapses on the road.

FEMALE CHORUS A & B: Still female girl woman wife mother daughter sister

BUT
My ravaged body will bring the water
My eyes will never tell
I will not speak
BUT
my silence

FEMALE DANCER: My silence will shelter me

ACTION: The MALE DANCE CHORUS lingers as the unseen, haunting presence on the road; The FEMALE DANCE CHORUS settle into fixed poses with their faces turned away from the audience, save one lone dancer, whose dance wafts on the road as memory.

FEMALE CHORUS *(in a round)*

A & B: I will take the road to water
I will take the road to water
I must go
We need the water
I will take the road to water
I will take the road to water
I choose to go
We need the water
I will take the road to water
I will take the road to water
I must go
We need the water

ACTION: *There is stillness in the village; THE FEMALE CHORUS looks toward the road. There is stillness on the road, except for the one lone dancer upstage center. Then, in the stillness, the FEMALE CHORUSES & THE FEMALE DANCE CHORUS turn their faces to audience;*
The MALE DANCE CHORUS breathes a hollow exhale. THE MEN Exit.

"TERESA"

Four women are seen in different areas on stage poised in stillness.
THE DANCER *reaches up, arms in a frozen spiral*

THE SINGER *stands looking out as if watching something*
THE REPORTER *holds a pad and pencil*
Opposite her, TERESA *sits in her tent-hut*

REPORTER: Imagine you see her Teresa is her name
She squats to prepare her teas
She laughs

ACTION: Teresa laughs.

REPORTER: Imagine you can see her
You say, "Where did your mother die, Teresa?"
She looks out
ACTION: Teresa laughs again
She laughs again
Then

TERESA: She died out in the wilderness and
I never saw her

REPORTER: Imagine you say, "And your father?
Who shot them, Teresa?"
She speaks

TERESA: Only the tea I make here is real
My eyes see nothing My head is empty

REPORTER: She looks out

TERESA: But my heart remembers

REPORTER: You say, "Teresa, your story is very important
You must tell it"
She looks to her tea Then

TERESA: Will you believe me if I tell you it is true?

REPORTER: You say nothing

ACTION: THE SINGER sings an a cappella vocal line to which THE DANCER dances then holds as Teresa continues.

TERESA: We were children
The Janjaweed came to look for people to kill and to occupy their villages
We heard the Janjaweed and we fled to the forest
The men did not find us but took our village
Then
Whenever the Janjaweed did find people it killed them

What I tell you is true will you believe me?
My father was fishing
When returning to our village Shots.
No fatherNo foodNo water
We were children We were afraid

ACTION: THE SINGER sings an a cappella vocal line to which THE DANCER dances then holds as Teresa continues.

One night
My mother left the forest with the others to get water
Before they reached the river Shots.
No motherNo fatherNo foodNo water
We were children We were afraid

Three days passed
The old men went out
Found my father on the way
Before they got to the river
Found dead women on the way

At the river they saw
Cloth dancing on the water Bodies floating beneath

The old men brought the water
We were afraid
After many many days I came here
My heart remembers
I grew up here

REPORTER: She is silent.

ACTION: THE DANCER dances Teresa's pain and memory. THE SINGER accompanies her. THE DANCER stops and is seen pulsing her breath. THE SINGER's vocal becomes a hum as Teresa continues.

REPORTER: You call to her,
"Teresa? I have heard your story
What would you . . ."

TERESA: I will tell you this because it's true
I have known hunger
Eaten fleas and carcass skins
I have known thirst quenched by dirt and sweat
I saw the bones the bodies of children like me
Dead in the desert
This is not my home I have no home
You see me laughing here?
What do you make of it?
No motherNo fatherNo brotherNo sister
No husband
No children
I have tasted bitterness Now I make my teas

REPORTER: Teresa?
Teresa?

ACTION: THE SINGER's vocalizing trails off and ends; she exits.
THE REPORTER checks her pad, looks out then exits.
THE DANCER finishes her movement, she exits.
TERESA drinks her tea and looks out at nothing.

"NOW IS NOT THE TIME FOR SILENCE"

FEMALE VOICES: Shall I tell you of my Darfur?
Beige-brown sand grains in my skin
'tween my toes 'n fingers
millions of thousands of hundreds of grains
embedded into the floor that is my desert
My feet remember

ALL VOICES: Now is not the time for silence

MALE VOICES: We must move this mountain

FEMALE VOICES: Your eyes see your ears hear
Carry my heart with you

ALL VOICES: Now is not the time for
MALE VOICES: polarizing ethnic difference
to substantiate hatred, inhumanity and genocide

ALL VOICES: Now is not the time for
FEMALE VOICES: fragile calm, frozen anger and
great global neglect

ALLVOICES: You have eyes, you have voices
MALE VOICES: Shall I tell you of my Darfur?
My home, my blood, my family
My fear, my love, my longing
My heart remembers. My hope remains.

ALL VOICES: When you are facing a mountain
KNOW You can move the mountain
Now is not the time for silence
CARRY My heart with you
Remember me
Remember
Me

VOICES exhale.

From the Local to the Global: The World as Our Stage

In 2010, from November 14–21, as an 85-minute production, *What the Heart Remembers* would run for eight performances on stage in the USF School of Theatre and Dance. Each performance would be followed by a post-show discussion with featured scholars, audience, and cast members. *What the Heart Remembers* received the 2010 Tampa Bay Area critics' award for "Best of the Bay" for theatre/dance performance. Travers received the same award for her choreography. Additionally, I received a commendation from the Kennedy Center Associate Theatre Festival for directing. In the summer of 2012, Travers and I adapted *What the Heart Remembers* for its premiere at the prestigious Edinburgh Festival Fringe in Scotland. The production was nominated for the Festival's Amnesty Freedom of Expression Award. The collection of the children's drawings is now housed in the Holocaust and Genocide Studies Center at the University of South Florida Library (Tampa), under the directorship of Mark Greenberg. A digital video disc of the production of *What the Heart Remembers* is archived in the media resource collection of the USF Library.

Notes

1. "Combining poetry, prose, narrative, song, dance and music, the *choreopoem* represents less a simple synthesis of these arts than an attempt to use them to energize and transform the human subject . . . the form demands that the performer have an organic, physical relationship to the text. For the choreopoem is less an object than an act and its performance is by definition a transformative experience for both performer and spectator." David Savran, *The Playwright's Voice: American Dramatists on Memory, Writing, and the Politics of Culture* (TCG Books, May 1999).

2. Following independence from Britain in 1956, Sudan became embroiled in two prolonged civil wars for most of the remainder of the 20th century. These conflicts were rooted in Northern economic, political, and social domination of largely non-Muslim, non-Arab Southern Sudanese. Competition for scarce resources played a large role. As nomads began to compete for grazing land, traditional reconciliation measures were no longer able to settle disputes, causing the region to become increasingly militarized. The complexities of desertification, famines, and the civil war raging between North and South Sudan contributed to a rise in regional tensions during the 1980s. Similarly, as oil was discovered in Western Sudan, the Sudanese government and international contributors became increasingly interested in the land in Darfur. http://www.operationbrokensilence.org/; http://www.ushmm.org/confront-genocide (accessed July 2009).

3. In 1948, the United Nations General Assembly voted unanimously to create the UN Convention on the Prevention and Punishment of the Crime of Genocide.

This recognized that "at all periods of history genocide has inflicted great losses on humanity" and that international cooperation was needed "to liberate mankind from this odious scourge." The international legal definition of the crime of *pre-genocide* is found in Articles II and III. In the present Convention, genocide means any of the following acts committed with intent to destroy, in whole or in part, a national, ethnical, racial, or religious group, as such: (a) Killing members of the group; (b) Causing serious bodily or mental harm to members of the group; (c) Deliberately inflicting on the group conditions of life calculated to bring about its physical destruction in whole or in part; (d) Imposing measures intended to prevent births within the group; (e) Forcibly transferring children of the group to another group. Article II describes two elements of the crime of genocide: 1) the *mental element*, meaning the "intent to destroy, in whole or in part, a national, ethnical, racial or religious group, as such," and 2) the *physical element* which includes five acts described in sections a, b, c, d, and e. A crime must include *both elements* to be called "genocide." www.preventdenocide.org (accessed July 2009).

4. Alice Walker, a poet and activist, who is mostly known for her award-winning book, *The Color Purple*, employed the term *womanist* in *In Search of Our Mothers' Gardens: Womanist Prose* (1983). Walker defined a womanist as "Womanish, the opposite of girlish . . . Being grown up . . . A Black Feminist or Feminist of Color . . . A woman who loves other women, sexually and/or non-sexually. Appreciates and prefers women's culture, women's emotional flexibility (values tears as natural counterbalance of laughter), and women's strength. Sometimes loves individual men, sexually and/or non-sexually" (xi–xii).

5. Founded by journalist and human rights activist Rebecca Tinsley, Waging Peace is a nongovernmental organization in the U.K. that campaigns against genocide and systematic human rights abuses and seeks the full implementation of international human rights treaties. Our current priority is Sudan. www.wagingpeace.info (accessed July 2009)..

6. This is the definition for "Voice" that I give student actors in my "Voice for Actors" course. I teach that voice is an acoustic activity, wherein speech is a motor activity.

This is the full choreo-poem as it appeared in the program for the USF premiere performance:

WHAT THE HEART REMEMBERS: THE WOMEN AND CHILDREN OF DARFUR

WRITTEN AND DIRECTED BY FANNI V. GREEN, CHOREOGRAPHED BY JEANNE TRAVERS

PROLOGUE:

"Village Portraits: Shall I Tell You of My Darfur"

Movement I

"Faces of a Man"

"Women and Children: Walking . . . Walking . . . Walking"

"Adam's Song"
"Children at Play"
"Road to Water"
Intermission
Movement II
"Adam"
"Teresa"
"Farchana"
"Lovers"
"Death, Burial and Sorrow"
"Hope and Resilience"
EPILOGUE:
"My Beautiful Sudan"

12

"I Come from a Dream Deferred"

ERICA C. SUTHERLIN

i come from a dream deferred
her last chance at love
with a lover who knew
there was no possibility of monogamy
i come from calloused hands
curler burns, coffee stains and frustration
i come from the center of the earth
my umbilical cord returns to the mother
i come from the dark, dank womb
of guilt regret aftermath and cycles
i come. i came. i am.
back alley abortions gone bad
postpartum depressed mothers crying
i come from the african slaves servants maids boy girl niggers coloreds
negroes blacks afro-americans
i come from the mutilated clitoris of keyan new guinea african middle
    eastern women
the bound feet and broken smiles of my asian descent
i come from the uzi toting bomb strapped spear throwing goddess
masked by warrior markings and fatigues
i come from the broken jaw bruised feminine spirit
who knew soon would be her last
i come from the voiceless women whose beauty cannot be revealed
branded cattle and land

for plowing and plundering of her natural resources
i come from the universal laws
the law of the land
jezebels and whores
temple prostitutes and queendoms
i come from the dirt on the bottom of your shoe
the victim of rape who never told
the molested female with trust issues
i hail from the spit and fire of racism
the shards of the glass ceiling
i come from that woman, those women
the classy well dressed put together hot stepping double look causing queen
i come from the big boned fat jokes big ass behind thick lips swollen legs
flat feet flabby arms small and wide waistline
i come from the soul the source the spirit the one the god that is and gave birth to the feminine.

13

On Becoming a Feminist

RUDOLPH P. BYRD

When I was eleven I ordered my father, at knifepoint, to leave our home.

The context for this pivotal event was a particularly violent argument between my parents—erupting, it seems, out of the languor of a summer afternoon in Denver. Filled with concern for my mother's well-being, I left my bedroom and assumed the position of witness at the threshold of my parent's bedroom, which, on that afternoon, was in chaos. When my father raised his hand and struck my mother's face, the world as I knew it changed completely. I did not hesitate to protect her. I went to the kitchen and returned with the largest knife I could find and ordered my father to leave our home. To my astonishment and relief, my father stepped around the knife I pointed at his chest and departed in silence. He returned sometime later, wary, somewhat contrite, and conscious—perhaps for the first time—of the necessity to contend with his firstborn and namesake. From that day to the last day of his life, I knew that I, in one sense, was at war with my father. I knew and he knew that his abuse of my mother would not go unchallenged. Needless to say, this tacit understanding brought us to an unexpected depth, one that continues to possess, even after his death, tremendous power and meaning.

My commitment to feminism thus began with resistance to the abuse of women. When I ordered my father at knifepoint to leave our home, asserting, "Get out and leave my mother alone," I was uttering one of the oldest sentences in the world. Other boys had said such things to their fathers. I did not want my father out of our lives because I loved him and needed his protection and guidance; what I wanted out of our lives was the violence.

As I would come to realize, it was in that moment that my commitment to gender equality crystallized. Such a commitment placed me, inevitably, in opposition to my father, who held—like many men of his class and generation—deeply flawed, patriarchal views of family and society. Views that he wrongly thought entitled him to abuse, physically and psychologically, my mother and doubtless other women.

My mother, Meardis Cannon, was the first feminist I had the privilege to meet. My mother's feminist consciousness registered in family life in a variety of ways: in her authoritative use of language, in the dignity of her own person, and most especially in the management of our household.

As the firstborn of five children, I quickly learned that my mother did not take gender into account in the division of labor. In the management of a household where my father was present but selectively involved, she routinely placed us where we needed to be, not where we wished to be or, heaven help us, where we thought we should be. As a male child, I cooked and cleaned as well as mowed the lawn, shoveled and salted the steps in winter, and, when I acquired my driver's license, did much of the shopping. In other words, there was nothing I did not do and there was nothing she believed I should not do by virtue of my gender. The result is that I grew up able to do many things well. I also did not regard the home as the domestic sphere of women but as a shared space in which I had, along with my siblings, many responsibilities and a particular investment.

My mother also reared me with a deep sense of egalitarianism. I regarded my siblings as equals in all things while I also fully acknowledged their complexity as individuals. Moving from boyhood to manhood, I valued the insight this rearing produced, especially in relationship to my two sisters who were, like my mother, all women to me. Reconstructing this early period in my life, I understand that my respect for women began with my respect for my mother—an abiding respect born of her feminist consciousness.

I believe that I would have resisted this vital principle, like other men, had it not been for my mother's instructive, inspiring example and also for my ability to transfer and apply knowledge from the domestic sphere to the public sphere. Always the questions were these: Even though they are strangers, why would you treat women beyond your kinship group any differently from your mother and sisters? Even though they are strangers, why would you not wish these women to have what you wish for your mother and sisters: a life free of male domination and violence? Then and now, I understood that these questions bore the imprint of my mother's hand, that is, the imprint of her feminist consciousness. And while she did not call herself a feminist, she understood, like all feminists, that the personal is political. For me, this is an insight, born, in part, of family life.

My development as a feminist was shaped not only by my education at home but also by my education beyond the home. In my college and university training during the 1970s, I was introduced to the work of Virginia Woolf, Toni Morrison, Jean Toomer, and Alice Walker, all of whom—most especially Walker—had a profound impact upon my development as a feminist. In their work, I discovered theories of resistance and oppression that expanded my developing understanding of gender and the dynamics of male domination and male privilege. A vital work from this period is Walker's *The Third Life of Grange Copeland*, her first novel, one that I read soon after its publication. The reading of this novel was a moment of self-recognition for myself and all the women in my family. The tragedy of Meme and Brownfield Copeland captured what the poet Robert Hayden called in "Those Winter Sundays" the "chronic angers" of our home. Walker's novel provided a fictional framework for the pivotal event that constituted my initiation into feminism. Above all, it provided a name for the problem that, as Betty Friedan writes in *The Feminist Mystique*, "has no name."

In my education beyond the home, I learned of the existence of an intellectual tradition to which I could declare allegiance and one that nourished my development as a feminist. I learned, in fine, that feminists are made, not born. The knowledge of the existence of such a tradition, and the knowledge that I could choose, through my work, to extend its power and reach had a lasting impact upon my choices and actions.

Of the men in history who have had a marked influence upon my development as a feminist, Frederick Douglass is perhaps the most important. I think of Douglass's pioneering support of women's rights at the Seneca Falls Convention of 1848, the lone black male in attendance and the only male to assume a leadership role at this historic convention. I also think of his complex alliance with Elizabeth Cady Stanton over the elective franchise for women, which led to the adoption of the Nineteenth Amendment to the Constitution in 1920. As the founding editor of *The North Star*, whose epigraph was "Right Is of No Sex," Douglass was keenly aware of the necessity of complementary social movements. "All good causes are mutually helpful," asserted Douglass in a speech delivered on March 31, 1888, at the International Council of Women in Washington, D.C.: "The benefits accruing from this movement for the equal rights of woman are not confined or limited to woman only. They will be shared by every effort to promote the progress and welfare of mankind everywhere and in all ages."

As I began my career in the academy, I continued to search for ways to develop as a feminist, a process that continued to take place mainly within the meaningful discipline of teaching and scholarship. And this process was enriched by the development of friendships with feminists. Of these friends and colleagues, Beverly Guy-Sheftall of Spelman College has had the greatest impact upon my development as a feminist. Our friendship has deepened through the coediting of *Traps: African American Men on Gender and Sexuality*, an anthology that is a testimony to our shared commitment to antisexist and antihomophobic struggle. Soon after our meeting in the early 1990s, Beverly and I discussed a number of projects; and when I proposed to her that we edit an anthology of writings by African American men on gender and sexuality, she immediately consented. Through this collaboration with Beverly—who is one of the leading feminists of our generation—I felt welcomed as a male to the transformative and progressive work of feminism, and in the process understood what my place and my work as her comrade in feminist struggle should be as a scholar and activist.

And what, precisely, is a feminist? A feminist is an individual committed to the goals of feminism which, as defined by bell hooks in *Feminism Is for Everybody*, is "a movement to end sexism, sexist exploitation and oppression." Significantly, hooks's definition of feminism underscores the important fact that the goal of feminism is the abolition of all forms of male domination, not the hatred of men.

Of the many things I feel called to do as a feminist, chief among them is the creation of a corpus that inspires knowledge of and disloyalty to patriarchy. *Traps* and, more recently, *I Am Your Sister: Collected and Unpublished Writings of Audre Lorde* (written with Beverly Guy-Sheftall and Johnnetta B. Cole) perform this strong function. Moreover, I understand that this fulfilling and subversive work must be done with and apart from women who are committed to the goals of feminism. In this regard, the example of Douglass within the context of the first wave of American feminism is most instructive.

As a feminist, I urge all men to embrace this progressive tradition that was advanced by Douglass. Why? Because we cannot, to paraphrase the black lesbian feminist Audre Lorde, dismantle the master's house with the master's tools. Notwithstanding its appeal of privilege and power, patriarchy is a bankrupt ideology. Based upon the ideology of male superiority and domination, it is antithetical to the historic goals of the black freedom struggle and the story of freedom told in all periods of African American history and literature, most powerfully in the slave narratives. Further, patriarchy blocks the process of self-actualization in men as well as women. It imposes upon men an identity based upon male domination. As an ideology based in privilege and violence, it is corrosive of relationships between men and women and also those between men. Finally, because of its intolerance of difference, patriarchy is one of the greatest threats to the creation and development of communities, as Toni Morrison has warned us, with her customary acumen and eloquence, in her novel *Paradise*. The sobering truth at the novel's center is that if women do not conform to the expectations of men, if they do not submit to the rule of men, the men will kill them. By contrast, feminism is a means of liberating women and men from the ideological trap of patriarchy through the choice of a politics that nurtures a vision of mutuality, equality, democracy, and nonviolence.

As a feminist, I stand on the watchtower of freedom with Douglass and his spiritual descendants. I am positioned here not only because I regard myself as a spiritual descendant of Douglass but, more important, because I am a direct descendant of Meardis Cannon whose feminist consciousness, even in death, continues to influence, to summon the language of James Weldon Johnson, "my forms of habit, behavior, and conduct as a man." I urge all men and women to join us here and live fully, mindfully, in the present as we prepare for a livable future. As Lorde reminds us, there is no separate survival.

Acknowledgment: I take this opportunity to honor the memory of the brotherhood that Rudolph P. Byrd and I shared in our scholarly labor together. As two black men telling the stories of our journey toward "becoming feminist[s]," we made it possible for other males—across borders of gender, class, and sexuality—to comprehend the life-saving, transformative power of Alice Walker's vision of womanism. I will always remember Rudolph's initial invitation to me to join in solidarity with the other black men who contributed to the publication of *Traps: African American Men on Gender and Sexuality* (2001). My dear brother, your Spirit of love lives on in the words you and your coeditor Beverly Guy-Sheftall—my sister in the struggle—spoke in the conclusion of the book's Preface: "*Traps* emerges out of our unwavering opposition to the most blatant forms of sexism: violence against women and misogyny." As Audre Lorde boldly declares in "A Litany for Survival"—"we [you and I] were never meant to survive." Yet, as pro–feminist-womanist black men, we made it over through the loving Spirit of womanism.

Permission to reprint: granted by Henry Leonard. This essay originally appeared in the journal: *Women's News and Narratives*, fall 2009, Director Dona Yarbrough, Emory University.

* * *

Acknowledgment: As the editor of this book project, I would personally like to thank Henry Leonard for his commitment to furthering the womanist legacy that Rudolph passed on not only to men of African descent, but to all males devoted to the struggle for human rights across differences of race, gender, sexuality, class, and nation-state affiliation(s)—*Gary L. Lemons*

14

Compelled by the Spirit

My Journey to Become a Womanist Man

M. THANDABANTU IVERSON

. . . I am sick
Of having to remind you
To breathe
Before you suffocate
—Donna Kate Rushin, "The Bridge Poem"
from *This Bridge Called My Back*

When We Are Called, We Must Answer

The epigraph for this chapter is an excerpt from "The Bridge Poem," by Donna Kate Rushin. It appears in the opening pages of *This Bridge Called My Back* (edited by Cherríe Moraga and Gloria Anzaldúa, 1981). The poem reminds all who read it of a recurring call to humanness uttered by generations of African American women, and echoed by millions of other women of color, throughout the torturous sojourns of our peoples in this "land of the free, and home of the slave." A marvelous Black woman who offered friendship and healing to all she encountered in our times at Oberlin College in the 1970s, Donna Kate Rushin spoke a healing word from her heart to Black males so that we might become more than our slave masters intended. We are still answering that call.

In this chapter, dedicated to Aaronette White[1] and Fay Bellamy (Powell),[2] I use the biblical injunctions of "doing one's first works over" and "counting up the costs," to examine the relationships and factors shaping my journey as an Afrodescendant male. Beginning with my relationships with my mother, father, and sister in Columbus, Ohio, during the two decades from 1947–1967, I question the ways in which an African American working-class family known for its exemplary role in racial uplift also became an oppressive site for the production of patriarchal masculinity and heterosexist battering and abuse. Illuminating what I have come to highly regard as the feminist impulses of my mother, I focus attention on how one Black woman's resistance was expressed in her education of her son.

My narrative then shifts from the pro-feminist foundation laid by my mother to my turbulent transition to early "Black" (male) consciousness. My four years at Hiram College (Hiram, Ohio) shaped me in ways that I am still unraveling, and my times in Cleveland and Oberlin, Ohio, set me firmly upon Pan African pathways. My times in Atlanta, Georgia, were momentous. Taken together, the rigors and revelations of graduate school years at Atlanta (now Clark Atlanta) University; the challenges of my first marriage (which ended in divorce); my introduction to Men Stopping Violence, Inc.; my close association with Black feminist women; and my work with pro-feminist men like Sulaiman Nuriddin, Paul McLennan, Omar Freilla, and Askia Muhammad Toure contributed to changes that I am still sorting out, and for which I feel deep gratitude. My reflections turn finally to ways in which my journey to feminist *and* womanist praxis continues to impact my teaching of Labor Studies and my human rights activism. In all that I do, I am still striving to yield to the Spirit, as the old Spiritual enjoined us, and to "change my name."[3]

Early Lessons on How and What to Represent

My most vivid memories of connections between social movement activity and my early daily life are images and sounds of my household and church communities in Columbus, Ohio. My immediate family—my father, mother, and my sister, Jeanie—seemed to always be associated with a palpable-though-somewhat-ill-defined notion of "Movement," as my father had sought a job as "the first Negro bus driver" in the city. In 1953, this simple act of trying to secure gainful employment had unsettled quite a few White folks, and enlivened a good many people throughout the Negro community; meaning that almost everybody seemed to know who my dad was. In those days, such widespread recognition also meant that almost everything I said and did became instant objects of scrutiny.

Folks seemed to always be measuring and assessing me; encouragement and criticism were ever-present rites to my passage. Either I was expected to be some sort of standard-bearer for others, or I seemed to be falling short of expectations. I felt a lot less pressure and much more pride when I looked at the *Call and Post* newspaper clippings my mom kept of my dad standing next to a huge bus that he appeared to be boarding. No matter where we went in the city, Negroes seemed to know my dad and my mom's husband. Oddly, I don't remember much talk at home about the struggles that I later learned were associated with my dad's new job. He seldom spoke about his job when he would finally arrive at home with that tired bend to his body and that furrow in his brow.

Beyond the mixed blessings of being part of a "Negro first family," one of the most riveting memories of my childhood is a sunny summer afternoon in 1957, when my mother had gone to the corner mailbox across the street from our house at 855 Lyman Avenue, in the newly developed section of what folks used to call "Hanford Village." I was busily doing something in my room, when my mom, who was quite pregnant with my new sister, called me to her side in the living room. As I entered the room, she was slowly paging through a small and familiar-looking *Jet Magazine*. Mom spoke to me in a warm-yet-authoritative tone. She was not angry, though I remember her as very grave. It was clear to me, even at ten years of age, that she was communicating to me something that she wanted me to remember for the rest of my days. Handing me the *Jet*, she told me to sit down and look at each of the photographs of the story unfolded on those pages. The story told of the brutal torture and killing of Emmett Till, a young Negro boy of thirteen or fourteen, who had gone "Down South" from Chicago for the summer.

Tragically, it turned out that while visiting relatives in Mississippi, he had made a dangerous mistake of whistling at a woman who was White. As my mom pointed toward me with an advising gaze—she knew better than I that I was already starting to gawk and wink at members of "the opposite sex"—she told me, "I want you to see what can happen to little black boys who mess with white girls." Together with her solemn counsel, the pictures seared into my boyish consciousness the terrible lesson Momma wanted me to learn. I can still see the images of the lifeless, bludgeoned, and bloated body of that young boy who had been so much like me.

My mother's lesson was not wasted. Though I do not remember ever telling her or my dad of my ways of applying that lesson, shortly after learning the story of Emmett Till's death, I had decided that at any time in the future, whenever I might see a White girl or woman, I would make sure to see everything about her in one swift, furtive glance—silently, and without any demonstrable intent of gazing as others could without fear of trouble. This decision stayed within my consciousness for some considerable time, at least until my senior year at South High School and my freshman year at

Hiram College, when I figured out that in some situations, I might actually be able to look at, and date, a White female and live to tell about it. Still, the lesson I had been taught at my mother's side had provided me with stern truths about how to behave properly—that is, how to represent myself, my family, and other Negro people.

What strikes me now, as I reflect upon that early counsel so gravely communicated to me by the person who had almost died birthing me into the world from which Emmett Till had been summarily and savagely expelled, is that mom had actually shared with me several lessons at the same time. As a Negro woman, worker, wife, and mother, she wanted me to survive in my future encounters with White people. And if I were to survive, she had prayed that I would become "a credit to my race," meaning that I would need to learn how to conduct myself so that others would be inclined to respect me—or at least, not view me as a flirtatious, mouthy, devilish, dandy of a person. She didn't spell everything out for me; she only pointed to the terrible price I might have to pay if I messed around with White girls. Her solemn instruction was meant to serve me as a guide for how to be *a person of color* in an unsafe White world and how to become *a person of color who would be a young man*. I could not then discern the distinction between these two messages bound together as tightly as the barbed wire that had been wrapped around young Emmett Till's body. Yet the searching gaze of my mother's eyes into mine made me feel the meanings of her words just as surely as if she had firmly placed her two hands on each of my shoulders.

Admonishing me in what she undoubtedly believed to be the appropriate race *and* sex etiquette for the times, Mom had been careful not to say any more than she had believed I could understand. Nothing had been explicitly stated about sexual relations or "carnal knowledge." My mom undoubtedly had considered such explicitness a lesson for another day, and her stern-yet-loving demeanor got my full attention. No less powerful had been the third, more muted, lesson: that if one didn't have the money and connections to get out of a dangerous racial (and sexually charged) situation, one had better wise up and "walk a chalk line." This was undoubtedly a valuable lesson about *class*, though again I say that I am confident that Mom was much more worldly wise than she felt inclined to spell out for me at that time.

The simplicity and power of those multiple and connected messages now cause me to marvel at the wisdom of this working-class Black woman from Zanesville, Ohio, who so carefully ordered my youthful steps without a high school diploma or advanced degrees and without being widely and well-traveled. Her "mother-wit" had been powerfully presented to me, and it was also she (among other wise guides in my youth) who shared with me most a sense of justice that was possible only by reaching, by one's humble actions, for a rectitude beyond the customary deeds of human beings. My mother taught me to "treat everybody right," and only then could I be confident in finding such justice. I have lived long enough to be immensely grateful to her for helping me to begin my life in ways that would enable me to have a chance to survive in an unjust social order without becoming cynical.

The Things You Remember Can Make You Want to Forget

Today I am still learning that, sometimes in life, what you remember is what you wish you could forget. I recall that it was a Sunday in June of 1959. I had just turned twelve. My mom, my dad, my baby sister, and I had returned to our house together from Mt. Vernon A.M.E. Church. I say "together" simply because Mom, Jeanie, and I sometimes attended Gospel Tabernacle, a Pentecostal church about a city block away. "GT" stood on the right, or eastward, corner at Ellison and Hildreth streets. The walk was short, but if you thought about the services and the feeling you got in the pews of each of the churches, the congregations often seemed rather far apart in those days. I think my mom liked to attend "GT" because there she felt less troubled by "mess." I remember that my dad's church seemed to have a number of Negroes who acted like (what Mom used to refer to as) "educated fools." Those folks would look at you sideways and talk to you like they knew lots of stuff that you didn't know. At Gospel Tabernacle, though, I think she felt more at home—like being at her former church home, in Zanesville, where the folks just seemed more "down to earth."

Anyway, we had arrived at home on one of those special June days, like Father's Day or Men's Day. I remember that we had returned home earlier than usual for a Sunday, because my godfather, Rev. Richard Nathaniel Nelson had cut his sermon short. He would do that on some Sundays when his Spirit-filled message or the choir's singing would lift folks up so high that there was a feeling of fullness in the church, and it just seemed to make sense to let folks go home and spend the rest of the day in peace.

I also recall that Mom had on a pretty blue dress with white polka dots, and a white necklace that I imagined to be made of pearls. Her hair was really pretty that day, and I remember hearing her talking to Dad in the living room. Jeanie, I think, was asleep in her crib. Dad had been sitting (actually, he seemed more to be lying down) in his comfortable old grey lounge chair with his stocking feet resting on that matching grey hassock. I don't remember hearing him say much. The baseball game was being televised on the console located against the wall at an angle where Dad could watch both the game and hear Mom, too.

Suddenly, I remember feeling this dreadful tension in my body, like when you are walking home on a familiar dark street and hear the growl of dog that you can't see. Mom's voice had gotten louder, as she was now calling my father by his first name. The next thing I remember seeing, as I darted into the living room from our bedroom, was my dad leaping up out of his chair. As he put both of his feet on the floor, his hand (turned sideways) was slicing across Mom's neck in the larynx area. She grasped her throat as her pearls scattered and bounced all over the floor. Gasping for air and crying out desperately to me, she shouted: "Run! Go to Aunt Alice's and tell her to call the police!" I bolted between Mom and her attacker and was out the front screen door and off the cement porch in a flash. I kept sprinting up the street until I was inside Aunt Alice's front door. Shortly after she had called the police, I remember seeing the white police cruiser in front of our house, and two White men with guns walking up to our front door. I had remained outside . . . That's as much as I can remember about that sunny Sunday afternoon, some 53 years ago.

Today I understand that the preparations my mother had made for her survival had reflected her considerable courage and keen intelligence. She was not a weak woman. At five feet, eleven inches, she was tall, well-formed, and sturdily built. Yet she was not physically matched to fight my father. He was taller, quicker, and quite strong. He had been a welterweight boxer with amazing hand speed in the CCC Camp prior to enlisting in the U.S. Army. Momma had known that she would probably be obliged to one day speak her piece, again, and she had known that there would no doubt be a cost. She had also known that she refused to live in utter fear of reprisal for speaking truthfully. She had thus devised a strategy that she hoped would temper probable future attacks from my father and also position me away from harm as well. This was not bad tactical planning for a woman who had little recourse for self-defense against battering in days before such assaults had even been named in our community, and at a time when Christian wives were expected to simply be "subject" to their husbands' desires.

Despite the denials that threatened to smother my mom's spirit and her own affirming sense of herself as a person, *my mother was not a victim*. Standing alone and shelterless in the gales of my father's furor, seeing no means of escaping, she had devised a way to resist that she hoped would enable her to survive. Amid every storm and its unreliable wake, she had loved my father, and for some forty-odd years she had patiently sought for the means to help him without being destroyed in the process. Fortunately for her, and for us all, she managed to hold onto her faith in God without completely succumbing to the patriarchal interpretations of ministers in our community that rendered women mere handmaids and footstools for men.

It is also important, I think, to note that my mother—who never spoke specifically to me or anyone about "feminism" or feminist and/or womanist ideals or ideas—she nonetheless had given some serious thought to the radical messages that she wanted her son to learn and apply in his (my) own interactions and relationships with girls and women. She had apparently wanted to provide me with a moral code that could help me to evade the usual ways of interacting with females as a male because, from her experiences, she had seen very little respect being shown by males to girls and women. Her watchwords had been quite simple: "If you want other boys and men to respect your sister, you must remember that every girl you meet is somebody's daughter and somebody's sister." I do not know how she had arrived at those specific words, yet I have remembered them for my entire life. With something akin to a prophetic simplicity, Mom had given me advice that had challenged me to put all females' well-being in the forefront of my considerations. That positioning, in itself, revealed the possibility that I could become a man who could be different from many that she had known. Her words also signaled her own deep yearning for more equitable relations of power for her own daughter—if not also for herself. The more I mine my memories of my mom, the richer I become in my appreciation of her thought process.

As I look back on that day I experienced domestic violence in my family (so long ago and yet like yesterday), I realize that I did something good, something right. Although I, like millions of other Black males, had been born into *a complicated hierarchy in which I had begun to learn certain meager rewards of patriarchal privilege as well as the pains of race and class oppressions*—on that day, I stepped onto a narrow path that could lead me toward my own humanity. In taking a stand against the battering of my mother, I acted to save her, and I had acted in a manner that I hoped would help lead my father toward a more humane vision of himself. In fact, on that day I witnessed his abuse of my mother, I began a long and complicated journey toward a manhood that would not be predicated on the domination of girls, women, other boys, or even other men. I had no earthly idea, though, how the blows and the burdens of that afternoon would pummel my spirit and mind for years to come. Yet, I had helped to save my mom, although I did not fully understand then how challenging my climb to humanity would be. Sometimes the things that you remember are the very things you wish you could forget.

Remembering Other-Mothers Soul Sisters

Very shortly after my graduation from Hiram College, in 1969, I went to Cleveland, Ohio. This was, indeed, one of my first "leaps of faith"—though I certainly would not have described it in such terms. My experiences with race, class, and gender oppressions at Hiram College taught me two essential lessons. One of my lessons was that, notwithstanding the good intentions of many people, there were great and perilous injustices in this country and the world. The second lesson was that I was more than up to the intellectual and emotional challenges of trying to help set this unjust world aright. In Cleveland, I began working as a fifth-grade elementary schoolteacher. I must readily admit that I was not the best-prepared teacher, pedagogically speaking. However, I had a genuine love for all my students at Adlai Stevenson Elementary School. Most of all, I was eager and willing to learn as much as I could to become an effective agent of change.

I was truly blessed to meet four Black women: Thelma Dockens (my principal at Adlai Stevenson); Shirley Hughes (my mom's friend, who opened her home to me and provided me with a kind, familial setting in which I began to grow as an independent young man); Norma Jean Freeman (a marvelous activist within Cleveland's Black Movement)[4]; and Linda Ware Johnson (another activist who would, years later, become my sister-in-law). Each of these women demonstrated an incredible sense of herself and her community, and each one seemed to also have keen insights into the kind of Black man I was trying to become. Each of them provided me with validation that I was pursuing a righteous pathway, and each of them unflinchingly gave me constructive criticism when she saw me stumbling in my desired path. The mentoring and friendship that these women shared with me greatly reinforced my confidence in the earlier counsels of my mother regarding the ways of the world and the urgency of new standards for Black manhood.

At a time (circa the early 1970s) when the Black Freedom Movement was beset by incredible temptations and pressures from without and from within—not only by the seductions of "Black" capitalist opportunism, but also by a virulent sexism buttressed by denials of patriarchy in Black lives—these women helped me to understand the importance of the pro-feminist and womanist values my mother had planted deep within my consciousness so long ago. What my mother had communicated to me, in a very down-to earth manner, *as a matter of personal integrity*, was then communicated to me by these Black other-mothers and female mentors as *also a matter of politics for social justice*. Together these women illuminated for me the dynamics of unjust power relations in society and showed me pathways for opposing injustice.

At the time, I did not consider the gendered character of the lessons that these sisters unassumingly shared with me. I simply viewed them as kind, spiritually wise, thoughtful, community-minded, and self-reliant African American women. Now I understand much more fully the multiple lessons they were able to share, precisely because of the multiple kinds of injustices they themselves had experienced. Without ever using the word *feminism*, the commitments, conversations, beliefs, and behaviors these mentors and friends shared helped me to begin to view and value the lives of Black women and girls as no less important (in our struggle for a more just society) than the lives of boys and men. I only wish today that I had understood how prescient my mother had been toward my understanding the complexity of gender relations.

It Must Have Been the Spirit: Coming Full Circle, Facing My Past

In 1981, the year Ronald Reagan became president of the United States, I married a Black woman.[5] It was not the wisest decision that I had ever made. We had slim-to-no resources. We had decided to marry after a relatively short long-distance relationship, and there were many unresolved and challenging issues within the unexamined baggage in each of our lives. Still, we had thought that we were in love. We had both been politically "progressive" people, and we each had been very open to making whatever sacrifices would be necessary. We had had absolutely no idea of the extremely difficult journey we were embarking upon.

During the next seven years, we had both worked incredibly hard to make ends meet and nurture our family. Vera already had two young boys when we married, so the multiple obligations of being a husband, becoming a stepparent, maintaining a 3.5 grade point average in graduate school, and working any and every decent job that I could find had literally blown my mind. During our marriage, the unresolved issues and tensions in each of our lives had reemerged in intense and volatile disagreements, and I had begun to demonstrate the male-centered and dominating behaviors that

I had inadvertently learned while being reared as a child in a patriarchal, dominated home.

While it is true that my wife and I had entered our marriage with a lot of internalized experiential baggage, the most important truth was that I had made the grave error of trying to control my wife instead of controlling myself. The result of this impoverished, tension-ridden, and stressful situation was that my wife shot me one afternoon during an argument. She shot me in self-defense because she was afraid of me. Frankly, had I been her and had experienced the battering as she had received from me, I would have resorted in the same manner. The details of what followed after that tragedy are much too complicated to recount here. What is most pertinent to the overall account of my journey is that my wife and I finally decided, together, that if we were going to be friends, we could not remain husband and wife. We divorced amicably after seven years of marriage.

The lessons that I learned in the aftermath of that terrible afternoon with my wife have greatly contributed to changing the course of my journey as a pro-feminist and womanist-identified Black man. Admittedly, the exact chronology is a bit difficult to pin down; yet there are several developments that I must note. One of the most crucial realizations I had arrived at was that, despite the fact that I had loathed my father's dominating and controlling behaviors toward my mother, I had lived to repeat those very behaviors. This had not occurred because I wanted to treat the woman I married in a sexist and patriarchal manner. She was the first Black woman outside of my immediate family from whom I had ever really felt love.

Yet I had come to repeat my father's behavior because I had known no other way to behave. This is not to say that I had not been intentional in battering my wife. I am saying that it was a result of being reared in a home in which sexist and patriarchal relations of power were modeled. Moreover, because I had never engaged in the necessary work to come to grips with the behavioral consequences of those lessons in my own life, I was set on a path to act out the very behaviors that I had loathed in my father. It did not matter that I hated those behaviors that controlled and dominated my mother. Those were the only ways in which I had ever witnessed how my father related to my mom.

A second lesson that emerged from the turbulent years of my marriage was that the behaviors I had witnessed in my household had reverberated powerful traumatizing effects for *all* who lived within that space. This means that each of us—my mother, my father, and I—needed to find a path to healing as well as a path to different models of relationship-building. This requires deliberate effort and time; healing and constructive ideas and methods of building relationships do not simply happen. This is especially true for the persons and families of oppressed groups and people. There is nothing trivial, foolish, or frivolous about unlearning the abusive forms of relating that are spawned within oppressive social orders.[6] As a good friend of mine once said, "In a chittlin' factory, everybody comes up stinkin'."

A third lesson that I gleaned from my errors during marriage is that the patriarchal and sexist messages are not simply matters of childhood socialization, but daily oppressive structures are ongoing. Males in this society will do well to engage with other males in personal and collective ways of opposing the patriarchal and sexist models to which we are incessantly oriented. This is necessary work for any male who, like me, has grown up witnessing and learning models of patriarchal behaviors. It is also work that must often be done—if it is to be done most effectually—by males working with other males. This is not to suggest that males have nothing of significance to learn from women. Women and girls can teach males much that we need to know. My point here is that challenging and encouraging males to unlearn and resist patriarchy is a task that can often be more instructively done by males—simply because males often listen to males differently than they listen to females.

Radical Allies: They Led Me to the Water, but I Had to Wade

Following my divorce, in the process of trying to sort out what I wanted to abandon and what I wanted to improve in my life, I decided to return to my graduate studies in political science at Clark Atlanta University. Like many people who have lived through the trauma of domestic violence, marital separation, and divorce—I felt quite uneasy for some time. I was glad to be opening a new chapter in my life, yet I did not know how to go about it. I wanted, and needed, companionship. Yet I was deeply apprehensive that my controlling and dominating behaviors would once again contribute to my undoing in any relationship that I might try to develop with another woman. One of my female associates mentioned to me that there was a group within the Atlanta area called Men Stopping Violence, Inc.—organized specifically to encourage and challenge males to rethink and end their sexist behavior. After some debating with myself, I made the decision to call MSV and see what might happen.

When I reached MSV by phone, I was unable to speak with anyone, and the voice message prompted me to leave a message. This might well have been just another opportunity to return to the "safety" of my own complacency;

yet for all of my apprehensiveness, I truly wanted to begin whatever work would be necessary in order to become a different and better man. I had seen the terror, anger, and pain in my first wife's eyes when I had battered her. I could still remember how she had grabbed her head as she stumbled backward under the blows of my hand. I had decided that I would never again be guilty of mistreating a woman I had promised to love. With that earnest commitment and with a truly contrite heart, I left a phone message with MSV. Waiting to receive a response, I hoped to see if this organization would lead me on a new path to self-transformation.

At the same time I reached out to MSV, I was incredibly blessed to be in a graduate program at Clark Atlanta University where I began to meet Black women who identified as feminists. As I gingerly but thoughtfully began to talk to them, I began learning how their concerns seemed to echo some of the very concerns that my mom and my ex-wife had expressed about their lives as African American women. I began to rethink arguments I had had with my sister, Jeanie, about how she hated for me to come home because I really didn't know "how to treat people." In my graduate classes, I began to invest considerable time in just sitting and listening to women—sometimes talking with me, but most times, just talking to other women. What I began to learn, slowly and almost imperceptibly, was that the women around me—just like the woman who had reared me and challenged me to be a different kind of man—had keen minds and deep feelings. I began to understand that they were not only worthy of respect, but their lives could help me understand the world around me, as well as myself, more deeply than I had ever imagined—if I were prepared to be quiet and listen.

Gradually, over the course of several months, I purposely placed myself in situations from which I would probably have recoiled previously. I followed up on the phone message left by Sulaiman Nuriddin, a member of MSV. He invited me to begin dialoguing with other men in the organization that would help me address my own issues, as well as doing some needed, serious self-examination work. At the same time, I began working with a small but expanding group of Black males within the Atlanta University Center called Black Men for the Eradication of Sexism (BMES), led by a remarkable brother named Omar Freilla.[7] I also took every opportunity that arose to talk with and listen to feminist women.

In the life-transforming work I had begun with antisexist women and men, I would come to experience closer political and intellectual associations with particularly remarkable and brilliant Black women: Faye Bellamy, Njeri Jackson, Gejuanna Smith, bell hooks, Junee Hunt, Qiyamah Rahman, Aaronette

White, and Loretta Ross. I am deeply, deeply indebted, and I will always be grateful, to each of these women. They demonstrated love in ways that I had never witnessed or experienced—except at my mother's knees as a child. These women might very well have rejected me once they learned that I had been a batterer. Yet those that knew never turned me away. They patiently asked me to ask myself hard questions related to my self-image and ideas of manhood and masculinity. They suggested books for me to read and sometimes allowed me to join them in critical examination of those books. These women and the men I met in MSV and BMES became my family. They provided me the nurturing and critical space in which I could envision a new me. Along with them, I began to experience the power of transformative and liberatory relations and behaviors that move us together—and those with whom we would come into contact—to more critical space of personal, political, and social engagement.

There is one particular experience that I want to share that will help to reveal some of the personal struggles I engaged during this time of intense self-reflection and rebirth. As I was coming to the end of my graduate work, I had to home in on a few final courses that would enable me to complete the establishment of my subfields in political science. At one point, I had strongly considered adding liberation theology as a subfield to my specialization in comparative/African politics and political theory. Yet after some weeks of critical self-examination, I decided that it was actually feminist theory that I wanted to pursue. I enrolled in a graduate course on feminist theory, scheduled at Spelman College to be taught by noted Black feminist scholar Dr. Beverly Guy-Sheftall. The decision to take this course led me to a series of unexpected self-confrontations.

One of the most dramatic conflicts occurred one afternoon when I went over to the Spelman College Bookstore to purchase a copy of Audre Lorde's *Sister Outsider*, which was required for Dr. Guy-Sheftall's course. As I was walking the short distance from the West End MARTA Station to the Spelman campus and the bookstore, I began to notice some intense feelings of self-apprehension. Although I honestly regret having to acknowledge this, the truth is that I was quite nervous about having people see me purchasing a book by a well-known Black lesbian writer. In my course of graduate study, having become a fairly well-known African American male activist, as well as a student in Clark Atlanta University's Political Science Department, I was concerned about what others would think and say about me, if they discovered that I was reading work by Audre Lorde.

My apprehension was visceral, even a bit mind-numbing. Once I purchased the book (fortunately for me, I had thought, there were not too many people in the store that afternoon), I hurriedly and surreptitiously placed the book in my book bag, hurried to the West End Station, caught the train, and went home. I did not take the book out of my bag until I was safely inside my College Park apartment, with the doors locked and the shades drawn. Only then could I feel safe enough to begin reading Audre Lorde's book. Yet what I had feared I would find in the disapproving gazes of others, I soon found in my own horrified look at my own reflection in my bathroom mirror. I had been afraid that if others had seen me reading *Sister Outsider*, they might have regarded me as less than manly. What I discovered in reading my sister's words (especially those about how she had wanted to raise her son), was that the person I was did not yet measure up to the humanity expressed in Lorde's hopes for her son. My manhood was not at issue—it was my humanness that was flawed. I had gotten some very fundamental questions twisted, and I had a great deal of self-examination to do.

This stark encounter with myself forced me to rethink much that I had previously, and comfortably, accepted about myself. The feminist theory course became a semester-long period of self-interrogation, demanding that I give an account of who and what I had been in my marriage, and in every single relationship in my life. Reflecting on my previous behaviors and my patriarchal and sexist thinking—I struggled through many tearful moments during that semester, and certain moments afterward. Gradually, I began to feel that I was beginning to understand, and embrace, the same model of humanity that Lorde had set before her son. And one morning, as if the message had come on the wings of my mom's spirit, I realized that the model Lorde had placed before her son was the same model my mom—and many other Black women—had set before me. The realization was a light that has now become the beacon I have determined to follow.

What Difference Has the Model of Intersectionality Really Made (in My Life)?

I close this chapter with some reflections on the difference my encounters with feminists during the 1990s made in my political life (which includes my teaching and activism), as well as my personal relationships. During my years of graduate study in Atlanta, Georgia, I learned about two vital conceptions of oppression theorized from a Black feminist standpoint: "simultaneity" *and* "intersectionality." Since Black feminists and womanists have not only challenged African American males to rethink our political approaches to inequality but also our theoretical understandings of how varying forms of oppression operate interdependently, I think it is important to discuss them here, particularly related to my own process toward becoming a pro-feminist Black man. It is not uncommon today for many male (and female) academic scholars and activists, across differences of gender and race, to acknowledge a measure of indebtedness to African American women in general, and to Black feminists in particular, for their critiques of the interrelationship between sexism and racism. Yet, all too often, such acknowledgments echo the self-exonerating whispers of a confessional, for what they reveal is far less telling than what they leave unsaid. During the past several decades, despite Black males' repeated praises offered to African American women for their political contributions to social justice struggles, the significance of their contributions to liberatory theory contesting the harmful effects of sexism remains a highly contested and contentious matter.

Black feminists and womanists have been at the forefront of illuminating the simultaneous operation of different forms of oppression and discrimination within many different personal, political, and social spaces. The theoretical concept of interlocking oppressions encourages all activists for social justice to consider the interconnected ways in which race, gender, sexual, and class oppressions affect all of our daily lives. Once such interconnections are acknowledged, we must strategically begin to dialogue about ways to contest them *simultaneously*. Witnessing the painful effects of multiple forms of oppression means that we can no longer separate racism from (hetero)sexism, homophobia, (dis)ability, or economic status. As Black men, in particular, we must also reckon more carefully with the myriad ways in which these forms of oppression not only disfigure the lives of all females but also our lives specifically as Black males.

Moreover, the recognition of the *simultaneity* of oppression is not enough in and of itself alone; the *intersectionality* of all forms of domination must be understood as well in order to act against them. Such a complicated approach to analyzing and theorizing personal, political, and social realities calls upon us as Black men to understand—as numerous Black feminists and womanists have repeatedly noted—that if we are to become more adept at advancing activist strategies for addressing multiple forms of oppressions simultaneously, we must more adequately assess and reflect on their complex operation in our daily lives. We cannot confront oppressions politically when we ignore ways they act out in our personal lives and remain silent about them.

In the work that I continue to do, as a teacher, activist, and family and community member, I am called to remember the injunction uttered by Donna Kate Rushin decades ago when she first penned "The Bridge Poem": "Stretch or drown, Evolve or die." If we—who identify as feminist and/or womanist (across differences of gender, race, class, and/or sexuality—are sincere about opposing all forms of oppression, we have no choice but to reckon with the liberatory possibilities of bridgework for coalitional alliance building.

Finally, if I am further along my path to becoming the liberated man my mother envisioned, it is because of the Spirit of love and the women and men who helped to transform my self-vision. I cannot fully articulate the myriad ways in which each of them influenced me to become a more humane, self-reflective political and social actor. Yet, by calling out their names, lifting them up, and acknowledging their contributions to my growth, I hope that I have helped readers of my story to understand a little bit of what bell hooks meant when she told me—face to face—that "Feminism is for everybody!" For the men and the boys (of all races and ethnicities) I continue to encounter, I am trying to embody the changes and the healing that can come when I challenge them to open themselves up to the self-transforming power of feminism *and* womanism. My mom used to tell me, "Son, we people got a long way to go, and a short time to get there!" I agree. Come my brothers (*and* my sisters), won't you join the journey of womanist liberation with me?

Notes

1. Aaronette White, PhD (deceased) was a brilliant scholar, teacher, and mentor who greatly encouraged me to begin a feminist journey during the 1990s in Atlanta, Georgia.

2. Fay Bellamy Powell (deceased) was a stalwart activist within the Student Nonviolent Coordinating Committee (SNCC). Fay made a major contribution to the development of my feminist consciousness during the 1990s.

3. In African American spiritual traditions, changing one's name symbolizes the altering of one's journey and choosing a path more in keeping with the leading of the Spirit. Thus, as Roberta Flack's memorable rendition of "I Told Jesus" tells us, when we arrive at the point of accepting the will of the Spirit—when we can "tell Jesus it will be alright"—He will change our names, that is, the way we live our lives.

4. Norma Jean Freeman and her husband, Donald Freeman, are two of the most well-respected and visionary activists of the Black Freedom Movement, as it evolved within the Cleveland, Ohio, area. Norma Jean and Donald were both intellectuals and educators, and they were some of the leading members of what became known as the Revolutionary Action Movement (RAM).

5. Vera Johnson (Powell) is now deceased. Some considerable time before her remarriage and her untimely passing, I did all in my power to seek Vera out (as well as her two sons) and make amends. She and the boys graciously forgave me, and I forgave her. Several years ago she passed. Despite having been forgiven, I will always

regret that I did not understand how to be a better human being during the years of our marriage. She deserved a much better man than I could be at that time.

6. In evoking the concept of "oppression," I recognize that for many people in the United States, this concept is off-putting as a term for describing daily existence in this country. Yet for many groups, and for the persons who are members of those groups, *oppression* is precisely the term that describes the conditions of their lives. Feminist scholars such as Iris Marion Young have written *quitter* illuminatingly about the political and personal manifestations of oppression in daily U.S. life. See Young's "Five Faces of Oppression," in her volume, *Justice and the Politics of Difference*, 1990. During the past several decades, numerous scholars have joined in the effort to interrogate the personal and political consequences of unjust relations of power. See also *Feminism and Men: Reconstructing Gender Relations*, (Eds.) Steven P. Schacht and Doris W. Ewing, 1998; and *A Question of Manhood: A Reader in U.S. Black Men's History and Masculinity*, (Eds.) Darlene Clark Hine and Earnestine Jenkins, 1999.

7. During the 1990s, in Atlanta, Georgia, Omar Freilla and a number of other Black males in the Atlanta University Center formed a group to oppose sexist behaviors and ideas on the campuses and in the city. I was extremely fortunate to learn about this group and to begin participating in its discussions and actions. One such action was a conference, attended by at least 250–300 people, challenging and encouraging African American males to become feminist, or "pro-feminist" men in solidarity with Black women. It was at this conference that Gary Lemons and I first met.

Acknowledgments

When Gary Lemons invited me to contribute to this volume, I was of course honored. An incisive teacher and scholar, Gary is also one of the most intrepid feminists with whom I am acquainted. The fact that he is an African American male made his invitation even more intriguing. Yet as he shared his vision for this volume with me during several subsequent chats, the magnitude of his undertaking—and mine—loomed more challengingly with each conversation.

Gary asked me to tell a bit of my story as an act of solidarity and hope, I am sure. He wanted to provide me with a space, and an opportunity, within which to tell the truth about some of my journey as "a pro-feminist" Black male. He is, no doubt, as hopeful as I am that my telling will shed some light on the subject of how any male might make his way toward becoming a feminist and new sort of womanist man.

I agreed to write about my journey because, in giving voice to some of my experiences, I can "answer the call" of so many women of color, who have earnestly desired to see a new generation of men who are unafraid to live as "reliable witnesses" to the transformative, healing power of feminism. In witnessing to that power, we also yield ourselves more completely to its mission of societal and personal transformation.

Special thanks to:

Fay Bellamy (Powell); Sulaiman Nuriddin, Dick Bathrick, Ulester Douglas, and "Red" Crowley of MSV, Inc.; Akazia Hunt, bell hooks, Qiyamah Rahman, Loretta Ross, Beverly Guy-Sheftall, Aaronette White, Omar Freilla, and Paul McLennan.

Contributors

M. Jacqui Alexander, PhD, is a writer, teacher, creator, and founding Director of the Tobago Center for the Study and Practice of Indigenous Spirituality. She focuses on the sacred dimensions of experience, the significance of sacred subjectivity, and the shape and meaning of Kongo cosmology in the Caribbean. Her publications include *Feminist Genealogies, Colonial Legacies, Democratic Futures*, coedited with Chandra Talpade Mohanty; *Sing, Whisper, Shout, Pray! Feminist Visions for a Just World*, coedited with Lisa Albrecht, Sharon Day, and Mab Segrest; and *Pedagogies of Crossing: Meditations on Feminism, Sexual Politics, Memory and the Sacred.*

Dora Arreola, MFA in Directing, is the founder and Artistic Director of an all-women ensemble from México and the U.S, Mujeres en Ritual Danza-Teatro. Arreola created Mujeres en Ritual in 1999 to explore issues of women at the border region of Mexico and the United States. Arreola is coauthor of the book *Mujeres en Ritual: Género y transformación/Gender and Transformation.* Her artistic practice is making performance a collaborative and critical process to develop interdisciplinary and cross-cultural work. Arreola has more than twenty years of professional experience as a theatre director, choreographer, and performer. She is currently an Associate Professor of Theatre at the University of South Florida. She has received grants and commissions from the Ford Foundation, Cultural Contact, National Performance Network and more.

Andrea Assaf is the founding Artistic/Executive Director of Art2Action, Inc. A performer, writer, director, and cultural organizer, she has a Masters in

Performance Studies and a BFA in Acting, both from NYU. She's currently Artist-in-Residence and guest faculty at the University of South Florida. Andrea is an acclaimed performer and director, who tours original work nationally and internationally, including venues such as OSF as part of the National Asian American Theatre Festival, La MaMa, the Kennedy Center Millennium Stage, and more. Awards include: 2017 Finalist for the Freedom Plow Award for Poetry & Activism, 2011 NPN Creation Fund commission, and 2010 Princess Grace Award. Andrea serves on the Board of CAATA and Alternate ROOTS, and is a member of RAWI for Arab American writers.

Kendra N. Bryant, PhD, is a poet, painter, and teacher whose work appears in *The Inside Light: New Criticisms of Zora Neale Hurston*, 2010; *Trayvon Martin, Race, and American Justice: Writing Wrong*, 2014; *Solace: Writing, Refuge, & LGBTQ Women of Color*, 2016; and a handful of academic journals and texts. She currently teaches in the Writing and Rhetoric Program at Florida International University, Miami. Kendra can be reached at www.drknbryant.com.

Rudolph P. Byrd, PhD, was the Goodrich C. White Professor of American Studies and founding Director of the James Weldon Johnson Institute at Emory University. Byrd was also the founding Co-Chair of the Alice Walker Literary Society. For almost a decade, he was the Director of the Department of African American Studies at Emory. His publications included *The World Has Changed: Conversations with Alice Walker* (2010); editor for the second edition of the novel, *Cane*, by Jean Toomer, coedited with Henry Louis Gates Jr.; and *Traps: African American Men on Gender and Sexuality*, coedited with Beverly Guy-Sheftall (2001). Rudolph P. Byrd died in 2011.

Atika Chaudhary earned her MA in Literature from the University of South Florida. Her research and writing focus on the intersectionality of race, gender, sexuality, and class from an autocritographical, womanist, and feminist standpoint. She is also interested in exploring the complexities of identity in the context of language and transformation.

Paul T. Corrigan teaches writing and literature at Southeastern University in Lakeland, Florida. He lives in the Peace River Watershed, where he walks to work. He writes poetry and scholarship on poetry, pedagogy, and spirituality. More information can be found on his website, paultcorrigan.com.

Fanni V. Green, a self-described "artist-activist," is an actor/writer/director/preacher/storyteller. Professor Green teaches acting and voice/speech/

dialects and directs in the School of Theatre and Dance at the University of South Florida in Tampa. An avid gardener and accomplished cook, Green is currently writing a one-woman performance piece on violence and aging. Her words to live by are: "Rejoice, Pray, Give Thanks."

Beverly Guy-Sheftall, PhD, is the Anna Julia Copper Professor of Women's Studies at Spelman College and is the founding Director of its Women's Research and Resources Center, the first of its kind at a historically Black college or university. She also serves as the Chair of Comparative Women's Studies. Guy-Sheftall's publications include *Words of Fire: An Anthology of African American Feminist Thought* (1995); *Traps: African American Men on Gender and Sexuality*, coedited with Rudolph P. Byrd (2001); *Gender Talk: The Struggle for Equality in African American Communities*, coedited with Johnnetta B. Cole (2003); and *Daughters of Sorrow: Attitudes toward Black Women, 1880–1920* (1990). In 2013, she was featured in *Makers: Women Who Make America*, a PBS documentary.

Susie L. Hoeller is an international business attorney. She has been recognized by the *National Law Journal* and the Dallas Bar Association for her pro bono work for refugees. Hoeller is currently an advisor to New Zealand Trade and Enterprise and an adjunct instructor at the University of Tampa Sykes College of Business. Susie is a graduate of Vanderbilt Law School and Colby College. She was born in Chicago and raised in Montreal, Quebec, Canada.

Ylce Irizarry's research specializations include Chicana/o, Latina/o, and Hispanic Caribbean Literatures. Her book, *Chicana/o and Latina/o Fiction: The New Memory of Latinidad* (University of Illinois Press, 2016), received the MLA Prize in Chicana and Chicano and Latina and Latino Literary and Cultural Studies. Her recent scholarship appears in the journals *Symbolism* (2017) and *Centro* (2015) and in the edited book collection, *Junot Díaz and the Decolonial Imagination* (Duke University Press, 2016).

M. Thandabantu Iverson is an independent labor and human rights educator living in Denver, Colorado. A second-movement activist since the 1960s, Iverson readily acknowledges the transformational power of intersectionality in his life.

Gary L. Lemons, PhD, is a pro–feminist/womanist professor of African American literature. His book publications include *Black Male Outsider, a Memoir: Teaching as a Pro-Feminist Man* (SUNY, 2008); *Womanist Forefathers, Frederick Douglass and W.E.B. Du Bois* (SUNY Press, 2009); *Feminist*

Solidarity at the Crossroads: Intersectional Women's Studies for Transracial Alliance, coedited with Kim Vaz (Routledge, 2012); and *Caught Up in the Spirit! Teaching for Womanist Liberation* (Nova Science Publishers, Inc., 2017).

Layli Maparyan, PhD, is the Katherine Stone Kaufmann '67 Executive Director of the Wellesley Centers for Women and Professor of Africana Studies at Wellesley College. She has published two books, *The Womanist Reader* (2006; as Layli Phillips) and *The Womanist Idea* (2012); her third book, *Womanism Rising*, is forthcoming. In addition to her books, Maparyan has published over 35 journal articles and book chapters on topics as diverse as the history of psychology, social identity and identity development, gender and sexuality studies, Hip Hop studies, womanism, and activism.

Erica C. Sutherlin is a candidate for the MFA in Film and Television Production at the University of Southern California. As an artist, Sutherlin has shared her creative talents with the entertainment industry, as an Equity actor, theatrical director, poet, screenwriter, and aspiring filmmaker. In the field of education, she has groomed, trained, and mentored hundreds of young artists aspiring to achieve greatness. Sutherlin is a trailblazer, breaking down barriers and opening doors for all people.

Index

Abraham religion, 26
Achebe, Chinua, 59
ACT-UP, 24
aesthetic(s), 173, 176–178, 182
Affirmative Action, relation to ivy-league study, 78
Afrekete at Spellman College, 110–111
African American studies, 24
African American womanists, 133
Africana studies, 24
Afrikanity, 24
Afrocentrism, 24
agency, 176
agnostic, 24, 27, 34
Ain't I a Woman: Black Women and Feminism (hooks), 65
Alarcón, Norma, 82; critique of exceptionalism, 90n3
Alexander, Jacqui M., 11, 12, 33, 101
aliens, 31
all-inclusive love, xi
Álvarez, Maribel, 174, 183n4
American immigrant, 124
Andemicael, Iobel, 141, 145–146
Angels, 28
Anglo-American corporations, 125
Anglo-American(s): exclusion practices, 72; as problematic term, 90n7
Anglo-Cleansing, 127
Anglophone, 133; Quebecers, 131
Anglo-Saxon, 124, 126
antimiscegenation laws, 126
Anti-neoliberalism, 24
Anti-Vietnam War protests, 125
Anzaldúa, Gloria, vii, ix, x,12, 31–33, 61–62, 64–66, 74, 84–85, 90n8, 136–140, 145–146, 180, 183n10, 216
Arcus Foundation, 12, 95–97
Arcus Project, 98
Arreola, Dora, vi, 7, 12, 13, 171–183, 187, 235
Artista-activista, 139
Art2Action Inc., 7
Assaf, Andrea, vi, 3, 7, 13, 173, 178–180, 183n8, 183n9, 184–187, 235–236
atheists, 27, 34
Atlanta, Georgia, 217, 229, 231, 232
Atlanta University Center (AUC), 96, 110
Audre Lorde Collection, 97
Audre Lorde Papers, 98
Audre Lorde Project (Phases I and II), 96
autocritography, 58, 83, 88; defined by Awkward, 90n12
autoethnography, as practice of resistance to silencing, 83
Awkward, Michael, 58, 90n12

Baha'I, 23, 74
Baldwin, James, 104
Bambara, Toni Cade, 7, 10, 56–66
Banks, Brenda, 97
Barnard College, 99
Basque region of Spain, 73
Bathrick, Dick, 233
Bedi, Kiran, 27–28

Bellamy (Powell) Fay, 216, 227, 231, 233
belonging, 72–73; relationship to citizenship, 75
Bennett College for Women, 101
bilingual red "Arret/Stop" signs, 128
Bisexual, Lesbina, and Gay Organization (BLAGOSAH), 99
Black feminism, 24
Black feminist, viii, 229, 230
Black feminist standpoint, 229, 230
Black Freeman Movement, 223
Black LGBTQ, 97
Black Lives Matter, as human rights group, 75
Black Male Outsider, a Memoir: Teaching as a Black Feminist Man (Lemons), 4, 53, 65
Black Men for the Eradication of Sexism (BMES), 227–228
Blackmon, Samantha, 146
Black Pride movement, 100
Black Studies, 104
Bonila-Silva, Eduardo, 145
border (U.S.-Mexico), 172, 174–182, 184, 186
borderlands, 177, 180–181, 183n7, 183n10
Borderlands/ La Frontera: The New Mestiza (Anzaldúa), concept of tolerance for ambiguity, 74, 84, 90n8
border studies, 32
Boriqua/o, as term, 74, 84
Breaking the Silence: The Audre Lorde Black Lesbian Feminist Project (Alexander and Guy-Sheftall), 95
B.R.I.D.E. at Bennett College for Women, 110
"The Bridge Poem" (Rushin), 162, 167, 216, 230
British, 125
British crown, 126
Brown, Michael: victim of police brutality, 89n2
Bryant, Kendra N., x, 10
Buddhist/ism, 26, 32
building bridges, 136, 139, 145
Building Womanist Coalitions: Writing and Teaching in the Spirit of Love (Lemons), vii-viii, x, 2–5, 7, 16–17
Butoh, 172
Byrd, Rudolph P., x, 11, 15, 97, 214, 236

Call and Post, 218
Camp Pride Summer Leadership Camp, 111
Campus Pride, 111
Canada, 124–126, 129–130
Canandian Army in Montreal, 127–128
Canadian Prime Minister Pierre Elliott Trudeau, 127
Canadians, 125
Candomblé, 25
Cannon, Meardis, 211, 214
Cardona, Nancy, as model of womanism, 81
Carrillo, Noé, 173
CASCADE at Howard University, 110
Catholic Church, 126
Caught Up in the Spirit! Teaching for Womanist Liberation (Lemons), 2
Center for Contemplative Mind in Society, 25
Charter of French Language, aka Bill 101, 128–129
Chaudhary, Atika, xi, 6, 9, 12
Chicago, 124
Chicana/o, as term, 70
Chicana feminist theory, 32
children of Darfur, 188, 190–194, 206
Christian, 133
Christianity, 24–25
cisgender, viii
Cisneros, Sandra, 76
citizenship, second-class, 73; function, 75; relationship to privilege, 75
civil rights activists, 125
Clark Atlanta University, 101, 217, 226–228
Clark Atlanta University Political Science Department, 228
Clery Act, 117–118
Cleveland, Ohio, 222
Cleveland's Black Movement, 223
Clinton, Bill, 133
Coalition of Activist Students Celebrating the Acceptance of Diversity and Equality (CASCADE), 99, 111
coatlicue state, 31
Cole, Johnnetta Betsch, 97–99, 213
collaboration, 173, 177–179, 181, 184
colonization, 173; decolonizing, 176; postcolonial, 181
Colonize This! Young Women of Color on Today's Feminism (Hernández and Rehman), vii, 57, 59, 60–62, 66–67
COLORS at North Carolina Central University, 110
Columbus, Ohio, 216, 217

Combahee River Collective, assertion of distinction between feminism and woman of color feminism, 90n11
"coming to voice," x
Committee on Institutional Cooperation (CIC), end of endowment, 90n10; as source of academic merit funding for minority students, 78
conocimiento, 31
"consensus reality," vii
conservatives, 29
contemplative pedagogy, 26
contemplative practice, 26ff.
Cooper, Anna Julia, 32
Cornielle, Ángel Salvador: assassination of, 73; use of strategic silence, 73
Corrigan, Paul T., x, 6, 12
Cosmos, 24
Crenshaw, Taryn, 102
Crowley, "Red," 233
Cuba, 127

dance, 172, 173, 176–177, 178; movement (creative/physical), 172, 173, 177–180
Davis, Angela, 60–61
de la Cruz, Sor Juana Inés, 173
Department of Women's Studies, University of South Florida, 54
descendants of African slaves, 124
desire, 176, 184
Dillard College, 101–102
Dion, Celine, 131
divination, 31
divinatory traditions, 26
Dogon, 25
dominicana, as term, 74
Dominican Republic, 72, 73
double consciousness, 24
Douglas, Ulester, 233
Douglass, Frederick, 15, 212
dream(s), 30, 33, 176, 185
Du Bois, W. E. B., 2, 120
"Dunkin Donuts" franchises in Montreal, 128

Eastern Europe, 123, 124
Eastern religions, 26–27
Edinburg Festival Fringe in Scotland, 205
Ellis Island, 123
El Teatro Campesino: exclusion, intellectual, 77, 79; intra-ethnic, 74–75; relationship to United Farm Workers' movement, 86
embodiment, 175, 176, 181
Emory University, 97, 214
"empathetic imagination," 59
empathy, 136–139, 141–142, 144
Employment NonDiscrimination Act (ENDA), 111
empowerment, 172, 182
English Canadians, 127
English-speaking minority, 125
Equality Forum & Research Project/Resource Guide to Coming Out for African Americans, 111
exploitation, 174–175, 176, 177–178

Felix Berumen, Humberto, 175
female body, 140
feminicide (*feminicidio*), 173, 174
feminism, viii, ix, x-xi, 182, 223
feminism: as oppressive, 84; as pedagogy, 71; as replication of patriarchy, 81
"feminism is for everybody," 231
feminist, 171, 172, 173, 177, 181, 182
Feminist Mystique (Friedan), 212
Feminist Solidarity at the Crossroads: Intersectional Women's Studies for Transracial Alliance (Vaz and Lemons), 54
Feminist Theory: From Margin to Center (hooks), 65
Feminism Is for Everybody, 213
Fisk University, 101
Florida, 4, 132
Foley, Neil, experiences of intra-ethnic exclusion, 80
Foote, Julia, 32
France, 26, 125
Francophones, 125
Frazier, Rev., 100
Freeman, Norma Jean, 223
Fregoso, Rosa Linda, 177–178, 183n7
Freilla, Omar, 216, 227, 233
French, 125, 128
French-Canadian(s), 125–127, 129, 131; bankers, industries; merchants, 125; politicians, families, workers, 126; providence, 128
French Crown, 125
Friedan, Betty, 212
Front de la Liberation du Quebec (FLQ), 126–127
Fronteras Deviades/Deviant Borders, 13, 173–181, 183n8, 184–187
fundamentalist Christians, 27

Garro, Elena, 173
Gates, Jr., Henry Louis, 58
Gay & Lesbian Liaison Unit (GLLU), 110
Gay and Lesbian Studies, 96
Gay Questions, Straight Questions, 110
Gender Talk: The Struggle for Women's Equality in African American Communities (Cole and Guy-Sheftall), 98
Georgia State University, 96
GI Bill, 124
Gilbert, Susan, 82
Glate, Thomas, 96
GLBT movement, 96
Govender, Pregs, 27
Green, Fanni V., x, 7, 8, 14
Greenberg, Mark, 205
Green movement, 24
Grotowski, Jerzy, 172
Gubar, Susan, 82
Guitierrez, Nova, 139, 141, 145–146
Guy-Sheftall, Beverly, 11–12, 15, 32, 97–98, 213–214, 228, 233

harassment: ageist, 82; ethnonational, 82; linguistic, 82; sexual, 81
Hayden, Robert, 212
HBCU campuses, 11, 101–104, 107, 108, 111–112, 114, 115–116, 120
Hebrew Israelites, 25
Hernandez, Daisy, 71
Hill, Lauren, 90n3
Hilltop, The, 99
Hip Hop, 24
Hiram College, 217, 219, 223
Hispanic: authenticity, 73; as identity, 71; relation to education, 73; as term, 84, 90n4
Hoeller, Susie, 12
Holmes, Barbara E., 33
Holocaust and Genocide Studies at the University of South Florida Library (Tampa), 205
hooks, bell, 15, 59, 60, 65, 68, 213, 227, 231, 233; cultural criticism, 77, 82
Hope, Donna, 98
How America's Immigrants Became White, 124
Hudson-Weems, Clenora, 30, 123
Hull, Akasha Gloria, 30
Human Rights Campaign (HRC), 111, 112, 133
Hume, Kathryn (Kit): pedagogy, 87; scholar and doctoral advisor, 75, 79
"hunked," 124
"hunkies," 124
Hunt, Akazia, 233
Hunt, Junee, 227
Hurricane María: US response as example of racism, 90n5
Hurston, Zora Neale, 16–17, 48, 99

I Am Your Sister: Collected and Unpublished Writings by Audre Lorde (Guy-Sheftall and Cole), 97, 213
Ifa, 25
Illibgiza, Immaculée, 27
India, 28
Indigenous spirituality, 31
In Search of Our Mothers' Gardens: Womanist Prose, 1, 68, 132
International Council of Women, 212
International Federation of Black Prides (IFBP), 100
intersectionality, 181, 229–230; difference between studying and experiencing, 73; as popular area of study, 73
invisible realm, 28, 31
Irizarry, Ylce, 10
Islam, 25
Iverson, Thandabantu M., x-xi, 15

Jackson, Njeri, 227
Jackson, Rebecca, 32
Jet Magazine, 218
JFK (John F. Kennedy), 125
Jim Crow, 123
Johnson, Kendra, 98
Johnson, Linda Ware, 223
Jones Act, imposition of US citizenship, 90n5

Keating, AnaLouise, vii, 32, 61–62, 64–65, 137
Kennedy Center Associate Theatre Festival, 205

"LaBelle Province," 132
La facultad, 31
"*La Güera,*" social construction of whiteness and social mobility, 70–71
Lambda Student Alliance, 99
"La Regie de la langue francaise," 128
Last Generation, The (Moraga), 86
Las Vegas, Nevada, 4, 131
Latin America, 131, 142

latina/o, as term, 84; defined, 90n4; relation to term latinx, 90n14
Latinas and Latinos, 145
latinidad, as expression of ethnic identity, 76
latinx, as term, 90n14
Lavender Report, 99–100, 111
Lemons, Gary L., vii-viii, x, 53, 88, 146, 215, 232
Le Moyne College, 73; as liberal arts institutions, 76, 77, 78
Leonard, Henry, 215
Lesbian and Bisexual Alliance (LBA), 98
lesbian/queer studies, 32
Levesque, Rene, 127–128
LGBT, 11, 96, 98, 100–120
LGBTQ, 98, 118
LGBT Studies, 103
LGBTT, 102
liberation, 33
Light, ix
"A Litany for Survival," 214
literacy, relation to social inequity, 83
Lopez, Yolanda, 84
Lorde, Audre, 4, 68, 79, 95, 104, 120, 213–214, 228–229; theory of the master's tools, 80
Loving in the War Years: LSA que nunca pasó por sus labios (Moraga), 85
Lugo, Alejandro, 181, 183n11
LUXOCRACY, 32
lynching and murder as a means of social control, 126

Maathai, Wangari, 27
Madison, Soyini D., 55
"maitres chez nous," 126
Maparyan, Layli, ix, 1, 10, 123
maquiladora(s), 174, 175, 178, 180
Martin, Trayvon, 70, 89n1
Martinez, Jackie: as Chicana Studies scholar, 82; feminist theory instruction, position on representation, ethnic, 82, 84
master narrative, as theory of hegemony, 80
McCaskill, Barbara, 26
McLennan, Paul, 217, 233
McMillan, Sean, 99
MDW NTR, 25
meditation, 27
Men Stopping Violence Inc. (MSV), 217, 226–227
mestiza consciousness, 71
"mestiza rhetoric," 45
metaphysics, 31
Mexico, 13, 171, 172, 174–175, 177–178, 180, 182n, 183, 184, 187, 235
Miami, Florida, 131
microagressions, relation to zenophobia, 74
midwife, 136, 141, 146
midwives of empathy, 137, 143
migration (immigration), 173
Mirecka, Rena, 172
miseducation, 71, 75, 90n1
missionary, 177, 179
MLK (Martin Luther King), 125
Montreal, 124–128, 130–131; metro area, 125
Montreal Canadians, 132
Moraga, Cherríe, 11, 56, 136, 171, 172, 182, 183n12, 216; on applied feminism, 82; Chicana theorist, 73; co-editor of and contributor to *This Bridge Called My Back*, 70; on silence, 85
Morehouse University, 101
Morrison, Toni, 146, 212, 214
motherhood, 141
Muhammad, Askia Toure, 217
Mujeres en Ritual, 13
Mujeres en Ritual Danza-Teatro, 13, 171–183, 184, 186
multiculturalism and college recruitment: relation to campus climate, 77
mysticism, 31

National Black Justice Coalition (NBJC), 111–112
National Defense Act, 127
National Gay and Lesbian Task Force (NGLTF), 100
Native Americans, 39–40
Negres blancs d'Amerique (*White Niggers of America*), 126
Nelson, Richardson Nathaniel Rev., 220
Nepantla, 31
nepantlera, 136–138; male, 143; nepantlera, 141; troubled, 141
New England, 126
New School, 57
New York City, 125, 132
Nipper, Darlene, 100
North Star, The, 212
Nuriddin, Sulaiman, 217, 227, 233
Nussbaum, Martha, 136
NYU (New York University), 2

Oberlin College, 216
occult, 31

"October Crisis," 127
Ogunyemi, Chikwenye Okonjo, 123
Olin-Ammentorp, Julie: as academic mentor, 76, 85; as surrogate mother, 76
O'Neal, Wendi, 98
"Open the Door," 139–140
oppositional models, 32
oppression, 172, 175–176, 179, 181
Order of Interbeing, 26
Osorio, Pepón, 85
Outlaw Culture: Resisting Representations (hooks), 68

Page, Cara, 96
Palmer, Parker, 37
Paradise (Morrison), 214
Parti Quebecois, 127–132
patriarchy, 140
Pedagogies of Crossing (Alexander), 11
pedagogy, 181–182
pedagogy, modeling, 75; informed by feminism, 71, 73, 86; informed by womanism, 71, 83, 89; measurements of effectiveness, 88
Pennsylvania State University, 78, 81; educational opportunities, 87
performance, 171, 172–173, 175, 177–182
petite bourgeoisie merchant class, 125
phenomenology, as methodology, 83
Philander Smith College, 101
Phillips, Layli, 96
Plum Village, 26
poetry, 142
politics of invitation, 32
poor working-class English Canadians, 126
postmodernism, 38, 45
power, 172, 173, 178–179, 181
prayer, 28
predominately white universities (PWI's), 103
prisoners, 28
process (creative): artistic process, 171–173, 176, 178–182; community process, 179, 181; writing process, 179–180
Purdue University, 81

Quebec, 125–126, 128–130, 133; Canada, 124–126; donuts bag raids, 128; hierarchy, 125; nationalists, 132; province, 125; separatists, 133
Quebec "branch" of the Roman Catholic Church, 127
Quebecois, 130, 132; collective, 128; utopia, 128
"Quebecois" culture, 128
Quebec Parliament, 127
queer, 171, 172, 177, 178, 182
Queer Nation, 24
queer studies, 96

racism, 172, 178, 182
rage: assuaged by mentoring, 82; as response to harassment, 82
Rahman, Qiyanaah, 227
RAINBOW SOUL at Morgan State University, 110
Randolph, Antonio, 98
Rastafarianism, 25
Reagan, Ronald, 224
Regis inspectors, 128
religious identity, 29
Reyman, Busha, 60
RFK (Robert F. Kennedy), 125
Richard, Thomas, 172, 183n3
Richardson, Bernard L., 100
ritual(s), 171, 172, 173, 177, 178
Roediger, David, 124
Roman Catholic Church, 125–126
Rommel Alfonso Guzmán, Sergio, 177, 182, 183n6
Ross, Loretta, 228
Rushin, Donna Kate, 162–163, 215–216, 230

SafeSpace at Morehouse, 110
Safe Zone programs, 107
Santeria, 25
Scenes of Instruction, a Memoir, 72
secular, 34
segregation, 139, 145–146
Seneca Falls Convention, 212
separatist movement, 126
sexism, 171, 172
sexual orientation, 112
sexual trauma, 140
Showalter, Elaine, 82
silence, breaking, 175–176
silence, when unproductive, 74; relationship to literature, 81; resistance to, 83, 86; as response to exclusion, 75
simultaneity of oppression, 230–231
Sister Chan Khong, 26–27
Sister Outsider, 4, 68, 228–229
Slavs, 123
Slowe, Lucy Diggs, 99

Smith, Barbara, 25
Smith, Gejuanna, 227
solidarity, 172, 182
Sommer, Doris, concept of strategic silence, 90n6
Southern University, 101
Spelman College, 24, 97, 101, 103, 213, 228
Spelman College Women's Research & Resource Center, 95, 103
spirit, viii, x
spirit of love, xi
spiritual activism, 26
spirituality, 23ff
spiritual movement, 32–33
Stanton, Elizabeth Cady, 212
Statue of Liberty, 124
Stewart, Maria W., 32
Sutherland Springs, Texas, 4
Sutherlin, Erica C., 14
Suzuki (Tadashi), 172
Swan, Jesse, 143, 144–145, 146

Talking Back: Thinking Feminist Thinking Black (hooks), 59, 85
Teaching to Transgress: Education as the Practice of Freedom (hooks), 67
testimonio: authenticity, 83; construction of voice, 83; as narrative form, 83
theatre, 171–183; devised theatre, 173; improvisation, 173, 179; physical actions, 172–173; play, 176, 177, 178, 180, 182; political theatre, 173; script, 179–80; training, 172, 176, 177, 181
Thich Nhat Hanh, 26
Third Life of Grange Copeland, The (Walker), 212
This Bridge Called My Back: Writings by Radical Women of Color (Moraga and Anzaldúa), vii-viii, 7, 12, 55–57, 60–61, 64–67, 70–71, 78–79, 136–139, 142–144, 216
This Bridge We Call Home: Radical Visions for Transformation (Anzaldúa and Keating), vii, 11–13, 61–64, 66, 136–139, 141, 143
threshold theories, 32
Tiep Hien Order, 26
Tijuana, 172, 173, 174–175, 178, 180; Maclovio Rojas, 179; Zona Norte, 175, 178, 179, 180
Till, Emmett, 218–219
Tinsley, Rebecca, 192
Toomer, Jean, 212
Toronto, 128–129
trafficking: human/sex, 173, 174, 175
Train the Trainers, 107
Transformations: Womanist, Feminist, and Indigenous Studies series, vii
transgender, 175, 177
Transgenero ("transgender" and "transgenre"), 15
transgression, 174, 177
Traps: African American Men on Gender and Sexuality (Byrd and Guy-Sheftall), 11, 213–214
trauma(s), 176
Travers, Jeanne, 190–194, 205
Troyano, Ela, 85
Trump, Donald, 3–4

"undisputed metropolis," 125
unilingualism, 128
United Farm Workers, 86
United States, 125, 133
University of South Florida, 53, 71
University of Toronto, 101
U.S. border, 125

Vallieres, Pierre, 126
Vaz, Kim, 54, 70
voice: alteration of, 70; process of coming to, 83–85; silencing of as oppression, 70
Voudoun, 25

Waging Peace, 192
Walker, Alice, vii, x, xi, 1, 2, 9, 12, 15–17, 25, 32–33, 36–38, 48–49, 51, 53, 65, 85, 123, 132, 133, 136, 140, 146, 171, 183n2, 191, 212, 214
What the Heart Remembers: The Women and Children of Darfur, 14, 187, 190–194, 205
Wheatley, Phillis, 2
"white," 123
White, Aaronette, 216, 227–228, 233
White Anglo-Saxon Protestant (WASP), 124
white-flight, as response to diversification of residential areas, 72
white privilege, 123, 132
Will to Change: Men, Masculinity and Love, The (hooks), 15
wisdom traditions, 31
womanism, ix, 25ff, 53, 73, 76, 123, 132, 214, 231
womanist(s), viii, ix, x-xi, 1, 2, 17, 37, 39, 44, 48, 53, 123, 136, 140–141, 143, 171–186, 183n2, 191, 229–230
Womanist, The (newsletter), 26

Womanist Forefathers: Frederick Douglass and W. E. B. Du Bois (Lemons), 2
Womanist Idea, The (Maparyan), 1, 10, 23, 31
womanist idea, 123, 132
womanist pedagogy, 34
Womanist Reader, The (Phillips), 123; as encompassing humanity, 76; relation to feminism, 73, 76; relation to woman of color feminism, 78
Womanist warriors, 18
Woman That I Am, The (Madison), 55
women of color, 171, 174, 176, 177, 178, 179, 182
Women's News and Narratives, 214
women's origins, 123
Women's Research and Resource Center at Spelman College, 11
women's studies, 54, 70, 87
women's studies department, 54
Woolf, Virginia, 212
World War II, 124

X, Malcolm, 40

Yarbrough, Dona, 214
Yezierska, Anzia, 76
Yoruba, 25
Youngstown, Ohio, 124

Zanesville, Ohio, 219

The University of Illinois Press
is a founding member of the
Association of American University Presses.

University of Illinois Press
1325 South Oak Street
Champaign, IL 61820-6903
www.press.uillinois.edu